GASTROFASHION

D1612889

DRESS, BODY, CULTURE

Series Editor: Joanne B. Eicher, *Regents' Professor*, *University of Minnesota*

Advisory Board:
Pamela Church-Gibson, *London College of Fashion, University of the Arts*
James Hall, *University of Illinois at Chicago*
Vicki Karaminas, *Massey University, New Zealand*
Gwen O'Neal, *University of North Carolina at Greensboro*
Ted Polhemus, *Curator, "Street Style" Exhibition, Victoria and Albert Museum*
Valerie Steele, *The Museum at the Fashion Institute of Technology*
Lou Taylor, *University of Brighton*
Karen Tranberg Hansen, *Northwestern University*
Ruth Barnes, *Yale Art Gallery, Yale University*

Books in this provocative series seek to articulate the connections between culture and dress which is defined here in its broadest possible sense as any modification or supplement to the body. Interdisciplinary in approach, the series highlights the dialogue between identity and dress, cosmetics, coiffure and body alternations as manifested in practices as varied as plastic surgery, tattooing, and ritual scarification. The series aims, in particular, to analyze the meaning of dress in relation to popular culture and gender issues and will include works grounded in anthropology, sociology, history, art history, literature, and folklore.

ISSN: 1360-466X

Previously published in the Series

Helen Bradley Foster, *"New Raiments of Self": African American Clothing in the Antebellum South*
Claudine Griggs, *S/he: Changing Sex and Changing Clothes*
Michaele Thurgood Haynes, *Dressing Up Debutantes: Pageantry and Glitz in Texas*
Anne Brydon and Sandra Niessen, *Consuming Fashion: Adorning the Transnational Body*
Dani Cavallaro and Alexandra Warwick, *Fashioning the Frame: Boundaries, Dress and the Body*
Judith Perani and Norma H. Wolff, *Cloth, Dress and Art Patronage in Africa*
Linda B. Arthur, *Religion, Dress and the Body*
Paul Jobling, *Fashion Spreads: Word and Image in Fashion Photography*
Fadwa El Guindi, *Veil: Modesty, Privacy and Resistance*
Thomas S. Abler, *Hinterland Warriors and Military Dress: European Empires and Exotic Uniforms*
Linda Welters, *Folk Dress in Europe and Anatolia: Beliefs about Protection and Fertility*
Kim K.P. Johnson and Sharron J. Lennon, *Appearance and Power*
Barbara Burman, *The Culture of Sewing: Gender, Consumption and Home Dressmaking*
Annette Lynch, *Dress, Gender and Cultural Change: Asian American and African American Rites of Passage*
Antonia Young, *Women Who Become Men: Albanian Sworn Virgins*
David Muggleton, *Inside Subculture: The Postmodern Meaning of Style*
Nicola White, *Reconstructing Italian Fashion: America and the Development of the Italian Fashion Industry*
Brian J. McVeigh, *Wearing Ideology: The Uniformity of Self-Presentation in Japan*
Shaun Cole, *Don We Now Our Gay Apparel: Gay Men's Dress in the Twentieth Century*
Kate Ince, *Orlan: Millennial Female*
Ali Guy, Eileen Green and Maura Banim, *Through the Wardrobe: Women's Relationships with their Clothes*
Linda B. Arthur, *Undressing Religion: Commitment and Conversion from a Cross-Cultural Perspective*
William J.F. Keenan, *Dressed to Impress: Looking the Part*
Joanne Entwistle and Elizabeth Wilson, *Body Dressing*
Leigh Summers, *Bound to Please: A History of the Victorian Corset*
Paul Hodkinson, *Goth: Identity, Style and Subculture*
Leslie W. Rabine, *The Global Circulation of African Fashion*
Michael Carter, *Fashion Classics from Carlyle to Barthes*
Sandra Niessen, Ann Marie Leshkowich and Carla Jones, *Re-Orienting Fashion: The Globalization of Asian Dress*
Kim K. P. Johnson, Susan J. Torntore and Joanne B. Eicher, *Fashion Foundations: Early Writings on Fashion and Dress*
Helen Bradley Foster and Donald Clay Johnson, *Wedding Dress Across Cultures*
Eugenia Paulicelli, *Fashion under Fascism: Beyond the Black Shirt*
Charlotte Suthrell, *Unzipping Gender: Sex, Cross-Dressing and Culture*
Irene Guenther, *Nazi Chic? Fashioning Women in the Third Reich*
Yuniya Kawamura, *The Japanese Revolution in Paris Fashion*
Patricia Calefato, *The Clothed Body*
Ruth Barcan, *Nudity: A Cultural Anatomy*
Samantha Holland, *Alternative Femininities: Body, Age and Identity*
Alexandra Palmer and Hazel Clark, *Old Clothes, New Looks: Second Hand Fashion*
Yuniya Kawamura, *Fashion-ology: An Introduction to Fashion Studies*
Regina A. Root, *The Latin American Fashion Reader*

Linda Welters and Patricia A. Cunningham, *Twentieth-Century American Fashion*
Jennifer Craik, *Uniforms Exposed: From Conformity to Transgression*
Alison L. Goodrum, *The National Fabric: Fashion, Britishness, Globalization*
Annette Lynch and Mitchell D. Strauss, *Changing Fashion: A Critical Introduction to Trend Analysis and Meaning*
Catherine M. Roach, *Stripping, Sex and Popular Culture*
Marybeth C. Stalp, *Quilting: The Fabric of Everyday Life*
Jonathan S. Marion, *Ballroom: Culture and Costume in Competitive Dance*
Dunja Brill, *Goth Culture: Gender, Sexuality and Style*
Joanne Entwistle, *The Aesthetic Economy of Fashion: Markets and Value in Clothing and Modelling*
Juanjuan Wu, *Chinese Fashion: From Mao to Now*
Annette Lynch, *Porn Chic: Exploring the Contours of Raunch Eroticism*
Brent Luvaas, *DIY Style: Fashion, Music and Global Cultures*
Jianhua Zhao, *The Chinese Fashion Industry: An Ethnographic Approach*
Eric Silverman, *A Cultural History of Jewish Dress*
Karen Hansen and D. Soyini Madison, *African Dress: Fashion, Agency, Performance*
Maria Mellins, *Vampire Culture*
Lynne Hume, *The Religious Life of Dress*
Marie Riegels Melchior amd Birgitta Svensson, *Fashion and Museums: Theory and Practice*
Masafumi Monden, *Japanese Fashion Cultures: Dress and Gender in Contemporary Japan*
Alfonso McClendon, *Fashion and Jazz: Dress, Identity and Subcultural Improvisation*
Phyllis G. Tortora, *Dress, Fashion and Technology: From Prehistory to the Present*
Barbara Brownie and Danny Graydon, *The Superhero Costume: Identity and Disguise in Fact and Fiction*
Adam Geczy and Vicki Karaminas, *Fashion's Double: Representations of Fashion in Painting, Photography and Film*
Yuniya Kawamura, *Sneakers: Fashion, Gender, and Subculture*
Heike Jenss, *Fashion Studies: Research Methods, Sites and Practices*
Brent Luvaas, *Street Style: An Ethnography of Fashion Blogging*
Jenny Lantz, *The Trendmakers: Behind the Scenes of the Global Fashion Industry*
Barbara Brownie, *Acts of Undressing: Politics, Eroticism, and Discarded Clothing*
Louise Crewe, *The Geographies of Fashion: Consumption, Space, and Value*
Sheila Cliffe, *The Social Life of Kimono: Japanese Fashion Past and Present*
Linda Welters and Abby Lillethun, *Fashion History: A Global View*
Therèsa M. Winge, *Costuming Cosplay: Dressing the Imagination*
Jenny Hall, *Japan Beyond the Kimono: Innovation and Tradition in the Kyoto Textile Industry*

DRESS, BODY, CULTURE: CRITICAL SOURCEBOOKS

Rebecca Mitchell, *Fashioning the Victorians: A Critical Sourcebook*

GASTROFASHION

From Haute Cuisine to Haute Couture: Fashion and Food

ADAM GECZY AND
VICKI KARAMINAS

BLOOMSBURY VISUAL ARTS
LONDON • NEW YORK • OXFORD • NEW DELHI • SYDNEY

BLOOMSBURY VISUAL ARTS
Bloomsbury Publishing Plc
50 Bedford Square, London, WC1B 3DP, UK
1385 Broadway, New York, NY 10018, USA
29 Earlsfort Terrace, Dublin 2, Ireland

BLOOMSBURY, BLOOMSBURY VISUAL ARTS and the Diana logo are trademarks of Bloomsbury Publishing Plc

First published in Great Britain 2022

Copyright © Adam Geczy and Vicki Karaminas, 2022

Adam Geczy and Vicki Karaminas have asserted their right under the Copyright, Designs and Patents Act, 1988, to be identified as Authors of this work.

For legal purposes the Acknowledgements on p. xii constitute an extension of this copyright page.

Cover image: Six Course Meal, Spring/Summer 2018.
Photograph by Kristen Jan Wong. Courtesy of Leeann Huang.

All rights reserved. No part of this publication may be reproduced or transmitted in any form or by any means, electronic or mechanical, including photocopying, recording, or any information storage or retrieval system, without prior permission in writing from the publishers.

Bloomsbury Publishing Plc does not have any control over, or responsibility for, any third-party websites referred to or in this book. All internet addresses given in this book were correct at the time of going to press. The author and publisher regret any inconvenience caused if addresses have changed or sites have ceased to exist, but can accept no responsibility for any such changes.

A catalogue record for this book is available from the British Library.

A catalog record for this book is available from the Library of Congress.

ISBN: HB: 978-1-3501-4749-2
PB: 978-1-3501-4750-8
ePDF: 978-1-3501-4751-5
eBook: 978-1-3501-4748-5

Typeset by RefineCatch Limited, Bungay, Suffolk
Printed and bound in Great Britain

To find out more about our authors and books visit www.bloomsbury.com and sign up for our newsletters.

CONTENTS

ILLUSTRATIONS

ACKNOWLEDGEMENTS

We would like to thank Pamela Church Gibson for her valuable feedback when writing this book. Annette O'Sullivan for her cover design and Leeann Huang for giving us permission to use '*Six Course Meal*' (SS2018) on the cover. Our gratitude goes to Frances Arnold and Joanne Eicher for their unwavering support and belief in our book ideas. We acknowledge Massey University New Zealand and The University of Sydney for their ongoing support and to our friends and colleagues for providing us with a collegial environment in which our research can prosper.

INTRODUCTION: INSIDE AND OUT

When we go out to a fine dining restaurant, we dress up. There is something of an expectation in this, as if not to dress the part is an insult to the food and to the establishment that serves it. When we see exceptions to this rule, like the inappropriately dressed tourist in sneakers or the punk with green hair in a stylish restaurant, other guests can experience palpable discomfort, as if they were seeing violations of a social protocol. That is why there are dress codes still in place in some establishments, to ensure a tone comparable to the setting, and to avoid unsettling the patrons, who are all hoping to partake in that ritual of prestige and privilege that is the imbrication of food and fashion. Joanne Finkelstein writes in her study of *Dining Out* (1989), people dining at a restaurant understand the protocols and are aware of their role and of the behaviour that is required of the individual. The restaurant is a public space where diners scrutinize one another, examining the way that other guests are dressed, whether their manners are appropriate and if they possess the proper etiquette skills expected at a dining establishment. 'The restaurant is a window through which a prolonged gaze can be enjoyed . . . a diorama which allows a concentrated view of each other'.[1] The combination of attention devoted to dress that is in some way commensurate with the attention given to the preparation and presentation of the food is such a given that it seldom bears mention. Yet it is worth pondering that the rise of gastronomy, restaurants, fashion, and haute couture occurred together, and have always enjoyed a symbiosis. Historically, the rise of social refinements – in manners, speech, clothing, taste – are inseparable from those of food, which became far more than a source of nourishment, but a spectacle, a locus of community, and the display of wealth and privilege.

We first coined the term 'gastrofashion' in our book *Fashion Installation, Body, Space and Performance* (2019) specifically to describe the emergence of designer restaurants and cafés as a form of 'retailment', as fashion labels created branded environments that consumers could literally *consume.* The first of these opened in 1998, with Giorgio Armani's eponymous restaurant in Paris. Earlier on, Pierre Cardin had purchased the world-famous Parisian restaurant, Maxims, in 1983; considered one of the first forays into fashion retail extension and licencing (along with Christian Dior, Givenchy and Yves St Laurent). It is now de rigueur in the twenty-first century for top-line fashion boutiques to open restaurants and align their label with celebrity chefs.[2] Fashion brands have now begun providing the complete shopping and lifestyle experience by incorporating restaurants, bars and cafés where the millennial consumer can relax, refuel and socialize. These include Dolce & Cabbana's *Martini Bar and 1921Gucci Café*, Burberry's *Thomas,* and Prada's *Pasticeria Marchesi.* However, we wanted in this book to go further than just exploring designer eateries; we wanted to examine the relationship between food and fashion, as well as clothing, style, manners and dress in all its manifestations from the restaurant to the catwalk, the cookbooks, the diet fads, celebrity chefs and so on. We were also interested in food and fashion and its impact on cultural mores and appearances. Food and fashion transmit meaning and have their own systems of communication that often merge and coalesce. Roland Barthes warned us that food should not be seen as insignificant because food and culture are very closely related and influence regimes of taste and class.[3] We have also learnt from Claude Lévi-Strauss' seminal work on the food triangle, *The Raw and the Cooked* (1964) and Mary Douglas' *Food in the Social Order* (1984) that food (like fashion) is a code that expresses patterns of social relations, such as gender and sexuality. With this in mind, we wanted to explore the many points of connection between dress and gastronomy from the antecedents in the sixteenth to eighteenth century, to the present day, and the many ways food is deployed in fashion.

While food writers have written extensively on 'fashions' in food, there has been surprisingly little, except for passing comment within gastronomy literature, on the imbrication of gastronomy and the fashion industry. 'Imbrication' perhaps does not do the relationship justice, because it is many-sided. On the most basic, material level, clothing is what is put *on the body*, and food is what is put *in the body*.

Similarly, food became a means of distinguishing between groups and nations, and for brokering status and privilege and heritage. Clothing and dress become fashion, and food becomes gustation. There are precursors and precedents to this, which we will explore in the opening chapter, when we examine the relationship between the fashion system and the food system, gastronomy and the grand cuisine. The explosion of fashion and gastronomy that occurs in the eighteenth century must be considered a part of a larger complex, such as the social, demographic and technological circumstances that called them into being. An analogy from a later period can be called upon to illustrate this point. The growing popularity of the automobile in the early twentieth century created a new gastronomic culture of travelling to rural areas and outside towns. This was at the very time that clothing, or leisure wear began to simplify, to accommodate an active outdoor lifestyle.

Where food and fashion meet

The union of fashion and food, socially and politically, occurred in the cultural capital of Europe of the fifteenth century, in the Florence of the Medici. The ability to dress in finery, such as silks and furs, extended to the capacity for giving large banquets with rare and coveted offerings of food and wine. The spectacle of the greatest dome in the world, that of Brunelleschi, and the array of other artistic feats was mirrored in the manners and appearance of the highest echelons of society; it was not enough to be wealthy, one had to show cultivation and discernment. There were two very important Italian moves to France. First, Leonardo da Vinci entered the service of François I, after the latter had annexed Milan in 1515 and he worked, among other things, as director of events (which included banquets) in Amboise, in the Loire valley, until his death in 1519. The second was the marriage of Catherine de' Medici and Henri II in 1533, at a time when many several cities in Italy – Florence, Venice and Rome pre-eminent among them – were considered the leaders in taste, from art to food and courtly manners. (When Marie de' Medici married Henri IV in 1600, fittingly, the ceremony was held in Florence, which still at the time had a tenuous hold as the epicentre of European culture.) The court of the Medici in the fifteenth century is said to have introduced plates as a substitute for the bowls and eating boards used in medieval times, and in place of hands, diners used a two-spiked prong, the *forcina*, the incipient form of the fork, whose origins are obscure, possibly the Middle East or Catalonia. A painting by Sandro Botticelli for Lorenzo di Medici, the fourth panel of *The Story of Nastagio degli Onesti* (*c*. 1483) shows the banqueters using a *forcina* (Figure 0.1). The members of this banquet are all well-appointed, their clothing matching their gestures and prim demeanour. They are waited upon by handsome stewards in rich scarlet livery, who flank either side of the painting. They hold aloft dishes, which are bound by a strip of white linen that seems to be holding them in tow. What the contemporary observer may take for granted, but which is notable, is that the tables are covered in a white cloth. Here clothing, manners and food are in seamless unity.

Particular social structures in medieval times (manners and dress) were moulded by social attitudes. Sumptuary laws were imposed on dress by rulers, designed to make fashionable dress the prerogative of the élite, and so control behaviour and maintain existing class structures. In 1336, an English Sumptuary Law was passed regulating the number of courses at dinner and in 1364 a statute was imposed by the monarchy concerning diet and apparel. In *The History of Manners*, Volume One of *The Civilizing Process* (1982 [1939]) Norbert Elias traces how certain behaviours (table manners) and forms of speech were transformed by increasing the thresholds of shame and repugnance in court etiquette. Restraints imposed by complex social networks of social structures (food and dress) aided in the development of self-perception, or identity. In this

Figure 0.1 Sandro Botticelli, *The Story of Nastagio degli Onesti* (Fourth Episode) Tempera on panel, *c.* 1483. (Wikipedia Commons, Public Domain.)

feudal system, clothes were an indication of wealth and class, and fashionable dress was influenced and dominated by kings and queens. Any violation of these laws would result in harsh penalties such as the loss of property, fines or even death. In chapter nine of this book, we look at the ways that etiquette books (beginning in the Middle Ages) served as guides for appropriate manners, just as cookbooks were a guide to an aspirational lifestyle that gave one entry to a particular social class.

As the kitchens grew bigger and a space devoted to dining became more intimate than the Grand Hall, eating was given over to the pleasures of the table, hence the 'dining room'. As to be expected, the centrepiece of the dining room was the dining table, which was bedecked with the lavish preparations presided over the master of ceremonies – the cook. The customs and codes of behaviour at the table caught on throughout Europe, but not until the beginning of the sixteenth century. Courtly manners, dictating how to dine and how to dress, were elevated to an object of observation and commentary, as attested to in one of the most popular books of its time *The Book of the Courtier* by Baldessar Castiglione, a nobleman in the ducal court of Urbino. Published first in 1528, it is set in 1507 and the book consists of several conversations about etiquette, appearance and codes of behaviour through to morality, that occur over the space of four nights. Its success meant that it led to several (what would be called) courtesy books dealing with courtly behaviour, including conversation and speech, grooming, and proper eating habits. The ideal courtier must be careful of the modulation of voice as well as conscious of gesture and bearing. Excessive behaviour was frowned upon, and one was expected to show prowess in physical pursuits such as hunting and fighting, as well as familiarity with the intellectual domain, including the classics and the arts. All of this should be carried out without contrivance. An accomplished female courtier was expected '[t]o set out her beauty and disposition of person with meet [i.e. appropriate] garments that best become her, but as feigningly as she can, making semblance to bestow no labour about it, nor yet to mind it.'[4] The courtier must surround herself with things befitting of her status and must reflect that she befits it accordingly. She is meant to wear her clothing and hold herself with effortlessness and panache, what Castiglione called *sprezzatura*, which is used more commonly for men to describe a winningly nonchalant confidence. Clothing and eating, together with speaking and dancing, were all important domains of demonstrating the capacity for the higher graces. These higher graces would not be confined to the body alone, but to also to the spaces of public pleasure and celebration, the table.

'Table' is the metonym in gastronomic literature to designate the manners, protocols, conventions and codes that are part of the rituals associated with eating, usually in the formal or social context. It is where eating is staged according to determined rules of decency, sociability and decorum. Food became more elaborate with the development of courtly life in the late fourteenth and early fifteenth century, which means that it is contemporaneous with a widening expectation toward ostentation and luxury. As an intermediary between the well-attired élite and the sumptuous meal, from the Renaissance onwards, the banquet plate became quite literally an important platform in signalling one's status. One could say that the increasing importance of the plate on the table grew in tandem with dress at table. One cardinal example can be taken in the household of one of the most admired and fashionable women of her time, Isabella d'Este (1474–1539) and her husband, Marquese Francesco II. (As testament to being one of the great fashionistas of her day, Isabella was used as a model figure by François I, who ordered a series of dolls with her clothing as prototypes of what women in his own court in Fontainebleau should wear.)[5] An inventory shows how complex and important dinner services had become; the artist Giulio Romano was enlisted to decorate the many plates, bowls, ewers, tureens, salvers, wine-coolers, cutlery and more that graced the noble household. In terms of precious metals, an estimate shows that this amounted to some 250 kgs of silver with close to 2 kg of gold used mainly for gilding.[6] Valerie Taylor observes that Giulio's drawing testifies to the extent of the holdings, which was, in turn, a reflection of the role they played in the life of the household. Not only did Isabella have a talent for appearances, but she would have been in influenced by the sheer quantity, in Taylor's words,

> of doctrines, treatises, guides, manuals, and cookbooks dedicated to the preparation and presentation of food that were published in the Cinquecento, which led Françoise Sabban and Silvano Serventi to classify this period as the "golden age of Italian gastronomy". Already in 1498, new eating trends were

> perceptible in Bartolomeo Platina's fundamental work *De honesta voluptate et valetudine* (1498), which recommended eating all kinds of vegetables, fresh fruits, fish, and chilled wines that had not previously been considered fit for consumption by the élite.[7]

Service had also become tightly controlled and codified, as a sequence of hot then cold dishes. This, which became known as *il servizio all'italiana*, was an indicator of the advancements in cooking and display that took place in Italy in this period. Together with the table service, the family and their guests would be flanked with side-boards (*credenze*) covered in white linen for the display, service and preparation of other foods.[8] Dining became more refined, such as the introduction of handwashing, and implements became finer such as fragile glassware and elegant cutlery that was stamped with the coat of arms of the host. It was in the gustatory domain that, in the open display of wealth and beneficence, the patron could indulge in her own carefully orchestrated self-promotion, assisted by an early form of what today we would call branding.

Haute cuisine and haute couture

Although restaurants, or their pre-industrial equivalent, originated in the mid-seventeenth century – the oldest restaurant in Paris, Le Procope boasts that it has been in operation since 1686 – they only became a component of everyday life as a result of the French Revolution. This has to do with several factors, most evidently in the relaxation of norms, rules and hierarchies, the opportunity of a wider distribution of wealth which precipitated a deeper and more widespread sense of entitlement and competitiveness. Since the very birth of lavish courtly life, since the reigns of Charles VI and François I, and most decisively the reign of Louis XIV, French society placed a premium on status. So did any country, or grouping, in civilization for that matter – but it was the intricacy with which it was held, wielded, manipulated and seized that made the French notion of status unique in the seventeenth and eighteenth century, with dress and food playing central roles. The other factor was conversation – where one could exercise *esprit* – and so salons, but also dinner-parties and restaurants, became a stage for duels of language and wit. It was during and after the Revolution that the tendencies toward production, consumption and discernment flourished, as they were open to anyone who could afford them. It was the Revolution that relaxed sartorial norms and it was the Revolution that witnessed the rise of the restaurant. With blunt precision, the gastronome Alexandre-Laurent Grimod de La Reynière (1758–1837) explains that:

> The Revolution, ruining all . . . former property owners, threw all the good chefs out onto the pavement. At that point, in order to make use of their

> talents, they transformed themselves into merchants of good cheer under the name of restauranteurs. One could not have counted a hundred of them before 1789. Today, there are perhaps five times as many.[9]

There were more chefs available on the market, and a greater number willing to patronize them. This did not stop the élite from competing to enlist the chefs for meals and functions in their own households, much as celebrity chefs (and comedians) are still today hired by the rich to cater to a small and privileged coterie.

After antiquity, books on cooking can be found dating to the fourteenth century, but what these writers cooked or recorded, let alone whom they influenced could not match the talents of Marie-Antoine Carême, 'The King of Chefs' and the uncontested father of French Cuisine. It was Carême that made French cooking the optimal standard for cooking throughout the world. While under today's standards this claim might sound tired and overly biased in its Occidentalism, Carême is acknowledged as refining and tying together many forms of cooking of the day. He gave dining a coherence and rigour that came with standards, rules, protocols aligned to notions of a higher order of status, manners and way of living. There had long been great cooks, but it is his celebrity that draws him close to the rudiments of fashion as we have come to know them. It is one thing to propound standards and opinions, however; it is another for people to listen and to follow them. For Carême was a consummate self-promoter and entrepreneur. Having lived through the French Revolution, he understood the power of mass appeal and what could be leveraged from it. His insights are relevant to this very day, where there is a disproportion between those who, say, read about 3-star Michelin restaurants and follow their recipes and those who visit them. While several cooks before him had laid claim to renovating the art of cooking and rendering it 'nouvelle cuisine' (not the first to do so, as we will find), Carême took pains to mark himself out as the inaugurator of the new beginning. His success was to bring cooking from mere service into the realm of art. One of the ways he achieved this was in responding acutely and subtly to the shift that the Revolution helped to instigate from pandering to a minority élite to responding to consumers within a growing mass market. Just as the mass of printed matter helped to fuel desire and astute in the world of fashion, as Priscilla Parkhurst Ferguson affirms, 'printed texts translated the aristocratic cuisine of the *ancien regime* for a more inclusive bourgeois public'.[10] Born in the eighteenth century, Carême's vision of cuisine was firmly set on the nineteenth century, and his own ambition matched his vision to set the rudiments for fine cooking, what would become known as haute cuisine, for the future. Carême was very much a man of his time, which was a time of competing opinions and loyalties, and a time when the showmanship of skill was a marketable, if not coveted, commodity.

Even if gastronomy and the sovereignty of French cooking owes its greatest debt to Carême, the cook who left the most lasting stamp on contemporary cuisine was Auguste Escoffier. For while fashion has its Rose Bertin and cooking its Carême, it was Charles Frederick Worth and Escoffier who elevated fashion and food to a new height, that was available to anyone with the money and wherewithal to seek it out. It is a curious coincidence then, but perhaps no surprise, that haute cuisine developed closely in the wake of haute couture, almost contemporaneously. The rise of the grand spectacles created by the 'world exhibitions', dating from the mid-nineteenth century, marked a new level of magnitude for consumption and display. Worth established the first couture House in Paris in 1868, and ten years later the Le Chambre Syndicale de la Haute Couture was set up to safeguard luxury fashion. Two decades after that, the first mega-restaurants, the Ritz (founded 1898) and Maxim's (founded 1893) in Paris opened their doors to diners. The restaurant as we now know it, while having its precursors in the dining halls and coffee-houses of the eighteenth century, is in truth a product of the modernist spectacle at the end of the nineteenth century, in which alimentation is but a means to an end. People would come in the main to be *seen,* where eating was simply an anchoring activity or an excuse. Fashionable venues necessitated fashionable clothes. In the modern restaurant it is evident that the body is a privileged site of power subject to social forces that affect the way that bodies are disciplined, represented, constructed and consumed. Whether exercised through regimes of dress, diet, and later, cosmetic surgery or bodybuilding, fashion and food inscribe the body into a system of signs. Fashion, like food, chose the body as a site of power, display and resistance.

Taste cultures

The growth of the culture of the eighteenth century lies in the interconnectedness of industrial sophistication and growth, the burgeoning of urban spaces, the broadening of discourse and opinion, which together ushered in possibilities of social mobility hitherto unseen. Mobility has to be seen from several angles, and its role in fashion is crucial. While mobility is also coterminous with the rise of the middle class, it finds its first pitch-point in the eighteenth century with a density and diversity of opinion that was not possible in previous eras of social stratification and is linked to population density and information flows. Fashion, as it arose as a field of cultural discourse, is a system that is brokered across individuals and social groups, together with economies that are both financial and subjective. Gastronomy, as it was to appear, develops in the same way. The nexus of commodity (the product) and opinion (judgement after consumption) in gastronomy, art and fashion are relatively contemporaneous, sharing their development in the eighteenth century with the circulation of printed matter, in the early forms of magazines and newspapers, the *feuilles*, *feuilletons* and *affiches*, as they were referred to in France.

In art, the first serious art criticism is found in the work of Denis Diderot (1713–1784), which was largely aimed at the *Salons* (1759–1771) of the French Academy, held biannually at the Louvre. These publications were circulated privately at first with the assistance of his friend Melchior Grimm, who was the lover of Louise d' Epinay who ran one of the most popular, fashionable and influential private salons. His commentaries comprised of ruminations of aesthetic standards as well as selective analyses of painting-by painting, which could be used much as an audioguide can be today. A generation later, his counterpart in matters of food was Grimod de La Reynière who was not only younger but of noble birth. Grimod is credited as the founder of the genre of writing known as *écriture gourmand*, a literature that, in the words of Beatrice Fink, 'focuses on the multiple aspects and possibilities of food and eating, much as other types focus on aesthetics, philosophy, or, say, satire'.[11] In other words, he made eating a serious business that transcended simple alimentation – so gastronomy is to eating what fashion is to clothing, while both former terms aspire to the status of art. Diderot and Grimod are salient figures among a field of others who responded to a time when matters of taste became a genuine concern: who decided it, who had it, who influenced it.

Taste – *le goût* – in art, literature, fashion and food was central to a popular discourse that was no longer governed, or decided by, the nobility but whose arbiters were critics whose knowledge (real or postured), powers of judgement, when mixed with the wit and acerbity of their pen, wielded staggering power. Until the mid-seventeenth century, 'taste' – and its Continental equivalents such as *gusto* in Italian and *Geschmack* in German – were used exclusively for food. The transition toward a broader sense of cultural discrimination in fact originated in a cookbook, one of the early tomes of the new cuisine, *Les Délices de la campagne* (Country Delights) written by Nicolas de Bennefons in 1654.[12] Wit – *l'esprit* – which also translates to 'spirit', was a key element in social life, which had become increasingly disposed to mimicking courtly behaviour. The judge and political philosopher Montesquieu, in his entry on taste in the *Encyclopédie,* stressed the role of *délicatesse*, which applied as much to food as it did to art and literature. The coarse *grossiers* were unresponsive and unreflective, while the *délicats* judged art and food with subtlety and grace.[13] Another valued quality was *finesse*, one that was then translated into other aspects of social transactions and ceremony, notably the consumption of food.

Pierre Bourdieu (whom we write about at length through this book) would later conduct a critique of taste by investigating how the French middle class asserted their 'distinction' through their eating habits and spending practices. By dividing consumption into a structure that contains three items – food, culture and presentation (clothing and accessories) – Bourdieu analysed the spending, preparation and presentation of food as a way of determining difference (including gender and class). His seminal book, *La Distinction* (1979), subtitled, *A Social Critique of the Judgement of Taste*, deals with other aspects of people's behaviours, such as music, visuals, cinema, literature and so on that are often attributed to people's taste. People make choices according to their preferences, which are predicated on their social background. The lower class (manual and industrial workers) have 'vulgar' tastes and the professional upper class (teachers and executives) have 'delicate' and refined tastes. There is a struggle – and what emerges in Bourdieu's social analysis of the French bourgeoise is that snobbery runs rampant, and that the aesthetic choices people of each class make are different from and in opposition to those choices made by other social classes. According to Bourdieu, the social genesis of taste is bound with the centuries-old struggle between groups for titles of nobility and marks of distinction. Everyone inherits a class position which is defined by a certain amount of economic and symbolic capital (mainly education); it is only to a very limited extent, he argues, that this inheritance can be modified by social mobility. While Bourdieu looked for a fixed formula underlying the taste preferences of each class, Lévi-Strauss and Roland Barthes looked for a code, a system or a grammar underlying the food (and fashion) choices of each class.

This book is about something we have known for a very long time, that food is more than alimentary sustenance. Our enjoyment, experience and understanding of food comes from appearances. And with appearances come better ones and not-so-good-ones. This gives way to preferences, patterns, trends, and in modern parlance, fashions. Food goes into our bodies, and it plays a critical role in bodily appearances. We compete for foods, we compete and transact appearances, we arbitrate on what is preferred, what is unusual, what is objectionable. Food and fashion – it is almost too obvious. But nonetheless, this book needed to be written, especially at a time when both food and fashion have become serious points of contestation, environmentally as well as ethically. 'Gastrofashion' is not just an aesthetic concept but one that circulates around many key points of our lives as socialized animals.

1

BETWEEN THE FASHION SYSTEM AND THE FOOD SYSTEM, GASTRONOMY AND GRANDE CUISINE

It is now something of a given within studies of fashion to note that the beginnings of fashion as a site of as a site of culture and as a point of envy and emulation begins with Louis XIV and his court. Innumerable courts across Europe, large and small, turned to Versailles as the apogee of seemly conduct and good taste, causing French manners and French language to be the benchmark of what was considered civilized. It is worth rehearsing this point, if only to remark upon the durability of this perception. For while many things have changed, Paris still remains the global epicentre of fashion – and food. However, in discussions of this phenomenon in studies of gastronomy and those of fashion, each are largely discrete, as opposed to recognizing that they worked in concert with one another. To be sure, the reason for the French dominance in both clothes and cookery is not ascribable to the court of Louis XIV alone, but what his court did set up was a series of expectations that not only foreigners but the French themselves competitively set out to meet, creating a culture of discernment and expectation – which also discrimination and execration, leading to the Revolution, which exerted its own dramatic changes in fashion and food. It is from this period onward, together with the upheavals of Napoleon's empire and the successive revolutions, that cooking evolved from a specialized practice involved in the spectacle of courtly consumption and wealth to an art, where cuisine became grand cuisine, laying the ground for what would be haute cuisine, the counterpart to haute couture.

Coffee-houses and the first restaurants

One of the sources of the Revolution is traditionally said to have been in the salons of the eighteenth century that were held by the enlightened upper classes to exchange risqué ideas that were tightly policed in public by Louis XV's vigilant censors. Another is the restaurant, and another still is the coffee-house, now the ubiquitous café, where people could meet, exchange anything from pleasantries to seditious ideas. Coffee began to be consumed as a popular drink in the late seventeenth century, dates are given such as 1672, at the stand of an Armenian who went by the name of Harouthion. (The first shipment of coffee is reputedly to have arrived at the port of Marseille in 1660.) What he sold was not only in the taste and stimulant qualities of the beverage, but also for its exoticism, a feeling no doubt encouraged by the proprietor's flowing dress, or *robe en Arménien*. One of the oldest surviving coffee-houses, and the first public café in Paris, Le Procope, was opened by a Sicilian, Procopio Cúto aka Francesco Procopio, who had been apprenticed to an Armenian known as Pascal, who was a *limonnadier*, among the first to sell coffee along with lemonade. Cúto was quick to monopolize on the Orientalist cachet, having his waiters wear Armenian robes and serving his beverages, along with other delicacies such as sorbet, in decorative porcelain. Procope continued to be a fashionable place to meet, especially for intellectuals and future Revolutionaries. During the Revolution, it was the first establishment to display the Phrygian cap publicly. Today, it wears its historical heritage on its sleeve. It is a material allegory of history itself, melding actual relics with facsimile and pastiche.

The Armenian robe was one of the progenitors of the banyan, or house-robe, a garment of a hybrid origin (Japan, the Middle East, India), and grounded in the Orientalist imaginary.[1] Coffee, which was one of the few commodities whose consumption is unaffected by economic crises, was relatively cheap, which made it then somewhat socially levelling, and has always been an intermediary in social interaction. From the sixteenth century until well past the Revolution, the banyan would not only be used as respite from formal clothing by both women but mostly men, but it was acquired by intellectuals as the domestic gear of choice, often coupling it with headwear such as the rounded cap, the *taqiyah* in Turkish or the *kufi* in Arabic, to softer hats decorated with a tassel, a less rigid variant of the fez. The cross-relation between coffee and Oriental home dress maintained itself with the flourishing of coffee-houses throughout Paris and elsewhere, which from the earliest days in the late seventeenth century, were typically decorated in the Turkish fashion, *à la turque*. In London, the first of such houses opened a little earlier, in 1650 by an Ottoman-Lebanese Jew known as Jacob. The Turkish and Ottoman themes persisted with another coffee-house that opened in 1652, called the 'The Turk's Head'.[2] This was not uncommon, or perhaps expected, given that the English coffee-house was referred to as a 'Turkish alehouse'.[3] In the early days of the Procope, as Pierre Andrieu comments, 'a waiter dressed as Turk brought out tiny cups of coffee', for passers-by or carriages bearing more notable people who bought them as they would from lemonade sellers, 'although nothing would have induced them to mingle with the

Figure 1.1 'To the blue bottles' (Zu den blauen Flaschen), (Schlossergassl) old Viennese coffee-house scene (*c.* 1900), by an Unknown artist. (Wikipedia Commons, Public Domain.)

men drinking the same coffee indoors.'[4] In an anonymous painting from the early eighteenth century of a coffee-house, the centre of attention is a Turkish man wearing a fez, a brightly coloured sky-blue vest and puffy orange knee-length britches serving coffee to an appreciative soldier (Figure 1.1).

The Orientalist charm of such images tends to belie, however, the less than sympathetic reactions to 'foreign' tastes and commodities taken together with foreign clothing. An anti-coffee-house pamphlet from the late seventeenth century raged against those who too-willingly embraced exotic fashions and foods: 'Like Apes, the English imitate all other people in their ridiculous Fashions. As Slaves, they submit to the Customes even of Turkey and India . . . With the Barbarous Indian he smokes Tobacco. With the Turk he drinks Coffee.'[5] Brian Cowan, in his detailed account of the British coffee-houses, mentions how the growing popularity in coffee-houses engendered a cult of participation in terms of ritual and dressing-up. To those sceptical of the consumption of coffee, such enthusiasts were deemed as participating in heathen practices, with all the implications of decadence that the Orientalist myths had to offer.[6] As coffee-houses flourished along with the appetite for tea and tobacco, by 1784 there were over three thousand grocers licenced to sell tea in London.[7] In the eighteenth century, a sign of gentility and good manners, and good tea, together with a beautiful tea-service were as important as fine interiors and clothing in welcoming guests. Serving tea and the more overarching rituals and conduct at table, as opposed to mere quantitative consumption, had become the signs of refinement and good breeding. Bickham explains that 'for the pernickety world of British polite society, in which knowledge of how to use a commodity according to a set of changing guidelines was as important as its possession, eating was a public performance.'[8] Increasingly, appearances related to food display and consumption were as important as those related to body and self for staking claims to social importance.

Despite the many unsavoury aspects that were an occupational hazard of seventeenth- and eighteenth-century dress, in the eighteenth century in particular, there was a growing emphasis on health and bodily well-being, adopting more relaxed and 'natural' from of dressing as exemplified in domestic clothing and informal *déshabille*. The stronger consciousness of an unconstrained body had been prefigured in changes introduced in upper-class eating habits. The demands that Louis XIV placed on his courtiers to maintain the highest order of dress (which also ensured that most would become financially straightened and therefore more needy and less powerful), he also expected a level of gustation that was far from the ordinary. Just as André Le Nôtre had engineered hydraulics for the fountains of Versailles on an unprecedented scale, horticulturalists and gardeners assured that many delicacies, such as strawberries, peas, asparagus, and the king's favourite, figs, could be obtained well outside of their regular seasonal availability. Bonnefons's *Délices de compagne* would serve not only as a guide to cooks, but to kitchen gardeners as well, for direction in horticultural care and yield. While the greater public still lived of very meagre fare, the many efforts of the Versailles gardens resulted in an awareness and a diffusion of food varieties among those who could afford them, and with all of that, an ever-broadening spectrum of foods that cooks had available to them.

If the coffee-houses were melting-pots of conversation and fomenting personal and political passions, the earliest restaurants served as much as places of respite and relaxation. For the word 'restaurant' derives from shops that sold bouillon, or soup, known as a *restaurans*, or *bouillons reconstituants* otherwise called 'restorative soups', which had become popular around 1760, roughly contemporaneous with the coffee-house. But if coffee had its adherents and attractors as to its nutritional or medicinal benefits, the 'places of restauration' were aimed at people's well-being, the centrepiece of the establishment being the huge pot on the stove where the hearty bouillon simmered. The providers of these were first referred to as *traiteurs* which is the equivalent of 'caterer', as they catered to people's hunger and attended to their well-being.

One claim to the oldest restaurant goes to Tour d'Argent which opened its doors in 1582. At that time it was a hostel for travellers who were too late for the curfew and for the nightly closure of the gates of Paris. According to Andrieu, it is worth noting 'that it was at the Tour d'Argent, in the reign of Henri III (1574–

1589), that forks appeared on the dinner-table.'[9] Writing in 1846, Eugène Briffault claims that '[t]he first restauranteur in Paris was a man named Lamy. He opened his dining room in one of the dark and narrow passageways that then surrounded the Palais-Royal.'[10] Another contender is Antoine Beauvilliers, who is cited in Brillat-Savarin's *Physiologie du gout* [Physiology of Taste] as a hospitable host to eager guests, who began as a pâtissier in the household of the later Louis XVIII, then moving to the Palais-Royale in 1787 on the eve of the Revolution. While restaurants made their transition around 1770, states Brillat-Savarin, Beauvilliers who set out on his own around 1782, was the first restauranteur worth noting.[11] Huis Grande Taverne de Londres [Grand London Tavern] at 16 rue de Richelieu comprised, as Andrieu describes it, of 'exquisitely decorated rooms, magnificent with sword and shirt-frill.'[12] The setting flattered the guests. Whichever one of these is true, and according to whatever criteria, certainly the Palais-Royal was one of the prime locations for the restaurant's origins. Owned by the king's cousin, Louis-Philippe, Duc D'Orleans, since it was a private domain, it was not subject to the regular state controls of people, or conduct of conversation, and for this is often cited as one of the main seedbeds of the Revolution. In fact, as Andrieu also states, it was in the Palais-Royale that the first outdoor seating (but not yet tables) became available, with the Café Foy. And '[i]t was at the Café Foy that Camille Desmoulins, two days before the taking of the Bastille, plucked a leaf from a chestnut tree and stuck it in his hat as a cockade to arouse the enthusiasm of the crowds.'[13]

An advertisement in 1767 stated that these places of restauration were aimed at 'those with a frail and delicate stomach or for those whose diet is not in the habit of eating two meals or supper'.[14] A delicate stomach was not considered a bad thing, as it was seen as belonging to a sensitive mind and a refined spirit. The restaurants distinguished themselves from taverns by setting care and attention at a premium (diners in restaurants originally dined alone).[15] Just as one of the contested sites of the Revolution would be the body and dress that voided the cumbersome complications of the upper classes, the earliest justification for restaurants were for physiological care and betterment. In both cases, the emphases that justified the practices in dress and in food had a moral justification attributed to them.

Such places grew in popularity over the successive decades leading to the Revolution where, as we touched on already, they increased at a heady rate. One statistic has it that just before the Revolution there were around 1,800 cafés, but by 1807, at the height of Napoleon's power and prosperity, the number had risen to some 4,000.[16] (Of course, these statistics vary according to whether one includes cafés, restaurants and establishments of this kind together or separately.) The rise was exponential and dramatic. It caused an equally sizeable change in the social fabric on a number of levels, such as what became more accessible to a wider range of people, and how these people comported themselves in public spaces. Certainly, for the middle classes who controlled and carried out the Revolution, the democratization of culture was widespread and decisive. For those who could afford it, the system of availability was key. On a day-to-day level, food and clothing were the two areas of conspicuous consumption.

The prolific dramatist and social chronicler Louis-Sébastien Mercier describes how the Revolution made dining more available to people who could otherwise not afford it, sometimes to the detriment of public manners. The spillage of the cooks from the manor houses and plush city *hôtels* into the open market must have created a glut from which the lower classes, when they could afford it, benefitted, but much to the consternation of others. In their availability, refined foods and rare wines became demystified and objects of fashionable fascination.

> The moment when a simple worker earns, by the power of paper money, two hundred *écus* a day, he becomes the *habitué* of the restauranteur, leaving the cabbage with bacon in favour of chicken and watercress, renouncing the tin pint, even if a big one, for the sealed bottle for 40 *sous*. He still regularly needs his coffee and small shot (*le petit verre*). The poor darling (*Le bon chère*) thus becomes insolent, lazy, libertine, voracious and greedy (*avide et gourmand*).
>
> The slightly upper classes are consequently surpassed by the greediness (*gourmandise*) of the plebeian. The sale of emigrant wines has caused the gourmets to multiply. Desks stuffed with assignats have allowed even the thinnest clerk to savour rare wines (*vin de l'hermitage*), the wig-maker's apprentice is not the only one among the equal [citizens] who can boast of having tasted a delicious Madeira.
>
> The cooks of princes, parliament advisors, cardinals, canons and farmers-general have not been inactive for long after the emigration of the imitators of Apicius. They have become restauranteurs and have announced that they are going to profess and practice for any paying party *the science of the gullet*, as Montaigne calls it.[17]

The sudden availability of so many restaurants to a market that had historically knew nothing of the kind, or had to look over their shoulder for it, also meant that the cooks were playing to a captive audience. They created fashions in food and were alternately forced to follow them. As Mercier observes, the nouveau riches assembled from the weavers and bakers 'have made fine dining fashionable', causing cooks to redouble their efforts to promote themselves and to find new sources of satisfaction.[18]

The intensity of the years during the Red Terror, and the years after it, known less frequently as the 'White Terror' was one of both consumption and display. While the lower members of the former First Estate had access, in theory, to a gamut of goods, services and food that had been beyond reach, there were also balls and banquets that were like cathartic masques in dedication to the spate of violence that blazed before Robespierre was ultimately deposed and executed at the end of July 1794. These were known indelicately as the 'Victim Balls' or *Bals à la victime*. Here the women would dress in Greco-Roman style, with a tendency toward suggestiveness. In Mercier's words the dancers at such parties 'modelled the form of their appearance on that of Aspasia [a former lover of Pericles]: naked arms, an uncovered breast, the hair turned into braids around their heads – fashionable hairdressers complete their work before antique busts.'[19] They remain scantily clad *à la sauvage* even during winter weather. The food on offer matches the extravagance of the celebrations. Mercier comments on the profusion of fruits of all seasons, fruit ice creams, and 'orgeat [a liqueur of almond, sugar, and rose-water], lemonade, liqueurs from the islands flowing in abundant fountains'.[20] However one wants to take all of this, as hyperbole or reportage, what is certain is the persistent air of hysteria that marked the time. The body, which had only just a little earlier been a site of death and suspicion, became one of hedonism and display.

By the 1830s, restaurants and cafés were the nodal points for socialization in Paris, for 'going out', as havens, and as meeting points before or after appointments. One such establishment was Tortoni's not far from Procope. Andrieu offers a vivid vignette of the literary bohemian illuminati that assembled there with what is most likely an impressionistic recollection of what they wore that is nonetheless worth quoting:

> It was on the steps of Tortini's that Barbey d'Aurevilly, impeccably dressed like the best fashion-plate, would carelessly greet Dumas *père*, who introduced the fashion of soft shirts, pleated, and embroidered. Alfred de Musset, in af aultless bronze-green frock-coat and a big collar would be there, or Viktor Hugo in pearl-grey trousers and astrakhan waistcoat.[21]

Barbey d'Aurevilly was, after Brummell, one of history's great dandies, about which he wrote the most extensive account. Perhaps more than the salons of the century before, it was in the café and the restaurant that dandy-dom, *dandyisme,* could be staged, and where it was allowed its expression and evolution.

Food guides, cookbooks, nouvelle and grande cuisine

The circulation of knowledge about food, and the subsequent fashions and trends circulating around it, accelerated after the invention of the printing press. Indeed, together with Bibles, the most commonly produced publication were cookbooks.[22] It is safe to say that until the seventeenth century, competition from court to court, which was accompanied and implied in these books of instruction, regarding food superseded that of clothing.

From the Renaissance onward dining evolved together with increasingly more involved and sophisticated conceptions ceremony, constituted by deportment, dress and display. To reflect the demands of their masters, the head cooks, who were then more a mixture of today's chef and a butler, were in charge of procurement, organization and co-ordination from beginning to end. It was in the taste and the display that some of these chose to write down their experiences, usually in the form of food guide-books. These normally took the form of slender volumes which were accompanied by woodcuts. Understandably, the quality of culinary literature varied a great deal, and as it diversified and increased by the seventeenth century, it also became gendered. By this time there were cookbooks, in the words of Abigail Dennis, 'by and for the male chefs, and those written (largely) by women for female housekeepers'.[23] It was also this hierarchy that helped to bring in the notion that cooking could be elevated to an art beyond that of its everyday manifestations. This to some extent explains why there were comparatively so many more cookbooks beginning to be produced by the mid-seventeenth century. Such books reflected the competition between cooks and by extension, between courts such that, as Dennis remarks, '[a] sub-genre of courtly cookery books emerged, whose main purpose was to flaunt the exotic and unattainable dishes eaten by royalty'.[24] Some of these books amounted to treatises, which became a credo – whether seen as fashion or more as law – of proper gustatory habits. François-Pierre de La Varenne, for instance, in his influential *Le Cuisinier français* (1651), published two years before Bonnefons's *Delices de campagne*, called for what we today would call a more authentic and essentialist approach to cooking, where the object is to bring out the particular tastes of ingredients, as opposed to disguising flavours by infelicitous combinations or through an over-liberal use of spices. (Spices for some time had been a staple of upper-class cookery as they were a sign of status, comparable perhaps to artists who used blue from lapis lazuli to show the wealth of their patron.) Varenne also belonged to an epoch where the prestige of table was heightened and its attendant demands especially stiff. Varenne dedicated his *Le Cuisinier français* to his master, the marquis d'Uxelles with fulsome gratitude, stating that he had learned best of his craft under his patron's roof and to the satisfaction of 'a host of individuals of rank'.[25] The rules and ceremonies of behaviour, speech and appearance found their point of gravity at table. It was no surprise, then, that the nobility's assertion of itself as cultural actors and as leaders of taste increasingly converged on their kitchen and those who ran it.

If the word 'stiff' is anything to go by, we might take the measure of the importance that both prince and major domo had in the architecture of their etiquette in the example of Vatel. Vatel, the 'great Vatel' as he has come to be known, has now assumed something of mythic proportions in gastronomic annals. He was first the maître d'hôtel to Nicolas Fouquet, the disgraced former Superintendent of Finances best remembered as having built Vaux-le-Vicomte which would subsequently become the inspiration for Versailles. Having amassed for himself an enormous fortune from siphoning state revenue, Fouquet, with the stewardship of Vatel, presided over some of the most lavish banquets in the realm and by extension all Europe, leading to a fête for Louis XIV in 1661, which dangerous hitherto outdid the kind in pomp and grandeur. Vatel then moved to the services of the king's son-in-law the prince de Condé. Mme de Sévigné describes in her letters how one morning at 8 o'clock, aghast on receiving news that the fish for a state dinner had not been delivered, he knifed himself to death rather than withstand the disgrace.[26] And with such conditions came an increasing consciousness of table manners, the deportment of table, with 'table' as the metonym of all the ceremonies, codes and expectations surrounding eating in a decorous way.

It seems that those at the forefront of cookery and table – the combination of cooking itself and the entire staging of culinary events – had beaten tailors and couturiers to the post in the race for social mobility. Vatel's fate may seem a little ridiculous to us now – and it is hard to tell the degree to which de Sévigné is keeping amused astonishment in check – but it does reflect in the most dramatic terms the importance the higher serving staff drew from their patrons. While there is some degree of reciprocity to this, inasmuch as the patron drew prestige from the calibre of those in his employ he or she could attract, the standards of servility had a cult-like status, the affiliated house for which one served was the equivalent of what branding and celebrity is today. The tradition lives on today in celebrities hiring celebrity chefs as well as entertainers (comedians, musicians) to their private events, to designers being named upon the appearance of flavour-of-the-month celebrities at publicized events such as the Emmys, Oscars or the Met Gala. It is perhaps not surprising that the most fortunate, talented, loyal (and servile) were rewarded handsomely for their service. Paul Metzner notes how many of the cookbook writers had the ennobled 'de' before their name, and they all occupied senior household positions. They were educated and entitled themselves and may have been distant relatives of the minor nobility.[27]

If figures like Varenne, Bonnefons and Pierre de Lune begin to describe a genealogy of the celebrity chef, the chief forerunner to Carême was Vincent La Chapelle, who became enlisted as the chief kitchen steward of the court of Louis XV by Mme de Pompadour. La Chapelle had already made his name cooking for prominent court tables in London, Holland, Saxony and Portugal. While in London in 1733, La Chapelle began writing *The Modern Cook* while in the service of the Earl of Chesterfield. It would later become known under its French title, *Le Cuisiner moderne* (The Modern Cook) after it was expanded with two further volumes in the Netherlands, while in the service of the prince of Orange. La Chapelle's culinary treatise contained recipes and engravings of dishes, food arrangements and table settings. Le Cuisiner moderne is one of the books that would advocate the importance of 'nouvelle cuisine', effectively beginning a series of rebirths, new beginnings, and revisions, pattern of ostensible rejuvenation already familiar to the realm of fashion.

Although there was plenty of traditional hearty and rich fare, there were also recipes that were delicate and low in fat. It is credited with ushering in *nouvelle cuisine*, a break from the excessive eating toward a more considered, and restrained gastronomy in which quality and technique were at a premium. Occurring just before the circulation of much more modest illustrated flyers (*feuilletons*) on what represented desirable forms of dress for the day, La Chapelle's books were a lavish compendium of illustrations of food. His books are, in Dennis's words 'in some way foreshadow the vicarious pleasure offered by modern cookbooks, although the emphasis is obviously on the spectacle of luxury'. Or, we would add, that cookery magazines, which are usually accompanied with articles on interiors and filled with advertisements for gadgets and appliances, are just a 'bourgoisified' version of the same, reflecting desiring-images based on wealth and status. The effort that La Chapelle put into his work, and the attention it received was testament to the hold that French cuisine was beginning to have across Europe with travellers and prospective cooks gravitating to Paris, which by the early eighteenth century became the Rome of gastronomy.

While La Chapelle is more often cited in modern histories of gastronomy, there were other writers who vied for the attention in a market with a growing hunger for cookbooks and books about food. Most notably François Marin, writing under the nom de plume Menon, who began his career 1739 with a three-volume work, *Nouveau traité de la cuisine* (New Treatise on Cuisine), and is best known for his second book, *La Cuisinière bourgeoise* (The Bourgeois Cook, 1746). Menon would go on to write eight books, ending in 1786 with *La Science du maître d'hôtel confiseur* (The Science of the Pastry Chef). Menon had what we would today call a holistic approach to gastronomic practices of his day that went well beyond the preparation and presentation of food. Several of his titles make clear that action, strategy and deportment were just as important. His books were as much about ways of acting as they were about food itself, like style-guides for gastronomic mores and manners. For instance, in his *Nouveau traité*, there is a diagram showing the careful arrangement of dishes that are described in the course of the books. *La Science du maître d'hôtel cuisinier, avec des Observations sur la connaissance et la propriété des aliments* (The Science of the Food Chef, with Observations on Food Knowledge and Ownership) is self-explanatory, reflecting that food, eating and the culture of table was building its discrete taxonomy and codes that could be paralleled to rules of behaviour and appearance.

Just as the fashion system is established according to a principle that taste is something made available to everyone – what we might so far as call democratic – a recurrent theme in Menon's books is that food and cooking is a social mission that is on par with the arts as a safeguard of culture. In this regard, as Beatrice Fink observes, his views would echo Rousseau's views on the social contract, written shortly after.[28] As testament to their intellectual seriousness, the prefaces to such tomes were generally lengthy, using the model of a philosophical treatise. In *Le dons de Comus* (1739) Menon states that 'cooking, like the other arts . . . is perfect through the genius of the people, gaining in delicacy in the proportion to their decorousness'.[29] Uncannily this is a sentiment that would also chime with Winckelmann's influential thesis in *Geschichte der Kunst des Altertums* (History of Ancient Art) of 1764 in which he makes a corollary between the quality of a civilization and the quality of its art. The role of discriminative taste takes a prime role here, where the cultivation of one's gustatory sensibility would undeniably, as it was suggested, flow on into other matters such as the taste for clothing or art. There were also moral imperatives at stake here in both the burgeoning disciplines of gastronomy and in art history. Marin/Menon stipulated that he represented the triumph of 'modern cuisine' over 'old cuisine' presaging the rhetoric of decadence prevalent in the Revolution: 'Old cuisine is that which the French made fashionable all over Europe' whereas 'Modern cuisine, [is] built on the foundations of the old, but with less awkwardness and less apparatus, and with as much variety, is simpler, cleaner, and perhaps more scientific.'[30] In short, it is more frugal and calls for more skill. This means that it is ripe to become even more fashionable as it demands discernment on the part of both preparer and consumer, something to which we will shortly return in the rise of gastronomic criticism at the beginning of the next century.

The period of the early to mid-eighteenth century during which La Chapelle and Menon were penning their treatises (and organizing their illustrations) witnessed a distinctive rise in the volubility of public opinion about things cultural, well before art and gastronomical criticism would itself take shape with the likes of Diderot and Grimod. In his sweeping social history of art, Arnold Hauser remarks that the number of people interested in art for the sake of discussion over purchasing was already noticeable in the Salon of 1699, but by

> 1725 the *Mercure de France* already reports that an enormous public of every house and every age is to be seen in the Salon admiring, praising, criticizing, and finding fault. According to contemporary reports, the crowds are unprecedented, and even if most of them only want to be there because visiting Salons had become a fashion, nevertheless, the number of serious art lovers is also growing. That is indicated, first of all, by the mass of new art publications, art journals and reproductions.[31]

While this observation is focused on art, it would be naïve or obfuscating to consider this to be an isolated phenomenon. The Salon was an easy common rallying point, however what Hauser recounts is a steady rise in the volubility in discursive flows, of the right to opinion and the growing transactability of taste. This meant that people were not just looking, tasting, wearing, they were talking about it: weighing up, contesting, arguing.

As such, and because it appealed to the members of the middle classes that were rising in volubility, according to some accounts, *La Cuisinère bourgoise* was the most popular book of its kind in the latter half of the eighteenth century.[32] He was not the first to appeal to the middle classes, François Marin in a book contemporaneous with La Chapelle's, *Les dons de Comus: ou l'art de cuisine* (The Gifts of Comus, or, the Art of Cooking, 1739) advised that if the middle classes became more au fait about cooking and sourcing produce they too could eat in a grander style.[33] Although transposed into a somewhat eccentric philosophy of eating and well-being, traces of books such as these can be found in Rousseau's *Julie, or the New Héloïse* (1761), a highly influential book in its time. S. Wertz observes that 'Rousseau was one of the first novelists to elevate food to an important aspect of human life and living'.[34] Predating Rousseau's book by only a few years, in the updated preface (1758) to his *Dons*, Menon also preached temperance and forbearance. In the words of Beatrice Fink, 'the preface defends simple fare as a means of ensuring reasonableness in social behaviour and of checking the effects of conspicuous consumption'.[35] These were signs that the bourgeois table with a primacy on reasonableness was beginning to take hold. While a variety of writings to this end were increasingly in circulation, it was owing to Rousseau's writings that people developed a morality of food consumption that insisted on moderation and faithfulness to the essential characteristics of ingredients (as opposed to covering it with spices). 'Temperance of the senses by reason is Rousseau's view of health.'[36] Such directives against gluttony, flouting class privilege and the consciousness of excess and waste are still inherently with us in attitudes we have toward wastage in the present day – they are also pregnant in the pieties of food fads. What one consumed thus became more than a necessity, it became ideologically indicative not only of class but one's attitude to the body and to sociability. Rousseau also introduced consciousness of the different kinds of fare such as between urban and rural, as well as the importance of 'the communal bond that is present in family life and symbolized in the rituals of food and eating'.[37] Like fashion, food fell under the diffusion of luxury, as food rituals and practices became a reflection of taste and attitude.

The growth of the middle classes in the sixteenth century, who identified with one town and region or another, helped to nurture the symbiosis of signs of outward identity and gustatory tradition. It was food that was the most accessible and dynamic modulator of locality, and it would be food that would become the most powerful and pervasive expression of that locality's authenticity – a relationship that would reach high stakes in the great French wines which were inextricable from their unique *terroirs*. There had long been a tradition of naming dishes, sauces, and condiments in honour of the courtly patron, and as the acknowledgement of the importance of the cook rose, so the possibility of the lending a name to a 'signature dish', itself a new concept related to authorship and individuality. Although it did not originate with him, Rousseau nonetheless helped to encourage pride in the local produce and fare, lending impetus to the naming of food whence it originated or where it was popularized: *sauce Bordelaise*, *tripes Lyonnaise*, *salade Niçoise*. Carême, in his preface to his *Cuisiner parisien*, cites a far more extensive list as evidence of the superiority of French cuisine. It is a list long enough to suggest that a great family or a great town or city must be accompanied by a certified associated dish.[38]

As we know by now the rise of modern art and modern fashion cannot be viewed without considering the dialectical configuration of financial and discursive economies, as well as economies of self and society. The art of the eighteenth century was a significantly paired down version of the grand and tumultuous courtly art of the previous century, admitting in significant quantity art about sensibility (Greuze) and significantly bourgeois-inflected themes such as domestic genre scenes and still-life (Chardin). The court artist Boucher depicted fantasy village scenes with shepherds and shepherdesses, or intimate domestic scenes, many of which showed people sharing food or drink. Equally, what was incipient but still unheard of a century before, gastronomy began to jostle with the other arts, warranting not only recognition of its most eminent practitioners but now also its own history. The accelerating and widening recognition of the art of gustation prompted 1782 Pierre-Jean-Baptiste Le Grand d'Aussy to publish what is recognized at its first history *Histoire de la vie privé des français* (The History of French Private Life). As the title suggests, his intention was to write on the gamut of domestic life including interiors and clothing, but he became so interested in the section of food that it became all-consuming.

Cookbooks, to inclusion in philosophical novels, to social histories – all of this coalesce into a philosophical discourse of food. At the very same moments from the early to mid-eighteenth century onward, food discourse rose together with the rise of the fashion system. To be clear, by 'fashion system' we do not suppose that fashions were not in circulation before this time, but rather that fashion evolved into a discursive function that was not confined to class. While people were talking more freely about art, they were also arguing more persuasively about the clothes they were putting on their back and the food in their gullet. The popularity of Menon's books was as a result of middle-class consumers, while the fashion system implied that there was a market for fashion that had expanded significantly beyond the élite. One of the ways that Louis XIV had kept his courtiers in check was to burden their budgets with demands that they be sumptuously clad. While there were still items that discriminated between class and wealth, fashion was something more available, and more subject to a collective taste that involved the middle classes.

Critical gastronomy

While writings – and disputes – about food preparation, consumption and manners had gained momentum in the seventeenth century, it was only after the Revolution that the most comprehensive writings on gastronomy surfaced, in the form of the massive eight-volume work by Alexandre Balthazar Laurent Grimod de la Reynière, appropriately titled the *Almanach des gourmands*, published between 1803 and 1812. It would take Brillat-Savarin's *Physiologie du goût* a little over a decade later to establish the contours of gastronomic philosophy. Rather, the content of Grimod's almanac is more rambling, containing recipes and instruction, with the chief purpose of bringing the diner to a higher level of awareness in affairs of table. It is filled with anecdotes, jokes, asides, comic verse as well as more serious tracts of instruction. His position is clear: faced with the availability of good food and wine, and a panoply of other services and professions relating to food – from restaurants to farms to suppliers and shop-owners – there is something of a moral responsibility to the industry, and to the individual. Parkhurst Ferguson refers to his *Manuel des amphitryons* [Manual for Hosts], as a 'culinary "catechism"'.[39] Grimod exhorted that gastronomy be embraced as a discrete field of knowledge and activity, even suggesting that there should be professorships in the area in the lycées. Grimod styled himself very much as the prophet on the mount, boasting that he had never donned an apron. The public was responsive with some 22,000 copies being sold within the four years of the *Almanach*'s publication. The contributions of Grimod and those in his wake were decisive for making gastronomy what it is, for as Parkhurst Ferguson presciently states, despite the fact that 'writing anchors every cultural field, the transitory nature of culinary products renders the gastronomic field absolutely dependent on a textual base.'[40] Ushering in gastronomic 'literature', it would soon enter into literature, especially in the realist novel of the nineteenth-century as we will see in the following chapter.

It is from Grimod that we use the word *gourmand* and 'gourmet' today, which he had brazenly taken from 'gluttony,' the second of the Seven Deadly Sins. (At the time the 'friend' was typically sued for a food and wine connoisseur.) It contained the first accounts of wine tasting under the presiding attention of a 'jury des dégustateurs', as well as reports of the best restaurants to visit in Paris. It also contained gossip, tips on nutrition including aphrodisiacs and recommendations about kitchen utensils and devices. Beatrice Fink explains that

> [t]he *Almanach* and its companion piece the *Manuel des amphitryons* are at once a food-world source of information, practical guide, treatise on manners, and handy reference tool. The Almanack's gossip content and conversational style liken it to a gazette, its periodic nature to journalistic writing. More importantly, however, it creates a link between the world and word of food,

> thus inscribing cuisine and *savoir-manger* in *écriture* and poeticizing the gastronomic act. Animal and vegetable ingredients of dishes, ostentatious table trappings, and behind-the-scenes machinery are brought to life metaphorically and analogically. Imagery as ornate as period surtouts and pièces montées permeates the text, along with mythological and literary references. Protagonists of the host/guest ritual become three-dimensional in mini-dramas of social confrontation.[41]

This means that Grimod's work was decisive in bringing food consumption into the epicentre of sociability and the meaning of the newly socially-mobile classes. Fashioning a set of dos and don'ts for what was considered applicable and desirable. This said, it is also tinged with nostalgia and regret for the glory years of the ancient régime – the unstable economy after the Revolution, continued privations, the ongoing wars of the Revolution then Napoleon had left many misty-eyed for the past. Grimod showed that in food as in the world of clothing and manners, the intrinsic and the extrinsically specular were all intertwined. For instance, his *Manuel* details various rules of service, including the succession of dishes. Food was to be experienced, just as clothing worn, its alimentary characteristics were surpassed in the name of appearance and ritual. The road to pleasure was not a simple affair: it was governed by rules that served as a grammar of participation. Similarly, the fashion system developed through a set of codes that were then used for both conformity and divergence.

Grimod's *Almanach* and its ensuing anthology *Manuel des amphitryons* (1808) must be seen as a product of a number of convergent shifts in society which were not only economic and demographic – in terms of the availability of luxuries and the blossoming culture of consumption for the sake of status – but also philosophical and discursive. While Rousseau's influence and those of La Chapelle and Menon are clearly felt, Grimod's books can be compared with Diderot and D'Alembert's encyclopedia, except that he kept solo authorship. In this he was more like Samuel Johnson, who, while more systematic and ordered in his *Dictionary* (1755) seldom spared the reader an opportunity to have his own views felt over that of a consensual objectivity, a notion that was only coming into being at the time of the *Dictionary*'s publication.

What Grimod almost single-handedly helped to inaugurate is that the enjoyment of food no longer lay in the opinion of single courtly patron served by the skilled practitioner. Instead, it became the more intricate process that it is today with the discriminating and educated gastronome – the fashion expert – who mediated dynamically and with utmost sophistication between the skills of the cook on the one hand, and the tastes and desires of the public on the other.

2

GOOD TASTE IN THEORY AND PRACTICE: THE LANGUAGES OF SPECTACLE AND CONSUMPTION

The nineteenth century was the time when food and fashion gathered its language and entrenched themselves as fundamental to modern life. It is now a philosophical commonplace that the distribution of language reflects the priorities and practices within a given society. While occurring a little later in the century for fashion, by the mid-nineteenth century the names for foods, and the many things associated with them, had grown exponentially. Thanks to Grimod and Carême, followed by Brillat-Savarin and Fourier, food was no longer a simple matter of alimentation (*alimentation*), it was a practice at the epicentre to a civilized life. Afforded with its own discrete philosophy, gastronomy came with its own imperatives. These imperative straddled abstract notions as well as those related to codes of consumption and appearance. And while philosophy is also always prone to its fashions, the fact that the practices of food preparation, presentation and eating are social and material affairs, they were subject to far more widespread modes of debate. Fashion theory accords itself the value of being a material practice, while the same can be said of gastronomy, except of course according to different physiological conditions. In the nineteenth century, fashion and food became the fashion industry and the food industry, enlarging into separate but always interconnected, symbiotic worlds. This chapter traces the languages of food and fashion and how these coalesced at the end of the century into their own spectacles. Food and fashion formed the stage in which modern society in its transition from the old to the new played itself out, culminating in the Savoy restaurant, the Ritz and the Carlton. These luxury establishments were in many respects swansongs to the older age and entrée into the new. The Belle Époque is still looked on nostalgically as a time of lavish parties, flamboyant hostesses and a team of colourful personalities from the *grande monde* to the *demi-minde*. Grande cuisine as it came to be introduced at the beginning of the century coalesced into a le grand style. Its particular form of hedonism differed from all other times because it was built on spectacle and public consumption, food and fashion.

Gastronomy and *gastrosophy*: the culture of food

'Gastronomy', was a term that grew out of the Revolution to denote a level of finesse and culture, the art of alimentation as opposed to mere eating. The equivalent, arriving only a little earlier is fashion as opposed to dress or mere clothing. Both cases are modern terms born from free-market consumption. To be fashionable and to indulge oneself gastronomically presumes a culture of surplus-wealth as opposed to subsistence. Fashion is made to appear as opposed to clothe, and gastronomy is made for taste first, for sustenance second. Both cases speak to a system of signs whose values exist above and beyond material conditions.

Gastronomie originates in *Deipnosophistae* by Atenaeus which had been translated into French in 1623, but only enters into discourse at the beginning of the nineteenth century. Before Grimod's *Almanach des gourmands* (1803–1812) was the lengthy poem 'La gastronomie' by Joseph Berchoux from 1800, which went through several editions. Here Berchoux sets out gastronomy as its own individual art from, as announced in the opening dedication to a Mme Larcher-D'Arcy. He lists a number of arts in the figural sense such as 'the art of making great men' and 'the art of pleasing' what he says is missing from this list is 'the art of eating'. He 'addresses her' as 'a gastronomic poet' who will show her to 'dine *en artiste*/Which is to dine very delicately [*très légèremens*].'[1] The end of the second canto is an exhortation that belongs with such earlier treatises on culture and deportment as Castiglione's *Book of the Courtier*: 'To dine prosaically [*sand façon*] is a perfidy.'[2] The implication runs parallel to the alignment of morality and beauty in aesthetics of the same time. Here beauty of eating is encoded with a moral duty to one's well-being. Berchoux also pays dramatic lip service to the trend instigated by Rousseau and entrenched (Émile ate a simple vegetarian diet) by not denigrating the simple fare associated with the poor – which included cabbages, turnips, basic broths and bread with unrefined flour – and poking fun at examples of historic excess such as Nero's sybaritic behaviour, Trimalchio's Feast, as well as all the unspared delights of Apicius. Underlying all of this was drawing out the complex contours of refinement over mere consumption, that is gastronomy as opposed to *gourmandise*, or gluttony. Imperceptibly but not altogether successfully, the effort lay in jettisoning the old trappings of class privilege in favour of something acquired and learned, and better still, the product of innate talent. This period was, after all, the age of concept of genius. These were those who did not just have, they were the ones who knew, the connoisseur. But as we know about the historical tale since then until today, those who knew were nothing if they had not mixed with those who have.

As they coalesced throughout the nineteenth century, the connoisseurs (from the old French *conoistre*, 'to know') of art, fashion and food became recognizable figures of society, and pillars of what constituted the cultivated and the refined in a culture. They were those who judged and gauged how a culture modulated and represented itself according to appearance and consumption. In short, they were the commentators on taste, and together with the artists, haute couturiers and the haute cuisiniers themselves, the taste-makers. They began as journalists and critics, if they were not informed consumers of personal means (who could afford to bestow on themselves any title they wished), and in the following century, historians and theorists – fashion being a notable last in the list of creditable disciplines of serious study. In writing of the burgeoning of gastronomy in the early nineteenth century, Jane Levi comments that

> The gastronome became a recognizable and enduring figure of food-related expertise, bringing the gourmand into the modern age. The newly defined word marks some of the innovative ways that people were trying to think about food, as it embedded itself into the new society's ideas about fashion and taste. In this interpretation of the postrevolutionary period in France the idea of gastronomy fits into a general trend toward extending scientific thinking into multiple areas of the arts. Nineteenth-century gastronomy can thus be seen as a respectable, legitimate interest that came to represent what has been called the 'democratization' of an appreciation of fine food. It marks the increased accessibility to the bourgeoisie of ingredients, techniques, and information; evolving ideas about health and healthy eating; and new interpretations of good taste, hospitality, and manners.[3]

Levi explains how in the case of Charles Fourier these standards sought to reach philosophical proportions well exceeding those only adumbrated by Rousseau. Rather, Fourier countered what he believed to be the superficiality and aestheticism of Grimod and Brillat-Savarin, Fourier's cousin, by approaching attitudes to food in what in today's parlance would be called, holistic. To counter what he thought to be a limited experience and concept of gastronomy – mildly analogous to later evaluations of fashion as the 'feminine' trivialization of more serious masculine art – Fourier proposed the term 'gastrosophy' to embrace an understanding of food that took into account growth, procurement, exchange and distribution as well as preparation and consumption. He maintained that all categories of the aetiological art from the article of food itself to its consumption were mutually exclusive. This he contrasted with, say, Grimod, whose emphasis lay entirely in what was laid before him. For Fourier, for all its trappings, the notions of food set forward by Grimod was nothing but *gourmandise*, as it was all about sensory pleasure (remembering also that Grimod prided himself in never getting his fingers dirty), so retaining links to satisfying the most primitive instincts. In other words, Grimod's response to food was too dandified, and food required a sterner, more sober and far-reaching attitude. Instead, gastrosophy, was on a higher plane, and was a step to higher order of life, with political and religious overtones. As Parkhurst Ferguson affirms, '[s]eldom have the culinary and the social order more explicitly or more visibly tied and of greater moment than in Fourier's vision.' Despite his efforts to distance himself from them, what he did share with Grimod, Brillat-Savarin and even Carême was the desire 'to transcend the gross materiality of food, and, like them too, he was maniacally concerned with detail.' Further, as she succinctly advises, '[h]is gastronomical political economy endowed the proverbial land of milk and honey [France] with an elaborate, complex social organization grounded in visionary social science.'[4]

Fourier's ambitions for food to be 'read', as well as just consumed was consonant with many of the rising sociological discourses of his time, which insisted that modern life was a surface, or a complex of surfaces that, when subjected to the proper scrutiny, revealed hidden truths, not only of phenomenon of modernity itself, but one relating to the most primitive human instincts and most fundamental desires. He also anticipates the sexual binarization stigmatizing fashion, except with the distinction that the gastronome was primarily male. It was a blind spot that gastrosophy addressed, as Levi states, 'insisting that there be both male and female *gastosophes*.'[5] While gastronomy depended on knowledge, the knowledge of gastrosophy was more systematic and less prone to subjectivity and snobbery. In the words of Octavio Paz, 'in gastrosophy the number of combinations is infinite; pleasure, instead of tending toward concentration, tends to propagate and extend itself through taste and savouring.'[6] Fourier imagined an ideal society which he referred to as Harmony, where food approached in this holistic way played an integral part. But despite being seen as one of the pioneers of socialism, Harmony had its social divisions. The make-up of the middle-class table, for instance, was to a large part based on Menon's *La Cuisininière bourgeoise*.[7]

Once we have seen past some of these details and what we might now consider eccentricities, Fourier can be credited with being one of the chief forerunners to important food fashions that emphasize social welfare, and which placed food within a broad spectrum of production and consumption. Ecological sustainability is the most salient, which carries with it the sweeping moral imperatives instigated by Rousseau. Although it has been the gastronome who has survived over the *gastrosophe*, as Levi concludes:

In the twenty-first century, the gastronome can choose from multiple forms of expression, whether relishing backward-looking agrarian and artisanal ideas as preserved and promoted by groups such as Slow Food or futuristic techniques and creative presentation as developed by molecular gastronome, in both cases embracing elements of a nostalgia for a past that never was and projecting them into a possible utopian present.

We are not at all far off from the promises inherent to fashion of a better life and the possibility of alternative modes of being. It is always instructive to see how these prospective modes of being change over decades, or over just years, according to the pressures and myths of the historical present.

Brillat-Savarin and the elevation of the olfactory sense

If the gastronome outlived the *gastrosophe*, the name of Brillat-Savarin has well-outlived that of Fourier. Jean Anthelme Brillat-Savarin's *Physiologie du gout, ou meditations de gastronomie transcendante*, (The Physiology of Taste, or, Meditations on Transcendent Gastronomy) published in December 1825 just before his death, is something of a bible of gastronomy and the text that has helped it cement as a credo beyond that of an industry. As opposed to following a systematic logic, the book is a series of meditations and observations, including a dialogue and some axioms, following the tradition of essayists such as Montaigne or aphorists such as La Rochefoucauld, but also the great seventeenth-century sermonists Fénélon and Bossuet, and finally, Enlightenment *philosophes* such as Voltaire and Rousseau. Perhaps its most direct progenitor is the materialist philosopher Julien Offray de La Mettrie who wrote a series of books in acclaim of physiological pleasure: *La Volupté* (Sensuousness) in 1746, *Discours sur le bonheur* (Discourse on Pleasure) in 1751, and the *Art de jouir* (Art of Play; 'jouir' is also to ejaculate) in 1753, published two years after his death. What these texts share with Brillat-Savarin's treatise are, according to Fabrice Teulon, models for 'an economy of enjoyment [*jouissance*] based on the celebration of the senses and of the desiring body.'[8] Both suggest that a detailed, nuanced and systematic/'scientific' attention to one's sensuous fibre was of benefit to one's heath and moral well-being.[9]

Brillat-Savarin's *Physiology of Taste*, which has never been out of print, exists as two volumes, that begin with a series of gnomic statements, many of which have stayed with us, such as: 'Tell me what you eat: I'll tell you what you are.'[10] And: 'Table is the only place where one is never bored in the first hour.'[11] Born in 1755, he was very much a child of the eighteenth century, but given the late date of his book's publication, his influence was sedimented in the next. As Judith

Pike remarks: 'Brillat-Savarin's mythologizing of French cooking into the art of taste came about during a period when food was inextricably linked with nationalism and cultural identity.'[12] Between Carême before him and Escoffier after him, Brillat-Savarin is a kind of point of anchorage that keeps gastronomy firmly located in and as French before all else. Even in the global age, were practices are highly diversified and dispersed, eclecticism jostles with tradition, French-ness and food is still a tenacious combination where idea and reality are caught up with one another so as to be beyond reason. The very same is to be said of fashion.

Even if the Brillat-Savarin's tract is not systematic – how could it when dealing the olfactory senses? – it is extensive, and thorough, to the end of instituting gastronomy as a 'science' in its own right. 'Science' at the time holds a different meaning from now and can be interpreted a s afield worthy of serious and ongoing study whose semantics and relevance are well beyond those of the practicalities of eating itself. A magistrate, he also studied chemistry and medicine at the university of Dijon, which suggests that he subjected the empirical and justifiable to the practices of gustatory pleasure and taste. His background also helps to explain his many views which read like protocols and a call to order. 'the most indispensable quality of a cook is exactitude; it is must also be that of the guest.'[13]

The first volume is structured according to predictable themes beginning with meditations on 'the Senses', and covering appetite and thirst. By the end, with the meditation 'The Pleasure of Table', one begins to sense that Brillat-Savarin's ambitions are toward a metaphysics of gastronomic taste, which may first seem to be a contradiction in terms. This is because Brillat-Savarin is continually faced with the role of food in any living creature, and what food, with all its combination and mediation, has come to mean for humans. It is the food that we make and that we share and enjoy that is a vital constituent in our humanity. In this regard Brillat-Savarin's discussions are an intricate exploration of desire in relation to our physiology. That is its 'scientific' mission, prompting Luke Bouvier to observe that despite

> the 'scientific' or systematizing nature of such writing—its propensity for authoritative rule- making, for rationality, limits and propriety, its 'civilizing' properties in regulating the pleasures of the table—it also remains unavoidably a discourse of desire (and not just about desire), no matter how much the 'scientific' aspects attempt to master rationalize such desire, channel it into well-ordered economies, or even overcome altogether. This duality of 'science' and desire that characterizes gastronomic course is ultimately traceable to the underlying dualities of orality, which gastronomy so prominently mobilizes in its two interrelated forms: the orality of food and the orality of words.[14]

Such divisions or ambivalences prove to pervade Brillat-Savarin's work, which mirror our own ontology as living, sentient beings. Gastronomy as he highlights it brings us inexorably close to the connection and difference between physical experience and signification: a piece of bread can satisfy hunger and it can also elicit pleasure and fulfil desire. It can do so because it is especially good bread, but even when not, it may still give us pleasure. The difference in pleasures is of course impossible to quantify. But it comes closer when the ceremonies of table are observed and consensually shared, with consensus being the linchpin to any language of interaction.

In his explanation of the '[d]ifference between the pleasure of eating and the pleasure of table', Brillat-Savarin states that the former is a sensation that is 'actual' and 'direct' which we share with animals. Whereas by contrast, the 'pleasure of table is the reflected sensation that engenders the diverse circumstances of facts, places, things, and people that accompany a meal.' Further: 'The pleasure of eating involves, if not hunger, then at least appetite; the pleasure of table is more often independent of one from the other.'[15] The second volume is an even broader examination of the circumstances surrounding eating, which is treated less as a practice and more as a reflective experience: meditation 18: 'On Sleep', meditation 19: 'On Dreams', meditation 25: 'On Exhaustion', meditation 26: 'On Death', meditation 27: 'A Philosophical History of Cuisine'. It is telling that the final meditation, 30, is 'Bouquet'. This is a poetic meditation in every sense of the word, telling of an imaginary gathering of priests belonging to the cult of 'Gastéréa . . . the tenth muse [who] presides over the pleasures of taste.'[16] They prepare for a magnificent feast, attended 'kings and princes and Illustrious foreigners arriving for it from all over the world.' They have assembled 'to instruct in the great art of good eating, a difficult art, and of which the greater public still remain ignorant.'[17] What follows is a hallucinatory and sumptuously bounteous festivity:

> There, one finds, with bounty [*avec avantage*], everything that nature in its prodigality, has created for human sustenance. These treasures are centupled, not only by their association, but more still for the transformations that art has subjected them to. This enchantment has brought has united two worlds, confounded the realms, and closed the distance; the perfume that rises in these august preparations embalms the air and fills it with excitatory gaseous.[18]

The revelries conclude with the assembly disbanding with the satisfaction that they have begun the year with 'happy auspices'.[19] Thus, Brillat-Savarin avoids ending on a didactic note but on the contrary with lightness and joy in manner that makes the most of what is ineffable and abstract.

What ought we to make of this? Let us first digress. Our book, *Fashion Installation: Body, Space and Performance*, centres on the myriad space in which fashion has been situated since the Great Exhibition of 1851, which coincides roughly with the birth of haute couture, to fashion boutiques, fashion parades and launches. Apart from its grounding in history, the book's philosophical trajectory is to ask, 'Where does fashion occur? Where *is* fashion?' The apparently obvious answer would seem to be that fashion occurs in the garment 'itself'. However, the answer is perhaps less banal and more intriguing and enticing. Against the dominant, and doctrinaire position that fashion is an embodied practice, we contend that this is not the case, or rather the concept of embodiment falls short of the mark. Fashion occurs in the air, the atmosphere, as the nimbus of desire. We conclude on a note that chimes in spirit with the ending meditation of Brillat-Savarin:

> While fashion will always be associated with clothing, perhaps the quintessence of fashion is perfume, the 'air' that surrounds it, the blooms of seduction and desire that evoke and promise. Perfume either requires a body to wear it, or a person to smell it. It is always transient, but because the response to it is through the olfactory nerves, its effects can be the deepest, most sensorially visceral.[20]

The air and the atmosphere are the thresholds of the ineffable, where the excess that is fashion is encountered. Fashion involves clothing and dress, but clothing and dress does not always denote fashion which is what exists perceptually above and beyond them.

Of the many odd and eccentric establishments that sprouted up during and after the Revolution, one may have been on Brillat-Savarin's mind. These were the Frascati garden between the Boulevard Montmartre and the rue de Richelieu, which became famous under the management of a Neapolitan ice-maker by the name of Garchi. In the midst of the garden, pleasantly full of trees, stood a richly decorated building. In 1810 a guidebook, the *Nouveau Parisien* offers an idyllic description the kind of which would have captivated Brillat-Savarin:

> M. Garchi, famous for his ices, has decorated this house with the utmost elegance. It possesses a garden and pavement along the Boulevard. It is one of the most delightful spots in all Paris. The flowers, the scents, the lights, the charming women, the fashions, the dresses, all combine to make pleasure at which it is easy to imagine oneself at a fest of Venus. Frascati is the temple of frivolity, and to be in the swim one must visit it.[21]

It is easy to imagine oneself at a feast of Venus. Until the age of subcultural style was it not the ambition of boutiques since the House of Worth? This was all far beyond being a setting for an enjoyment of ice cream, it was a temple for a secular transcendental experience. In this G-rated brothel, ice cream was but a vehicle for a far more sensuous experience for which ingesting a pleasant substance was a catalyst, or a mere excuse.

Similarly, Brillat-Savarin makes a clear distinction at a very early stage of his discourses between satisfying the appetite and the pleasures of gustation. (We might also extend the metaphor with a prosaic fact that one is more conscious of the clothing one wears at times of staged gustation.) Barthes, in his celebrated essay on Brillat-Savarin elaborates on this first by alluding to his contemporary de Sade, and the practice of perversion which isolates the role of gratuitous gratification 'with no intention of procreation'. Sex and gustation have long been linked because of their relationship between sensory appetite and pleasure. The pleasure that is at the forefront of Brillat-Savarin's mind is well outside that of satisfying an appetitive need. True, one needs to procreate as one needs to eat but there is another order above this which is one hallmarked by excess. It is a celebration and refinement of excess that Barthes sees as amplified by the bourgeoisie's rising confidence and sense of itself. Brillat-Savarin is writing when 'the bourgeoisie knew no social culpability.'[22] This is where to settle for the simple satisfaction of gustation is to settle for too little and, worse, is to show indiscriminate ignorance of what culture (and industry) can afford. The modern (bourgeois) individual therefore

> must bring on stage, so to speak, the *luxury* of desire, erotic or gastronomic: an enigmatic, useless supplement, the desired food—the kind that B.-S. describes—is an unconditional waste or loss, a kind of ethnographic ceremony by which man celebrates hi power, his freedom to consume his energy for 'nothing.'[23]

Hence,

> [t]he question, however, remains unbroached as to why the social subject (at least in our societies) must assume *sexual* perversion in a crude, fierce, 'criminal' style, as the purest of transgressions, while *gastronomic* perversion, as described by B.-S. (and on the whole it can hardly be described better), always implies a kind of affable and accommodating acknowledgment which never departs from the tone of *good breeding*.[24]

These remarks essentially underscore much of what will be traversed in the rest of this book: the agonistic relation between luxury and good taste, the constant and dynamic intersection between gastronomy, desire and appearances, the 'ceremonializing' of culture and cultivation. Most of all – how all of these qualities are not vulgarly reducible to brute things, but rather reside in those who perform who are also those consume and appreciate, or who consort and interact with those who do, with those 'who know'.

Balzac and Brillat-Savarin: tastes, sights and moods

Balzac was drawn to Brillat-Savarin at a very early stage in his career, to such an extent that it inspired him to write *Physiologie du marriage, ou meditations de philosophie éclectique* (Physiology of Marriage, or Meditations on Eclectic Philosophy) which was published in 1829, only four years after the *Pysiologie du gout*. Balzac's preoccupations with food, encouraged by Brillat-Savarain and explored in rich detail throughout the *Comédie humaine* and other writings, were diverse. For food reaches not only into the realms of social interaction and enjoyment, but in Balzac becomes a basic barometer where taste and class meet. Where illusions, deceptions and dissemblance's lead to the perceptions of good taste and good breeding. Granting the individual merits and popularity of Brillat-Savarin's text, it is nonetheless safe to assert that its influence was bolstered all the more by Balzac's quick embrace of it, making of gastronomy something of a literary fashion among writers. The Brillat–Balzac connection, Philippe Dubois relates, 'launches a fashion where each [writer] essays his [sic] own small physiology, through to the Goncourt brothers who in the same vein published *La Lorette* in 1853.'[25] Moreover, Balzac measured gustatory pleasure against sexual pleasure, as a form of indulgence that was a means of augmenting feelings of agency and power.[26] If this is to be considered in greater depth, Balzac introduces the consumption and pleasure taken in food as something close to the nineteenth-century principles of using clothes to augment agency. The active appreciation of food, as with fashion, can remove inhibitions and take to places that, perhaps, in an earlier time, were far harder if not impossible to reach. As respective but complementary 'physiologies', the transformations are more chemical than just chimerical.

Perhaps the most famous statement to arise from Balzac *Physiology of Marriage* is the declaration: '*flânerie* is a science: it's the gastronomy of the eye.'[27] One ingests what one sees and rolls the sights and sounds as one would savour food in the mouth. Elsewhere Balzac takes up the binaries alive in Brillat-Savarin's conception of eating to sheds light on love, but with a slight twist, for the arts of love is one of elaborate ruses, deceptions and appearances – hence gastronomy:

> A piece of brown bread and a jug of water are right for the hunger of everyone; but our civilization has created gastronomy.
>
> Love has its piece of bread, but it also has the art of love, which we call coquetry, a charming word that only exists in France, where that science was born.[28]

In another, later entry, Balzac refers to gastronomy as 'an ecumenical discipline'.[29] In the first entry, in which flânerie is called 'the gastronomy of the eye', Balzac goes on to explain that: '*Flâner* is to play, to gather the qualities of the spirit, to admire the sublime tableaux of sadness, love and joy, portraits gracious or grotesque; it is to look into the depths of thousands of lives: to be young is to want and possess everything; to be an old man is to live the life of the young, to be married to their passions.'

The analogy of the eye devouring a myriad number of people for appraisal is an enactment of a form of consumption that is eminently modern. *Flânerie* and the figure of the *flâneur* would become immortalized by Charles Baudelaire in his 'Painter of Modern Life' (1863), the roaming, free-wheeler who takes in the sights of modern life. He would assess the appearances of passers-by, in a kind of urban odyssey of the mind. Inevitably, the 'gastronomy' in which the *flaneur* partakes, is that of the fashions that people wear. Baudelaire comments on the tantalizing effect of the generic black frock coat on men, which allows for scant differentiation between classes. When it comes to women, he asks:

> Which poet would dare, in the painting of pleasure instigated by the apparition of beauty, separate a woman from her costume? Who is the man who, on the street, in the theatre, in the forest, has not taken pleasure, in a most disinterested way, an expertly composed *toilette*, and did not take away with them an image inseparable from the beauty of the one to which it belonged, thus making the two, the woman and the dress, an inseparable whole?[30]

Baudelaire continues that such reflections return to 'certain questions relating to fashion and appearance' that trump 'the inept calumnies' of 'dubious' (*très-équivoques*) 'lovers of nature', in other words those suspicious of mediations of non-mediation.[31] What unites Balzac's with Baudelaire's *flâneur* is the trust in the senses over the truth. It is what is wrought in the imagination of what the *flaneur* encounters. The 'gastronomy' of this encounter was conscious of the care taken to construct for the sake of the richest and most lasting result. Fashion is essential because it is always about playing a part and making an impression. Bearing in mind that the good gastronome in Brillat-Savarin's conception favours quality over quantity, the modern *flaneur*, while a virtual consumer, is one who savours the best sights for inner contemplation or to turn them into poetry or art.

Balzac, who effectively launched his career with the *Physiologie du marriage,* together with *Le Dernier Chouan* (The Last Chouan), both in 1829, followed a year later with his *Traité de la vie élégante* (Treatise on the Elegant Life), which first appeared serialized in the magazine *La Mode* between October and November. It is a book that is in many ways tempered by the July Revolution, and the immediate time leading up to it, the revolution that toppled the last Bourbon king, Charles X, ushering in the 'bourgeois kind' Louis-Philippe. Although it is generally cast aside by Balzac scholars as something of a frippery, it was later inserted as part of a trilogy of treatises that Balzac wanted to comprise his 'Pathologie de la vie sociale' (Pathology of Social Life). In his treatise on fashion and manners he proposes a set of changes that precipitated the July Revolution. He suggests that dining attained its luxurious height during the reign of Louis XV in which it was the province of only a select few, while in his own day the pleasure of table amounted to two thousand times as many.[32]

As Hiroshi Matsumara points out, the place of germination for his treatise on fashion and manners germinated in an article devoted solely to the theme of table, which appeared in *la Mode*, several months earlier in May 1830, the 'Nouvelle théorie du déjeuner' (The New Theory of Dining). '*Déjeuner*' which is presently the verb and the noun for 'lunch', in the nineteenth century referred to the meal before midday, the 'repas léger du matin' [light morning meal], therefore more akin to what '*petit déjeuner*', 'breakfast' is today. Balzac suggests that to be in fashion is to preside of a certain kind of morning repast: 'The *déjeuner* is thus to be found today amongst disciples of FASHION [in English].'[33] It takes into account that 'in the life of the fashionable there is a sort of horror for the food bowl [*bol alimentaire*], a horror for the rest ends at six in the evening.' One must eat without having 'dined' per se. 'A *fashionable* [written as such] will have eaten, but without the right to say, 'I have had *déjeuner*.' He will have simply *taken something*, a trifle.'[34] The piece is perhaps a trifle ('*un rien*', a nothing), except for the fact that it shows the attention that Balzac placed in fashion and food, which is reflected in work to come. Further, because Balzac believed himself to be an effective social barometer, it does indicate, albeit in the most throwaway terms, how the bourgeoisie who were gradually toppling the old orders of the nobility, were fiercely aware of the habits of protocol and their role in both replicating and reshaping them. Through the lens of Brillat-Savarain and Balzac, Matsumma cites a number of factors that eventuated into the modern, bourgeois table which included the creation of standard eating times together with the rise of cafés and restaurants that lined the long boulevards that opened up in the middle of the nineteenth century.[35] Thus the restaurant becomes the forerunner of the fashion boutique, where places of eating and gathering are measured according to their fashionability and the need to be seen in them. The café and the restaurants were essential elements, rituals of visibility that the boulevards helped to encourage, and which was so abundant and celebrated in the Realists and Impressionist painting of the time.

A curious but not-so-often noted detail is that in many ways gastronomic themes bookend Balzac's writing career, from the earliest writings as we have just scene, through to his final novel, *Cousin Pons*. Gastronomy, or more precisely gastrolatry – food kept in disproportionate, idolatrous, esteem – is the character Pons' big weakness. He has delicate tastes and is the lover of fine things, especially rare antiques and fine food. He is defrauded of his antiques by some of his relatives, causing him to find consolation in food. Parkhurst Ferguson comments that, by setting gastronomy within tragic contours,

> Balzac broke with philosophical tradition that restricted expression of the baser tastes—touch, smell, and especially taste—to base-born characters and to the baser genre of comedy. Balzac's reinterpretation of the literary mode for such expression expanded and strengthened the connections between literature and gastronomy and, hence, between the gastronomic and literary fields.[36]

The valorization of a broader range of the senses will be briefly taken up again in the next chapter with the example of Baudelaire, for whom observation, especially as typified by the *flaneur*, was commensurate with material consumption, where sights, sounds and smells were all but devoured. If interpreting them was important, equally important was the immersion and participation in them. Just as clothing could be used by his characters to deceive, to seduce, or to dissemble (from Rastignac to Reupembré), in Balzac food is a fecund agent of more than sustenance: it provides a site of transaction, of retribution, assimilation, even intimidation along lines of class and knowledge.

Naming food and fashion

Among the characteristics of his many efforts to establish Gastronomy as a 'science', Brillat-Savarin goes into lengthy digressions that often entailed the coinage of neologisms, as if objectivity lay in such mystification. As Barthes observes, the neologisms are a reflection of Brillat-Savarin's love of language (Brillat-Savarin himself likes to point out to his reader that he knew five) where, in the need to dissect the nature of gastronomy, language ends up dissecting itself, or proliferating into multiple directions. Brillat-Savarin, as Barthes states,

> comes up with an astonishing classification of the tongue's movements as it participates in manducation: there are, among other oddly learned words, *spication* (when the tongue takes the shape of a stalk of wheat) and *verrition* (when it sweeps). A twofold delight? B.-S. becomes a linguist, he deals with food the way a phonetician would (and subsequently will) deal with vocality . . .[37]

Brillat-Savarin's writing is, in the words of Bouvier, 'a self-displacing discourse that proves incapable of mastering its own desire for language.' Ultimately, 'as with so much gastronomic writing, it is the irresistibility of storytelling that finally gains the upper hand.'[38]

Well before Brillat-Savarin's linguistic conceits, since at least the sixteenth century and the explosion of trade, foods and dishes have been subjected to a relentless campaign of colonization through the ownership that names bestow.

Names and their real or fabricated genesis are everywhere, many of whose links have been severed over time, from Eggs Benedict to mayonnaise. The former is supposed to have originated in a Wall Street stockbroker, Lemuel Benedict who in 1894 at the Waldorf Hotel ordered a breakfast combination as a cure for his hangover. Mayonnaise, which sounds French, whereas actually originated in Spain: in 1756, the duke de Richelieu took the port of Mahon and invaded Menorca, and his cook took his inspiration from the local fare, popularizing it back in Paris.

One does not need to look very far to see that the rise of any lasting discourse is wedded to rhetoric and obfuscation. If we leave out the tortured – literally and figuratively – rise of science itself since the Copernican Revolution, we could assert that it is in food, fashion and manners that misdirection and misattribution are built into their very evolution. This is evident when we consider the powerful and seductive hold that the attribution and possession have over the public and national consciousness: paprika did not originate in Hungary, and tulips are not indigenous to Holland. Similarly, Chanel did not invent the little black dress, it was Patou, but that does not deter anyone from giving her the credit. Meanwhile, the credit that Paul Poiret gets for flowing harem pants is not apocryphal but by his own gift for self-promotion. He simply rebadged and made more exotic the bloomer that had been about for over twenty years before, making what had been formerly branded as reactionary as desirable. What is more, he is cited as freeing women's bodies from corsets, but this also lives on as just freeing women's bodies. It takes reading more of the fine print to give the bloomerists and suffragettes their due. The reason for all of this is not that false or displaced attribution is a mistake ossified by time into a truth, but rather it is much more to do with marketing (at which Chanel was an adept). and thereby the making-familiar of an idea over idea and by dint of proliferation and quantity. The juicier story tends to win out over the drab one.

Fundamental to this ownership is dynamic of *representation*. The separation – tenuous to be sure, but unassailably present – between thing and quality is found in the discourses of fashion and gastronomy at the end of the eighteenth century, where fashion becomes distinct from clothes and gastronomy from food. In *The Fashion System* Roland Barthes relates that '[t]he description of a garment (i.e. the signifier of the vestimentary code) may be the site of a rhetorical connotation.' In this context, the imbrication of 'matter and language' Barthes terms 'poetic'.[39] Thus 'there is a poetic mutation as soon as we shift from real function to spectacle, even when this spectacle disguises itself under the appearance of the function.'[40] This may take its appearance in recourse to what Barthes asserts are inevitably poor literary allusions ('*petticoats—creamy and dreamy*'),[41] or with diachronic relationships: 'certain species clothing function as old signifieds "fossilized" into signifiers (*sport shirt*, *Richelieu shoes*): the mixed adjective often represents the initial stage of this process, the fragile moment when the signified is going to "take", to solidify into a signifier.'[42] It is in this process that fashion is a process whereby the garment is 'constructed', not in the physical but in the denotive, semantic realm.[43] Barthes outlines four kinds of themes around which this denotation takes place:

> nature (*flower-dress, cloud-dress, hats in bloom,* etc.); geography, acculturated under the theme of the exotic (*a Russian blouse, Cherkessk ornaments, a samurai tunic, pagoda sleeve, toreador tie, California shirt, Greek summer tints*); history, which primarily provides models for an entire ensemble ('lines, as opposed to geography, which supplies 'details" (*Fashion 1900, a 1916 flavor, Empire libe*); and last, art (painting, sculpture, literature, film), the richest of inspirational themes, marked in the rhetoric of Fashion by total eclecticism, provided the references themselves are familiar (*the new Tangara line, Watteau's déshabillés, Picasso colors*).[44]

By this stage it is perhaps no longer necessary to say that the resemblance to the way food is named is uncannily similar, or more, almost completely symmetrical with the model proposed here. What is distinctive is the oscillation, between specificity and arbitrariness, and yet it is in the naming and the repetition that value and identity is conferred.

As to be expected the codes relating to food names were passed down according to the codes of ownership and power. Foods were named according to region (in Barthes' topology, this relates to geography), or a distant place (exotic), to a moment in history, or in dedication to a personage which could be someone who owned the land from which the food came or was a patron of the cook, or it could be a special cultural dedicatee (art) such as 'Peach Melba', named after the famous soprano. 'Poetic' descriptors for food have proved to be more lasting and arguably not as kitschy as their sartorial counterparts. Eggs *à la neige*, for example, is an evocative analogy for egg whites whipped until 'stiff', resembling the whiteness and softness of clumps of powdery snow.

Regionality, or the consciousness of regionality, only comes to the fore at the end of the Middle Ages. (What was considered desirable for health and for pleasure has undergone several changes since then. For instance, in the court of Henry VIII, known for its gustatory feats, sugar played a central part in one or more of the procession of courses, since at the time it was a highly precious and valued commodity. It is also speculated that the court was almost permanently inebriated.) Cuisine, especially French, is stamped with regional registers, if the dishes no longer resemble what they were, or the exact link has been severed. For example: *tarte bourbonnoise, brouet de Savoie, sauce cameline à la façon de Tournai*. Italian food which developed in the earlier days of the courtly life of the Renaissance, is also richly stamped with regional registers: *alla bolognese*, *alla milanese*, *alla Fiorentina* are all add-on phrases known to anyone who has visited an Italian restaurant anywhere in the world, and it is just as telling that while the terms are familiar, the foods to which they are tacked on to are less so. In attribution and description, the list is potentially endless, and to this day, always evolving on the level of both the name and the dish. The famous combination *à la Provençal* that is garlic, olive oil and tomatoes is much more tenuous, although it carries an air of being steeped in tradition. Yet in the fourteenth and fifteenth century, the peasant Provençal diet was cabbage and may also have included lettuce, leeks, spinach and beans. For all accounts, the 'regionality' of what we now call Provençal cooking owes much to the vegetables from the Americas. As Jean-Robert Pitte explains: 'That is so with regard to green peppers and *piperade*, foie gras and corn, cassoulet and beans, *gratin dauphinois* or *potée* and potatoes. This phenomenon is identical in foreign countries: what would Italian cooking be without the tomato?'[45]

To return to Peach Melba. This was a creation of the great French chef, Auguste Escoffier dated at 1892 on the occasion of a special soirée at the Savoy Hotel in London to celebrate Nellie Melba who was then performing in Wagner's opera, *Lohengrin* at Covent Garden. Escoffier pride himself in catering to his female clientele with daintier dishes, and there is a long list of them that are named in their honour. (Once when asked about the secret to his craft, he replied rakishly: 'Madame, my success comes from the fact that my best dishes were created for ladies.')[46] Although perhaps one of the better known to us today, it was a far cry from an exception for Escoffier who was not only an inventor of foods but a shrewd inventor of names. (The list of 'ladies' to which Escoffier paid homage include the who's-who of actresses of the time: Réjane, Rachel, Mary Carden, Adelina Patti, Yvette, Sarah Bernhardt and more.)[47] Naming dishes after individuals of note had been in vogue since the seventeenth century. It was an honorific process that registered mastery and patronage, such as Sauce Soubise, however in Napoleon's time dishes were named after politicians or military victories, such as Chicken Marengo.[48]

But it was Escoffier who excelled in adaptation. In alignment with the tradition of invention, revision and adjustment set in train by Worth, Escoffier developed, improved or updated recipes from the great chefs before him, primarily Carême. If Escoffier can claim the lion's share of credit as a baptizer of dishes – not only for their quality but for sheer quantity – one of his most formidable predecessors in this trend was Adolphe Dugléré who was born in 1805 and worked until 1848 for the Baron de Rothschild, and at the age of sixty-two in 1867 became chef at the Café Anglais, and it is under his stewardship that the restaurant became famous.[49] By the 1860s, the Café Anglais as Andrieu relates, 'was the resort of artists, society lions, dandies and fashionable women – all, in short who sought to be in the mode.'[50]

In the year Dugléré began at the Café Anglais, a banquet was held for the Tsar, the king of Prussia and Otto van Bismark in which all the dishes had the names of statesmen, diplomats and heads of state, both living and dead.[51] As Pitte points out, the International Exposition, under Dugléré's direction, did much to raise this restaurant to one of international standing. Although he never wrote a book, he had a keen sense of glamourous and fashionable clientele, making the latter approach perhaps more *de riguer* than the former. As a result, to quote Pitte,

> [t]he most famous recipes in his register resulted from a publicity exchange with the establishment's best clients, who belonged to the worlds of fashion, art, finance and politics: *pommes Anna* was dedicated to Anna Deslions, the prostitute; *potage Germiny* to the Count of Germany, officer of the Banque de France; *poularde Albufeira* to Marshall Suchet, duke of Albufeira—this was a recipe that Carême dedicated to him, not to forget himself, *barbue Dugléré*. No chef today would dare dedicate a dish to himself, despite the temptation probably felt by some of them.[52]

No matter, we have branding and product lines for that. Chefs may occasionally indulge in this practice, but it is in dedication also to the time when it was more in vogue. For while in the Second Empire with the growth of haute couture, which quoted painting and where gowns became associated with wearer, food too had become a dedicatory art, shamelessly feeding off the importance of its patrons to nourish its own growing status as an art.

Meanwhile Escoffier, in the sumptuous surroundings of the Savoy in the early 1890s, was regularly charged with making a suite of new dishes for special parties. One such, for a group of Englishmen to celebrate a huge win in the casino in Monte Carlo included dishes such as: *Selle d'agneau de Galles aux tomates à la Provençale* (saddle of Wales lamb with tomatoes *à la* Provençale) *Sauce souveraine au suc de pommes d'amour* (sovereign sauce with the juice of love apples), *Salade de coeurs de laitue rouge des Alpes* (salad of red lettuce hearts of the alps), and *Asperges nouvelles sauce 'Coucher de soleil par un beau soir d'été'* (young asparagus with a 'sunset on a beautiful summer's evening' sauce).[53] The lumpy English translation give further indication of the extent of poetic licence being employed. For a famous multi-course banquet for which the diners paid the then astronomical sum of £15 a head, dishes included: *Laitances de carpes à la Luucullus* (carp milt *à la Lucullus*), *Timbale d'écrevisses Nantua* (crayfish timbale Nantua), *Poularde royale* (chicken royale – roast chicken with foie gras and truffles), *Aspegerges Argenteuil* (Argenteuil asparagus – purple asparagus), *Nageoires de tortue à l'Americaine* (Turtle fins in the American style), *Comtesse Marie* (Countess Marie – vanilla ice cream in strawberry ice), and *Gâteau regent* (Cake of the Regent – chestnut cake). Against all of this verbal fanfare, other more descriptive listings (such as *Mousseline d'ananas dans son fruit* – banana mousseline with fruit) would have sounded jarringly prosaic by comparison.[54] These are citable highlights, but not, as one would expect, isolated cases. Laurence Senelick draws attention to the 'cookbook published by Delmonico's chef in 1895 [that] teems with dishes named after Adelina Patti, Rachel, Arthur Sullivan, Ristori, Judic, Verdi, Meyerbeer, and many others. Hit shows were similarly treated – cold Eggs Frou-Frou, Mikado soup, even *noisettes* of roebuck Valkyrie.'[55] Without doubt, the kitchen had transitioned from halls of state to the theatre.

Escoffier, who struck up an amicable connection with the celebrated writer Émile Zola when he came to stay in the Savoy, had always had a natural penchant for verbal embellishments. Luke Barr reports that in his earliest restaurant days while working in his uncle's Restaurant François in Nice, it was a talent that was quickly harnessed in writing the menus. As he himself comments: 'I started looking for words that sounded gentle and pleasing to the ear while expressing a connection with the food being proposed. All well-presented menus should be evocative and increase the desire to partake of a skilfully prepared and presented meal.'[56] Barr asserts that for Escoffier a 'menu was a kind of poem . . . a poem of anticipation.' The invention of names mirrored the excitement of a new dish's creation. As Barr relates,

> Escoffier invented something new and *named* it: *La timbale Grimaldi*, *les filets de sole Walewska*, *les cailles Carmen*, *la poularde Adelina Patti* . . . Starting in the mid-1880s at the Grand Hotel in Monte Carlo, he's begun naming many of his culinary inventions for aristocratic and historic literary figures, but he soon found that flattering his contemporary celebrity guests in this way was a brilliant kind of advertising. A dish named for an opera star, after all, attached that star's glamour to the recipe prepared in his or her honour, and to the restaurant, too.[57]

Escoffier had the entrepreneur's instinct for branding, a process that confers prestige reciprocally, like a circuit: the idea of the thing as ideal and its zone of association, person or place. Both benefit from one another. Indeed, outside of the most savvy opera enthusiast, the once great soprano is now remembered for the desert, not the singing, while a Caesar salad is most probably thought of as having some lost reference to the great conqueror as opposed to Caesar's Palace in las Vegas, where it originated.

Thus, in his inexhaustible capacity for conjuring names, Escoffier seemed most at home with Barthes' third register in fashion-naming, being art and culture, except the names were tipped far more to status and celebrity. If oriented toward geography it was an allusion to something unverifiable and remote, luxurious, or grand, as in a work of architecture or natural phenomenon, like a landscape or mountain. This tendency to conjure through naming lives on not as much in gastronomy or clothing, but in what joins them, namely in perfume.

While perhaps branding is the commercial version of the associative attribution, it is the abstract attribution in perfume to celebrities – whether they lend their name or their visual image – that this relationship is most prepossessing. Once again, we return to the inexhaustible powers of representation, the wish images, the promises that exist both embedded in and permanently external from the fragrance (or the dish, or the garment).

Such are the ruses that persist in fashion and food, and which we are in no hurry to escape. But if many names were in honour of a dignitary of high rank such as a prince, a king or a queen, it must be known the associative or arbitrary naming of food and objects was a symptom of the industrial age of middle-class consumption, the transfer of wealth, from old money to new money. As the nineteenth century progressed, it became increasingly the case and increasingly hard to hide that this transfer of wealth frequently occurred with the transfer and acquisition of titles. The newly rich middle classes desperately wanted a share in the prestige. The height of these exchanges between the old and new worlds in all facets of life, mirrored in food and fashion, art and design, reached its peak in the golden age of the Belle Époque that is the last decade of the nineteenth century until the outbreak of the First World War. August Escoffier and César Ritz not only benefitted from the confluence of wealth, image and spectacle at this time, but they were very much the architects and impresarios of the sites of modern consumption and display.

3
FOOD, FASHION AND THE MODERNIST SPECTACLE

To be included in the rag-tag list of misquotes is that of César Ritz: 'The customer is always right' when he really said, 'The customer is never wrong' (*Le client n'a jamais tort*). It doesn't matter much, but like such sayings, the attribution has fallen away to become something equivalent to an unwritten law for marketers and service-providers. And like many such statements that have been embedded into everyday life, they have much to say for themselves historically, as we now see ourselves today drowning in digital ratings and 'likes'. For what we take for granted would have been unthinkable to have said a hundred years earlier. It reflects a frenetic new age of consumerism that is no longer brokered on lines of class but on that of money alone, where everyone with money is a prospective client, and where an establishment could measure itself against its capacity to meet the needs of the most demanding. To this day, the star ratings of hotels are built on these principles, based not only on cleanliness and luxury, but also on the capacity to deliver twenty-four-hour long service, or not.

The luxury hotel existed before Ritz, but it was Ritz, together with his friend and longstanding associate Escoffier that helped bring it to its apogee. Ritz evolved the hotel into a place to be seen, a new social theatre that eclipsed the theatre itself. Unlike the theatre however, the restaurant of the end of the nineteenth century was where not only one could dress for the occasion, but where consumption was not passive but active and participatory. In her close study of the first decades of the life of restaurants in the early nineteenth century, Rebecca Spang asserts:

> Like a theatre, a restaurant was a stable frame around an ever-changing performance, a stage where fantasies might be brought to life . . . The restaurant, like the theatre, was a privileged locus of ephemerality . . . In the restaurant, everybody observed from polite obscurity, and performed with blithe indifference. If, in some senses, the world of the grand Paris restaurants generalized the behaviours of the courtly *grand couvert*attendants followed an elaborate code of etiquette, being seen was as important as being satiated, a definite dress code determined who was admitted and who left at the door.[1]

Eating on a gastronomic scale, that is not according to incidental or prosaic alimentation, is always attended by a performative dimension which, like fashion can be used as a means of self-assertion – and aggrandizement. 'You are what you eat' and 'clothes make the man' conjoin on the level of performance, the spectacle of engagement, the casting of impressions. To know about this history is to see more keenly why since then fashion and food have been such easy complements to one another, the bedfellows of conspicuous capitalist consumption.

There were a number of interrelated factors that gave rise to the high-level hotels and restaurants, among them the growing efficiency and popularity of train travel. Railways made travelling long distances faster, safer and more affordable. As a result of trains countless resorts popped up all over Europe, no longer confining season sojourns to those who could afford to buy and maintain country estates. In fact, the hotels, resorts and spas came to rival the country estate to the extent that it was no longer as coveted: it was far more desirable to be seen at a chic hotel and at the right time of the year. (A lesser known detail about a popular remark, that after Mussolini came to power in the mid-1920s, he made the trains run on time, the trains in question were principally those to the ski resorts.) To mix with the hoi-polloi became increasingly less stigmatized. It was in the Savoy, under the management of Ritz, that Edward, the Prince of Wales transitioned from dining in private to public. Just as fashions had blurred the classes, the social spaces of interaction and consumption had opened as well.

The period of the end of the nineteenth century, the *fin de siècle*, in which Ritz and Escoffier made their names and altered service and gastronomy forever, is often referred to as the Belle Époque. However, the many literary, dramatic and filmic representations of the time tend to obscure that for the large part it was not entirely 'belle', as the distinguished historian John Merriman is quick to point out, with large gaps between rich and poor, and living conditions, for the most part what we in today's terms would judge to be squalid. Most people did not eat or dress with any distinction.[2] Merriman goes into considerable detail over the depredations and appalling conditions that workers had to face, often without a day of respite, and ridiculously low wages, necessitating extreme measures such as petty crime and prostitution to enable even the most basic existence.[3] Kitchen workers, textile labourers, tailors, seamstresses and laundry-women were subject to long hours and were exposed to dangerous hazards. (For a cook in the nineteenth century to live to the age of 48 as Carême had done was not at all bad given the daily exposure to smoke and other toxins.) Yet if the roaring 1890s until the outbreak of the First World War is singled out as a time of plenty and the conspicuous hedonism of the few, it must be seen as a postwar construction propagated by the nostalgia of the 1930s, 'and then', continues Merriman, 'above all, with the lingering sense of the "world we have lost"', urged on by Vichy France and the growing truth that France was no longer a great power. It is a construction, nevertheless, that serves as a bottomless resource for both the fashion and gastronomy industries. In truth however, 'the prewar period [was] the Belle Époque that never was.'[4]

As evidenced in the art and literature of the time, urban upheavals precipitated by swelling metropolises, and urban reforms and reorganization such as Haussmann's massive reconfiguration of Paris in the middle of the century, were accompanied by other changes such as the interaction between classes. To be sure, since the middle of the eighteenth century at least, the nobility had mixed with intellectuals and others of the middle class in private salons and likeminded gatherings, but the shift in social space, as well as shifts in the distribution in wealth meant that the kinds of distinctions that had been in place for hundreds if not thousands of years had come to be eroded. While art was still the province of the privileged and educated, matters of clothing and food provided the easiest, most proximate, and accessible access to culture or 'culture'. It was in fashion and food, the latter including hotel and restaurant culture, that struggles of social distinctions were waged, through deceit, misrecognition and misprision, but also by dint of who could offer the best bid. The parvenu(e) and the *nouveau riche* now all had stakes in the game, and it was through what they put on their body and what they put into it, that they were best able to lay claim to privileges, graces and pleasure that they now thought was their right and their due. But first, the decades leading toward this ostensibly golden age, and the birth of haute couture and haute cuisine.

The cook and the bourgeois table

Echoing Balzac's commentaries on food and fashion written at the cusp of the July Monarchy, Baudelaire, writing at its end in 1846, makes a series of commentaries in his art criticism on food and the senses, suggesting an expanded appreciation of art. As Philippa Lewis comments, the parallels between art and food have typically been taken up as a criticism of the bourgeoisie's more prosaic appreciation of art as something to be consumed on par with food and drink. It is a conclusion drawn from a widely held view of the time that the olfactory sense was inferior to that of sight, a prejudice that can be traced to Kant. However, in view of his contribution to *Le Tintamarre*, a weekly journal of 'industry, culture, and fashion, that blended publicity and satire', his 'gustatory' criticism must be considered in a more positive light, she argues. Involving several senses – one only need also think of his poem 'Correspondences' – he exhorts his readers to have a more enhanced experience. Taste 'is transformed into a playful yet productive trope by means of which Baudelaire can convey, and heighten, the pleasurable effects of visual art for a new and powerful readership.'[5]

Baudelaire was not alone, but rather was a more citable example of writers who appealed to a greater variety of the senses in accounting for the aesthetic experience. The artistic hierarchies in painting would become challenged by Manet and the Impressionists, and the challenge to the traditional hierarchies of the senses was part of the way Baudelaire and the generation after him sought to make better sense of the world. His friend Théophile Gautier, writing in 1861, refers to a configuration of colours as a 'cacophony' (*tapage*) and remarks on the heady effects of smelling the freshly varnished paintings.[6] Even if, as Lewis allows, references to food and drink in Baudelaire's later writings would be of shorter shrift, in his *Salon of 1846* and his contributions to *Le Tintamarre* allusions to taste are deployed as 'a means of expanding and varying experience, creating sensory coherences and correspondences.'[7] The many ways that food is troped throughout his art criticism shows that it is integrating into aesthetic reflections alongside its steadily rising place within social intercourse.

At the time of Baudelaire's writing, restaurants had already begun to transition into what we know of them today. Carême, it will be recalled, would present banquets in the most spectacular manner, and when the scale and budget permitted, according to a refined and painstaking architectural idiom, reflecting his architectural interests. Following the tradition of the court banquets for hundreds of years, dishes were brought out together, if only perhaps in groupings, although these groupings tended to vary according to the foods available and were not always from savoury dishes to sweet dishes as we order the sequence of dishes today. In the old style, guests were confined to choose from what was available closest to them, and it was generally the case that by the time the food landed on the plate it was lukewarm at best. Further, as against the way culinary etiquette is structured today, it was not expected that diners partook of all that was in front of them. It was part of the ethos of the rich and privileged that they were above basic worldly need – indeed to leave wastage was desirable. Again, in the colonization of a far more universal approach to gustation, this service was characterized as *à la française*. This would be used to distinguish from the simpler approach to be known *a la russe*, the plate-by-plate approach that is now taken for granted. Its name was attributed to the Russian Prince Kurakin who asked to be served this way in Paris in the 1830s. Apparently while working for Alexander I in 1818, Carême served food in this fashion but deemed it something unsympathetic to French cuisine. In the 1870s, the style became more popular by Félix Urbain Dubois who had served as chef to Prince Orlov in Russia. Germans were also inclined to this form of service which meant that it could also be called service *à l'allemande*.[8]

Although purportedly invented by a senior Russian nobleman, this form of service was understandably far more akin to a bourgeois table, to smaller gatherings, and to diminished consumption. It could be both public and private, had less pomp, and afforded greater control over the service, all of which was conducive to restaurants. As Parkhurst Ferguson relates: 'Whereas the banquet makes use of elaborate, often multilayered culinary creations to manipulate space in the service of a communal spectacle, the restaurant regulates time to effect intimacy.'[9] Service *à la française* was a also hierarchical system, since where you sat governed what you had access to eating, while the more regulated style of service assured equality for all, and as was increasingly the case, that diners had greater control over what they ate. There would continue to be banquets into Restoration France, but they were far more the exception as opposed to the rule. It was also true that the transition was uneven and gradual, as members of the upper classes found the old service hard to relinquish as it was so firmly tied, since the evolution of court ritual over hundreds of years, toward their own social importance. As Annie Gray indicates, 'à la Française was emblematic of a way of life, with deep structures and rationales that were not easily discarded.'[10] The change in forms of eating helps us to consider the concomitant changes in clothing that gradually transpired toward the end of the nineteenth century, given that greater numbers of the middle classes were inclined to greater movement and easier transition from place to place. *À la russe* was also, as Gray observes, a process sympathetic to the 'nascent food critic industry'. Because it was linear, it allowed for easier access and appraisal.[11] Thus the spectacle shifted from the grandiose to one whose attributes were most suited to commentary. What people wore, where they wore it, where they went, what they ate, now all formed a massive and mutating discursive organism. The transcendence of food from matter dreamed of by Fourier and Brillat-Savarin had occurred more on the plane of the languages of status and consumption. A special kind of theatrical texture could be afforded with the new form of service, as Senelick emphasizes: 'Instead of dumping all the dishes on the table at once, the orderly progression of courses was built to dramatic climaxes and a satisfactory denouement.'[12]

Allowing for the concerns of class, the new service could be manipulated to serve ends of social distinction. For even if Russian service could be used to more dramatic ends in the restaurant, in the hands of the wealthy it could amount to an imposition of ceremonial tyranny. Margaret Visser notes how this manner of service could be manipulated to show off how many servants a patron could afford, to the extent that not one of the guests 'was allowed to help themselves, or to pass or ask for anything: the numerous servants were there to be depended upon.' She goes on to state that one complaint of the wealthy was that, if it did enable one to show off the number of servants and the elegance of their livery, this level of show did not extend to the display of porcelain and silver. The concentration on dish to dish, however, meant that culinary skill lay not on a display *en masse*, but instead, '[u]nder the new system every course had to be a culinary triumph'. Moreover, with the tables less encumbered, the tables had more space for decorations, such as flowers.[13] Ritz would seize on such opportunities, with mind not only to the overall spectacle of the dining room, but to complement the gowns and corsages of the women who sat amongst a dazzling floral array. As Gray further notices, service *à la russe*, the architectonic panoply of gustatory display was undeniably displaced: 'the central edible focal point had been lost, diffusing the gathering and reducing the importance of the food to the overall dinner.'[14] This meant the occasion was more on the people, the conversation, what was worn and what was said. The central displays could at times be so overwhelming, however, as to obscure diners from those on either side.

Tourism

Before he became associated with the Savoy and the Ritz in Paris, César Ritz was the manager of one then several hotels and resorts in Western Europe, between which he frenetically peregrinated, thanks to the growing sophistication of train travel. Bertram Gordon argues that, beginning with the opening of Paris in the middle of the nineteenth century, then the growth of train travel, 'France became the centre of a far-flung empire, and Paris, as its capital, had few rivals in both domestic and international tourism.'[15] Tourism had always existed in many incipient forms, which were oriented around pilgrimages, first of the sacred type, and then secular such as visiting former battlegrounds. Mighty upheavals like the Revolutions of 1789, 1848 or the Paris Commune also tended to draw people to visit from the provinces.[16] But it was really Paris itself that was an international drawing card, and in this respect, it was due to the fashions and the busy culture of cafés and restaurants. After the Nazis annexed most of France, they proclaimed that it would be the pleasure-capital of the Third Reich once Europe had been conquered and subdued. This had its seeds already sown in perceptions coming out of the first half of the nineteenth century. In 1864 the railroad was extended, linking Paris with Nice, literally opening the country. Electric lighting was introduced in 1877, which made it easier and safer to walk at night, meaning that bars and restaurants (and brothels and whatever else) were more accessible than ever before. The gazette *La Grand Ville* boasted that 1840's Paris was 'the centre of the arts, sciences, fashion and – one could almost say – of civilization.'[17]

By the 1870s, France and adjacent countries such as Switzerland and Italy, had quickly evolved into facilitating an intricate network of hotels and resorts where the well-to-do could travel according to the season. For instance, San Remo or Nice would be popular stays in the winter, while Rigi-Kulm, Lucerne or Locarno on Lake Maggiore were welcome in the summer. Ritz worked as maître d'hôtel in the Grand Hotel in Locarno before moving to become manager at The Grand Hôtel National in Lucerne, and a little after simultaneously occupying the post as manager of Grand Hôtel in Monaco. His serial successes facilitated his purchase of Hôtel de Provence in Cannes and the Minerva Hotel in Baden-Baden, which was connected to the Restaurant de la Conversation. Thanks again to rail travel, Baden-Baden had expanded as a spa town: when not taking in the cures from it mineral waters, visitors were apt to bask in the comforts that the hotel could offer. As these salubrious establishments began to flourish, so did the facilitation of women and families, with *wagon-lits*, or sleeping cabins, and sumptuous dining cars. In 1889 the Orient Express connected Paris, the capital of the nineteenth century with Constantinople, the capital of an earlier age.

As with the markets for food and fashion, train travel did not differentiate between the classes, except along financial lines. There is an amusing and quite striking passage in Marcel Proust's *À la recherche du temps perdu* (1913–1927) of encountering an incongruous person in a carriage in which his narrator and girlfriend are forced to sit. The passage highlights the innumerable instances of discord that were encountered in modern public spaces, along lines of class, taste, and appearance:

> We hastened in search of an empty carriage in which I could hold Albertine in my arms throughout the journey. Having failed to find one, we got into a compartment in which there was already installed a lady with a massive face, old and ugly, and a masculine expression, very much in her Sunday best, who was reading the *Revue des Deux Mondes*. Notwithstanding her vulgarity, she was ladylike in her gestures, and I amused myself wondering to what social category she could belong; I at once concluded that she must be the manageress of some large brothel, a procuress on holiday. Her face and her manner proclaimed the fact aloud. Only, I had hitherto been unaware that such ladies read the *Revue des Deux Mondes*.[18]

Not only was she out of place, but her reading matter made her even harder to place. Vignettes such as these became an increasing order of the day in cafés, restaurants and train carriages, and in the restaurants in the trains themselves. We may also think of the art of Edgar Degas and the social melting pots of the horse-races, bars and even the stock-exchange. As testament to how travel had changed society, while in the Grand Hotel at Balbec, Proust remarks with irony at the signs of faux grandeur, linking it to the sort of thing that would please that new collective phenomenon, the tour group: 'They gave to this room with its lofty ceiling a quasi-historical character which might have made it a suitable place for the assassination of the Duc de Guise, and afterwards for parties of the tourists personally conducted by one of Messer's Thomas Cook and Son's guides.'[19] The English businessman Thomas Cook was one of the fathers of modern mass tourism. He also helped to usher in several enabling systems such as coupons and special tickets that allowed easy transactions of food, travel and accommodation across borders.

Trian cars, railways had become, like restaurants new venues of social mixing – in Paris one could no longer just point to the Palais-Royale as it was so easy to do a century before. The unease that this caused was longstanding and, in many cases, well-founded. As early as the 1830s, when restaurants had become an urban fixture, a small sub-culture grew of men and women passing as higher stations as they really were to swindle a free meal or make off with expensive cutlery. As Spang relates, that over and again,

> newspapers' tales of unpaid restaurant bills and stolen tableware opened with a description of the well-dressed and impeccably groomed culprit. 'A man of elegant and military bearing'; 'a very well-dressed gentleman'; 'two fashionable youths'; 'a handsome gentleman with his pince-nez around his neck and his riding crop in hand, accompanied by a young and lovely lady'; 'a young lady with the most modest air and wearing the most elegant hat'; throughout the 1830s, and uninterrupted flood of news stories revealed every one of these (and many more) to be the most common sorts of criminals, intent on dining for free and making off with the spoons to boot.[20]

A small industry erupted around the pretence of class that reaped its advantages from the disorder and diversity of public spaces. This was only compounded by the invention of the automobile, where the culprits could make a speedy getaway, especially in the growing number of country restaurants that erupted as a consequence of fast and fluid country travel.

On a more positive level, automobile travel, which immediately became fashionable, sedimented interest and advocacy of regional cuisine and regional restaurants. Travel, tourism and gastronomy are so firmly bound up that it is the manufacturer of tyres, Michelin, that bestows the highest honours upon restaurants throughout the world. Car travel encouraged less formal clothing that was more comfortable, while also playing a key role in the interest in regionality in architecture, wine, food and cooking. Cars and car racing became a widely popular pastime for the rich, and with it, the consciousness of healthy foods to go with the new love of streamlining and speed. By the time of the outbreak of the First World War in 1914, there were over a hundred thousand cars on French roads.[21]

Ritz and Escoffier: kings of their trade at the service of kings[22]

When we think of the modern service industry and haute cuisine, their foundations lie in César Ritz and Auguste Escoffier. They presided, and created, the best hotels containing the best restaurants of their time. They were responsible for many of the changes in social interaction within the élite spaces of spectacle and consumption. As we have seen many times already, since the sixteenth century at least, food had long been an occasion for its own kind theatre, but with the collaboration and friendship of Ritz and Escoffier, this was taken to its outer limit at a time, in the 1890s, that was most responsive to hedonism to the highest bidder.

Ritz was born to a peasant family in the region of Niederwald in the Valais in southern Switzerland. He made his way first as a waiter in Brig, then moving to Paris at the time of the 1867 Universal Exhibition. At age nineteen in 1869 he began as an assistant waiter at the Restaurant Voisin where he became acquainted with some of the cultural luminaries of the time, the writer and gourmand, Alexandre Dumas *père*, Edmond de Goncourt, George Sand and 'The Divine Sarah', Sarah Bernhard, who would be a faithful to the Savoy in London. Following his tenure at Voisin's, and having just escaped the Commune, he returned in 1872, to work as a floor waiter at the Hôtel Splendide, where he was quickly promoted to maître d'hôtel. In living up to its name, the Splendide arguably was the most luxurious hotel in Paris where Ritz waited on some of the richest and most prominent people of the time, being particularly impressed by the number of self-made figures, many of whom emanated from America. Combined with innate ability and the hunger to join those whom he served, Ritz refined his manner and became something of dandy. He was always impeccable in his hygiene and in his manners, which while in London earned him the epithet of 'the Beau Brummell of the hotel trade', after the notorious father of dandyism.[23] With a carefully waxed moustache and carefully combed hair, a voice that did its best to conceal his coarse Valaisian roots, he excelled in ingratiating himself to the monied, the fashionable and the noble. When the social focus shifted briefly from Paris to Vienna in 1873 as a result of the World Exhibition, Ritz found work at the restaurant Les Trois Frères Provonçaux [the Three Provencale Bothers], where he found himself among the crème de la crème of European royalty, from the venerable Kaiser Wilhelm I, the kings of Belgium and Italy and the Tsar of Russia. The great old families were there, and, again, the newly affluent of America, who would soon help nourish the fading fortunes of many old noble families in return for the illusory legitimacy that titles can bestow. From there he moved to Nice to become the manager of the Grand Hôtel. Kenneth James notes that at the time Nice was 'now the centre of fashion on the Riviera', crowded 'with a throng of gentlemen, whiskered and silk-hatted, and of ladies with trailing skirts and tilted sunshades.'[24] Escoffier would later say of Nice that it was a place where 'people know how to dine as they know how to dress or bow.'[25]

Ritz seasonally alternated between the Hôtel Rigi-Hulm (in mountainous Switzerland), the Grand Hôtel in Locarno, the Hôtel Nice and subsequently the Hôtel Victoria in San Remo on the Ligurian Coast. At San Remo in the winter of 1876–77, he was approached by Colonel Pfyffer d'Altishofen to run the Grand Hôtel National in Lucerne which Pfyffer had just built to rival others in its lavish appointments and offerings, but due to poor management, it was not doing so well. After the convulsion of the Commune, France was coming out of recession; it and its neighbours were readying for new seasons of pleasure. Ritz accepted the position and went about an overhaul. Ritz was always attentive to appearances at all levels, which included the way patrons appeared, or thought they appeared. To this end, in Lucerne he replaced the dowdy lighting with modern gas-lamps. Another measure was the restaurant, to which Ritz rallied for improvements, and eventually hired a talented chef, Jean Giroux, which helped to bring in more glamorous and seasoned clientele, however doing do also proved expensive. Balancing levels of quality and show with mercantile logistics would be an issue bedevilling Ritz's career. In 1881, he was snapped up from the National in Lucerne to run the Grand Hôtel in Monte Carlo. Taking Giroux with him, Ritz transformed the drab establishment into one desirable to a new and fashionable clientele, including the Prince of Wales. (food-fashion-fun-fact trivia: the Prince is credited with popularizing the convention of undoing the last button on a vest or cardigan, since for him it was to accommodate his widening girth.) The Prince was a well-known bon-vivant, womanizer and spendthrift but his patronage was one of the best stamps of approval that any restaurant or hotel could wish for, and it would be an association that Ritz would continue to draw sustenance from in years to come. (For the Prince to cease his patronage, if it was abrupt or without extenuating circumstances, could result in breaking an establishment, or at least severely setting it back). When Giroux was poached with a huge salary by the Hôtel de Paris in Monte Carlo, Ritz turned to Giroux's teacher, Escoffier.

Escoffier arrived in Monet Carlo in 1884 and was pleased and impressed with Ritz's working methods, which expected a productive symbiosis between hotel and kitchen, which was not common practice. Ritz set a premium on cleanliness and decorum, and similarly, Escoffier demanded that all the cooks under him began the day dressed in impeccable whites, and throughout the service were restrained and quiet – in stark contrast to the squalor and bullying that persisted in most kitchens. (Today, there is less squalor but there continues to be bullying as we know by some celebrity chefs, not to mention the prominent cases of exploitation through underpayment.) Portraits of both Ritz and Escoffier a little after they began working together, show them to be proud men with an acute sense of themselves and their own style. When not appearing in chef's whites wearing his toque, (normally ceremonially on Sundays), Escoffier, despite his own humble origins, always presented himself as the dapper bourgeois in clean linen, tie, and a frock coat cut at just above the knee. A portrait of Ritz in 1888 with his recently wedded wife Marie shows him to be the paragon of fastidiousness, with an upright posture, attentive dignified gaze, and a bowler hat nestled on his knee. His sense of himself extended to suffering for the sake of fashion: thinking that his peasant's feet were too large, he wore his shoes a size to small. With such foreknowledge, it is perceptible in his strain of his dainty shoes. Marie

Figure 3.1 Ritz with wife Marie-Louise in 1888. *Schweizer Pioniere der Hotellerie*; Schweizerische Verkehrszentrale, 1976. (Wikipedia Commons, Public Domain.)

stated that not only did he have his shoes made a half-size too small, but he also took pains to look after his hands, which he also thought betrayed his lowly origins. She praises both his 'physical charm and elegance' as well as his 'remarkable courage and capability' (Figure 3.1).

Ritz had become a master of assessing appearances. Summing customers and perspective customers up was, after all integral to his job. Even in matters of love he was sensitive to aesthetics. Kenneth James reports how, at a picnic party where César was with Marie before their courtship, he 'remarked that the ribbon on her hat matched the colour of her eyes.'[26]

At the end of the main service Escoffier would ceremonially visit tables in his kitchen whites, which would have been implausibly spotless, and into which he would have changed into a new set for the occasion. At this juncture it is instructive to pause to look at the lineage of this uniform, which Escoffier was far from being the first to use, but which, as in 'traditional' French cuisine, he played a large part in instituting. First the double-breasted white coat. It is not for nothing that it has military connotations, since in earlier times chefs of kings and princes were required service on the battlefield. (The pattern of service does often bear an uncanny resemblance to a Napoleonic battle of prelude, frenetic apex, receding denouement and relieved aftermath, each night slightly different from the next but to all the same pattern, except when there are no customers.) In military fashion, chefs may use special kinds of buttons, have a badge of their name and/or the establishment on their left breast, and may choose to have coloured ribbon on the collar or pocket to denote status. On a more utilitarian level, the double-breasted coat provides protection from the heat, and can quickly hide soiling by having the clean layer buttoned over the dirtied one.[27] The neckerchief, which today is more motley, would be worn as a stylized, somewhat crude cravat. This was originally to trap perspiration in the days when kitchens were exceedingly hot because of fire ovens and imperfect ventilation. There may be other reasons such as protection from differences in temperature as the cook moved from refrigerated rooms to hot grills.[28]

By far the most interesting are the speculative beginnings of the toque. A short article from the Culinary Institute of America suggests that it can be traced back to 'Assyria in the mid-century B.C., when King Assurbanipal lived in fear of being poisoned. He required the head cooks in wealthy households to wear pleated cloth headdresses similar to those of the royalty.' It was an identifier and was supposed to foster loyalty.[29] A *Toque*, in French, or *toca* in Spanish was a floppy hat for both men and women that was gathered into a belt or crown. Over the eighteenth century the headwear worn by cooks throughout Europe varied widely, such as in Germany where hats were pointed finished with a tassel, or in France where the caps were of a kind of stocking that was coloured according to one's place in the kitchen. It was a chef under Talleyrand, Boucher, however who made the standard colour white, and it was Carême who made it close to what it is now. While under the employ of Lord Stewart, after seeing a woman in the street wearing a stiff, white hat, decided to emulate it by inserting a rounded piece of cardboard into his own floppy hat. In appreciation, it was Stewart who gave it the name 'toque'. There were no doubt variants, but the toque became a sign of the status, importance, even personality of the chef. Writing in 1894, in his book, *La Cuisine Anglaise*, Alfred Suzanne was prompted, hopefully ironically, to propose a series of variations as reflections of character. For instance: 'He who wears it pluckily, inclined on the corner of an ear in a showy fashion, is a bit of a snob.' While: 'Another type, who wears it negligently and simply atop his head, is either a reckless individual or a philosopher. It is notable that the toque, placed forward and pulled down over the eyes, protects the head of a thinker.' Outside of grand hotels and restaurants, the toque has been replaced with a simple hat for the sake of hygiene.

Back to Escoffier and Ritz. Before they ventured to London, they alternated seasonally, and comfortably, between Monte Carlo and Lucerne, following their leisured clientele. It was in the mid-1880s that, in James' words, they 'learned the effectiveness of sumptuous treatment in attracting high society.' This meant investing large sums of money and energy in the sumptuousness of the spectacle: extra candles, more flowers, better musicians. Meanwhile Escoffier could develop his talents where no ingredient was deprived him. It was also the time when his inclination toward naming dishes gained momentum, from the Maharajah to the Earl of Derby.[30] In keeping with the cult of celebrity, Escoffier made a practice of visiting tables graced by important dignitaries and was especially bewitched by beautiful women. One such case was in winter 1885 when he visited the table of the Russian Prince Kotchoubey who was sharing a table with his mistress, the Hungarian dancer Katinka who was deemed 'the most fashionable demi-mondaine of Europe of the time.'[31] In the ensuing conversation, Katinka confessed to some of her likes and dislikes so that when she dined in the restaurant again, they were promptly catered to and formalized on the menu. These sorts of exchanges became a regular occurrence, assuring that the best and most glamorous clientele continued to visit, but also established a dynamic where Escoffier built on his reputation through auspicious association. Indeed, his veneration for Sarah Bernhardt would become legendary: after watching her play he would rush to the hotel to supervise the preparation of her supper.

What Ritz and Escoffier managed to establish and design in the hotel in Lucerne was what was then considered the new style, but one that holds in various ways until the present day, conventions that we how take for granted. James describes the achievements in service and the appearance of staff in the following way,

> They [Ritz and Escoffier] had introduced the *service à la Russe* and the *à la carte* menu to the restaurant, and an imaginative cuisine served with an efficiency not found elsewhere. They had dressed the waiters in white ties and aprons, the headwaiters in black ties, and themselves in morning coats—familiar now, but astonishing then. Auguste himself is often pictured in a *toque blanche* and kitchen whites, but mostly dressed as a banker; he had to be seen, even in the kitchen, in his frock coat, striped trousers and carefully knotted cravat.[32]

By their own design Ritz and Escoffier had sloughed off the centuries-long stigma associated with those in service to become members of what we know call the 'service industry'. The level of their ingenuity and skill meant that they were sought out by the most privileged, to the extent that it had to be acknowledged, if only tacitly, that people like them were essential to the maintenance of their own power and image. This was unprecedented, and a clear sign of a new age of upward mobility and the cardinal role of food and fashion in such change.

Proust: the tribulations of class and the lure of food

It is much more than a conceit to pause with the work of Proust, and it is far from a digression. His work, embodied in *À la recherche du temps perdu* is the most intricate and subtle records of the dramas surrounding the transition of social class and status in France or of anywhere in Europe in this time. An unparalleled observer, a crucial dimension of his work revolves around appearances, a large part mistaken or misjudged. He played particularly well with the tribulations of class, gender and desire and the how expectations of these are played out, were exploited or mishandled.

Moreover, when Ritz established his eponymous hotel on the Place Vendôme in Paris, he became one of its most regular clients, dining there several times a week. As his first major biographer, George Painter explains,

> he was now 'Proust of the Ritz.' The great hotel became his second home, a substitute for the palaces of Cabourg, Venice and Évian which he would never see again, and the salons of the Faubourg, scattered by the war, whose surviving inmates now dined in strange company around him. At the Ritz he again found the movement and enigmas of a miniature world, the comfort and security of family life, the satisfaction of his lifelong craving for reciprocal service and gratitude. He worked in his cork-lined bedroom, but went to the Ritz to live, 'They don't hustle me, and I feel at home,' he said.[33]

Upon its renovation in 2016, the Ritz named several rooms in honour of its most famous regulars including Ernest Hemingway and Coco Chanel. The 'Salon Proust' serves madeleines for its high tea and has a copy of the famous portrait of Proust by his friend Jacques-Émile Blanche of 1893 in a white cravat held with a gold pin and a Wildean white lily in his lapel.

In later life, at the time of his Ritz years, Proust had relatively modest tastes in fashion as in food, although he was known due to his hypochondria to dress overcautiously, which usually meant a fur overcoat while dining. Proust attended a dinner at the Ritz in 1918 given in honour of Lord Derby who commented that 'of all the impressions my wife and I took home from us from Paris, Monsieur Proust was the most indelible.' This apparently pleased Proust when he was told about the comment until he learned that Derby had also said: 'Yes, he was the first chap we'd ever seen dining in a fur coat.'[34]

Proust's novel relates with detailed relish the ambitions of the middle and upper-middle-class to ascend to the most coveted ranks of society, their gaffes, and solecisms. In addition to the salon, the hotel and restaurant are the appropriate stages where these tensions can be highlighted based on the differences between the reactions of the middle classes in comparison with the aristocracy. For instance, in the Grand Hotel at Balbec class distinctions are felt in the differing manner of allocating gratuities, which in turn also drew a distinction between different kinds of service staff and their assessments of the guests. The narrator begins with the lift-boy, who falls into a panic when he is not given his customary tip, being insensitive to the social subtleties behind the situation:

> Because of Albertine's presence I had not given him the five francs which I was in the habit of slipping into his hand when I went up. And the idiot, realising that I did not wish to make a display of largesse in front of a third person, had begun to tremble, supposing that it was all finished once and for all, that I would never give him anything again. He imagined that I was 'on the rocks' (as the Duc de Guermantes [opined of the figures who stood at the apex of the social set] would have said), and the supposition inspired in him with no pity myself but with a terrible selfish disappointment.[35]

The lift-boy's obliviousness to what could be a sign of impecuniousness then causes the narrator to muse more broadly on tips as a litmus test for both patrons and those who serve them.

> From this point of view the staff might be divided into two categories: on the one hand, those who drew distinctions between the guests, and were more grateful for the modest tip of an old nobleman (who, moreover, was in a position to relieve them from 28 days of military service by saying a word for them to General Beautreillis) than for the thoughtless liberalities of a flashy vulgarian who by his very extravagance revealed a lack of breeding which only to his face did they call generosity; on the other hand, those to whom nobility, intellect, fame, position, manners were non-existent, concealed under cash valuation. For these there was but a single hierarchy, that of the money that one has, or the money that one gives.[36]

This state of affairs has its advantages, however: 'It is the convenient feature of a big hotel . . . that . . . at the sight of a hundred-franc note, still more a thousand-franc one, even though it is being given on that particular occasion to someone else, the hitherto stony face of a servant or a woman will light up with smiles and offers of service.'[37]

The 'woman' to which Proust refers is one of the innumerable would-be courtesans who snuck in the best establishments to find their prospects of one profitable night or at best become a *femme entretenue* (kept woman). One of the great figures is the enigmatic and sly Odette de Crécy who seduces the social dandy and art connoisseur Charles Swann and captivates the young Marcel with her grace, lavish interior decoration and her gowns. The narrator uncovers that she is most probably the subject of the painter, Elstir's, *Miss Sacripant* and most probably his lover, and most probably the lover of his libertine uncle, Adolphe, whom he remembers as a child. Odette is less a character unto herself than a vehicle throughout the novel for an increasingly unstable and fragile class system, which was being infiltrated by all sides, and for which the lines of entry were becoming more indistinct and more traversable. For in some tragi-comic gesture, Odette, once at the pinnacle of the social ladder ends her days as the second wife of the once formidable and socially venerated Duc de Guermantes. Were it not so real a circumstance after the First World War, the juxtaposition would be as comedic as it was preposterous.

The 'women' to which Odette once belonged had transformed herself beyond the newly opened Savoy which had begun to boom under Ritz. France at the time had different names for such women, which were more than synonyms, but signified a kind of unspoken and unquantifiable hierarchy. There were generically and evasively named lovers and mistresses which were more directly called *Les Grandes Cocottes* who may have preferred the label to *courtesan*, which was yet still more flattering than *prostituée* (noting in addition that the equivalent of 'whore', *putain*, is the most offensive French swear word). In his description of Ritz's reckoning upon the situation of the women 'of doubtful reputation and uncertain revenue', to use the words of his wife Marie, that flocked into the lobby and restaurant of the hotel, Luke Barr writes:

> These were no common prostitutes, some of them were in fact celebrated for their great beauty and their aristocratic lovers. They were notorious and darkly glamorous, moving easily between the worlds of the theatre (some of them were dancers and actresses) and high society. They were the height of fashion. It was only natural that they would flock to the Savoy, and Ritz welcomed them. But then there were the other, less glamorous courtesans, wearing large hats and noticeable quantities of makeup, women whose presence Ritz considered a threat to the hotel's good name and reputation. They had begun to appear in the lobby and restaurant with increasing frequency.[38]

The solution? Ritz mandated that evening dress be worn in the dining room and that only accompanied women were allowed access. Amusingly, hats were forbidden. As Barr adds: 'An extravagant hat worn in the evening, Ritz had discovered, was a sign of trouble.'

Proust's characters are to a greater or lesser extent modelled on real-life figures, most of whom he knew, or composites of several figures. The character of Odette, for instance, was based on the famous Belle Époque courtesan, Laure Hayman who, like Odette, among other parallels, kept a collection of porcelain (Figure 3.2). Few characters come out well in the novel, and the character of the manager of Grand Hotel at Balbec is a memorable cameo, and yet another

Figure 3.2 Portrait of Laure Hayman, 1882, Julius Leblanc Stewart (1855-1919). (Wiki art, Public Domain.)

remarkable portrait of the fault-lines, rivalries and tensions between classes, and the need to uphold appearances, despite the myriad deceptions inherent in these appearances. Although less than flattering there can be no doubt that one integer, immeasurable as it is, relies on Ritz himself, who went to great lengths over his own appearance and who over the years had become falteringly polyglot. Proust relates that the manager – who is never bestowed a name – had a strained voice owing to 'the divers accents acquired from an alien ancestry and a cosmopolitan upbringing',[39] pointing to roots in Swiss peasantry and his subsequent education amongst the cognoscenti of post-Commune Paris. He is described as attired in 'a smart dinner-jacket' and having 'the air of a psychologist' who, whenever the 'omnibuses discharged a fresh load, invariably took the grandees for haggling skinflints and flashy crooks for grandees!'[40] For the modes of travel, as with dining itself, were increasingly shared amongst high, middling and, occasionally, low. Like many of his kind, despite his background and his salary, the manager learned to identify with the highest echelons of those whom he served and looked down on the upwardly mobile classes who betrayed their class and their wealth in careless comments. His snobberies are not those of the upper classes, but rather a new class of snobberies gleaned irregularly and intuitively, some of them no doubt wide of the mark. He is a wonderful portrait of the many tacit judgements at this time, placing restaurants and hotels as centres for where these were made, the higher the level, the more prone to error:

> Social position was the one things by which the manager was impressed—social position, or rather the signs which seemed to him to imply that it was exalted, such as not taking one's hat off when one came into the hall, wearing knickerbockers or an overcoat with a waist, and taking a cigar with a band of purple and gold out of a crushed morocco case—to none of which advantages could I, alas, lay claim. He would also adorn his business conversation with choice expressions to which, as a rule, he gave the wrong meaning.[41]

Proust takes great mileage from the manager's ridiculous malapropisms, which, as far as we know, was something not shared with Ritz himself. As well as a source of humour, which is seldom far away in Proust special commentary, the manager's various gaffes ('he was always using expressions which he thought distinguished without noticing that they were incorrect – "of Rumanian originality"') are also signs of the pitfalls that result from the too hasty insertion of one class discourse into another.

What he lacked in the fineries of semantics, the manager excelled at co-ordination, control and vigilance. The narrator recollects his meals in 'in the vast hotel, generally full, of the Grand Hotel,'[42] where the manager presided with 'his glittering eyes' that 'saw everything and controlled everything'. His attention to detail 'ensured for the "dinner at the Grand Hotel" perfection in every detail as well as overall harmony. He felt, evidently, that he was more than the producer, more than the conductor, nothing less than the generalissimo.'[43] Nothing seems to escape his observation: 'I felt that even the movements of my spoon did not escape him, and were he to vanish after the soup, for the whole of the dinner, the inspection he had held would have taken away my appetite.'[44]

Another character with identifiable roots is the headwaiter of the restaurant at Balbec, Aimé who owes himself to the headwaiter at the Ritz, Olivier Dabescat. As Proust's other great biographer Jean-Yves Tadié affirms, the Ritz was far from being a place to eat or decamp from home, it was also where Proust could brush up on certain details that he needed to fill in the gaps in his writing at the time. 'During each meal' states Tadié, 'Marcel would interrogate this waiter [Dabescat] on the clientele of the Ritz, which knew at the time had knowledge of the high English aristocracy, the prince des Galles and his brothers, king Alphonso XIII, the king of Portugal, the queen of Rumania.'[45] Not only did the Ritz, under the care of Dabescat, provide Proust with sanctuary during the War, it was for him a research centre, where he had access to the best of the best whether in person or by word of mouth. As Philippe Michel-Thiriet adds, together with the society dandy Montesquiou, Dabescat 'was one of Proust's sources of society gossip, Dabescat knew everyone in Paris and would reserve "the best table" for one guest or another, to the point where a person of social standing could be determined by the table allocated by Dabescat.' When Dabescat was away on holiday in August 1918, Proust opined in a letter to the Princesse Souzo that without him, the Ritz 'has lost its keynote'.[46]

While there are numerous other incidences in which the experience of food interlocks with class and appearance, let us conclude this section with the narrator's observations in the restaurant at Rivebelle. It gives a bracing account of the experiences of the time, which no doubt made the business, and the times, so exhilarating not just for the lucky clients, but for those who were especially at the top of the service ladder such as Escoffier and Ritz. Proust captures the pace and the panoply of a fashionable restaurant at the peak of its activity:

> Several of the waiters, let loose among the tables, were flying along at full speed, each carrying on his outstretched palm a dish which it seemed to be the object of this kind of race not to let fall. And in fact, the chocolate *soufflés* arrived at their destination unspilled, the potatoes *à l'anglaise*, in spite of the gallop that must have given them a shaking, arranged as at the start round the Pauillac lamb. I noticed one of the waiters, very tall, plumed with superb black locks, his face dyed in a tint that suggested certain spectacles of rare birds rather than a human being, who, running without pause (and, one would have said, without purpose) from one end of the room to another, recalled one of those macaws which fill the big aviaries in zoological gardens with their gorgeous coloring and incomprehensible agitation. Presently the spectacle settled down, in my eyes at least, into an order at once more noble and more calm. I looked at the round tables whose innumerable assemblage filled the restaurant like so many planets, as the latter are represented in old allegorical pictures.[47]

Proust continues to describe these marvels, including a vignette of a 'wealthy amphitryon [i.e. gastronome], having managed to secure a famous author, was endeavouring to extract from him . . . a few insignificant remarks at which the ladies marvelled.' The dizzying description ends in bathos, as the interests of finance underscore those of the senses: 'Seated behind a bank of flowers, two horrible cashiers, busy with endless calculations, seemed like two witches occupied in forecasting by astrological signs the disasters that might from time to time occur in this celestial vault fashioned according to the scientific conceptions of the Middle Ages.'[48] Yet it was the genius of Ritz not to forego one for the other. In truth, his resolute need to preserve the integrity of the spectacle, raised the hackles of many who watched the pennies.

The Savoy and the modern theatre of gastronomy

Ritz was gradually, after numerous entreaties (and a handsome salary), lured away from the Lucerne and Monet Carlo Hotels to go to the new Savoy in London by a Richard D'Oyly Carte. Significantly, D'Oyly Carte had made his reputation and small fortune as a promoter of light opera, specifically as a promoter of the duo, Gilbert and Sullivan, through the Savoy theatre that opened in 1881. At the time, it was the most advanced theatre anywhere in the world and boasted being the first public building illuminated by electricity. Emboldened by his success, and urged on by Gilbert and Sullivan, he resolved to build 'the most perfect hotel in the world', which would boast advancements commensurate with the theatre next to it. In short, Ritz worked for someone who was a showman and impresario first and foremost. Leaving aside ceremonial occasions, the theatre was where women showed themselves at their best, and it was the theatre, especially at this time in the 1880s and 1890s, that witnessed the most profound mixture of classes, in which demi-mondaines jostled with Duchesses and courtesans with Countesses with ever-greater fluidity. The hotel and its restaurant would become the next stop in the evening passage of self-display and indulgence. After five years of building and preparation, the Savoy opened in 1889, and the guest list for the Grand Opening resembled a Royal Wedding and included royalty such as the Shah of Persia, the German Kaiser and the King of Greece. The hotel boasted the most modern amenities, including electric lighting and a bathroom in every room, a service unheard of until then.

Understandably, all of this came at a price, and the loans required for such an undertaking were barely being met. The staff were competent, but obviously lacked the singular flair that was required. Since it takes one to know one, D'Oyly Carte the impresario saw the impresario in Ritz, who was at first reluctant since in Lucerne and Monte Carlo he was close to being his own free agent. With a handsome salary, he acquiesced, and shortly brought Escoffier with him, as well as a small coterie of other faithfuls, including an old friend, a Master of Wine, Echenard, down to his head cashier, Agostini. Restaurants and hotels were thus resembling other forms of modern cultural production such as the couturier or the theatre troupe, in which the leader was apt to bring a trained and loyal entourage with him or her. The critical mass of skill and loyalty also acted as a form of insurance against any capriciousness that the monied backers may wish to exhibit.

The vaunted modernity of the Savoy was much on par with what Ritz and Escoffier wanted to offer. Escoffier had embraced the growing trend to dispense with cubicles that had been the norm since the earliest restaurants of the eighteenth century in favour of an open-plan dining room, with service in the Russian style which accommodated Ritz's passion for copious flower arrangements. Escoffier also introduced the *prix fixe* or fixed price menu, which allowed for greater order, efficiency and affordability. It was also a response to English customers who for the large part did not understand *à la carte* menus which were traditionally written in French. English clients balked at the names of dishes which were not always indicative of what the dish was, and who may have been unsure of the proper balance of dishes. The *prix fixe* was a readymade suite of meals that could also be paired with wines – the *nouveau riche* or unseasoned (and non-francophone) diner was thereby spared the risk of betraying any ignorance and loss of face. He also broke down the kitchen into different sections that discharged discrete skills and service that were then brought together in the main service (*pâtissier, rôtissier, saucier*, and so on), a Fordist assembly-line principle that is now the basis of commercial kitchens throughout the world. Escoffier's eye for detail did not stop there: he kept a careful record of what noteworthy people ate, so that he was abreast of their preferences and aversions, and so that he might replicate the dish, or present a delectable modification of it, upon their return.[49] It was the equivalent of tailor-made food, and an enormously flattering touch which earned him an almost cult following in his time.

In surveying the conditions sympathetic to their arrival in London, Kenneth James makes a series of observations about the freedoms in dress that echoed those Ritz and Escoffier sought to institute in the hotel, where freedom was the order of the day. Before this time, dining out was an activity confined almost entirely to men, but in the 1880s, this state of affairs changed drastically. In 1880's England, social mobility met physical mobility, especially when it came to women. One of the many signs was the casting of physical encumbrances.

> Twenty years earlier they had rid themselves of part of their iron cage, the crinoline. There was at first some gross distortion of the figure with the bustle, worn even while playing tennis. There remained the steel and whalebone wasp-waisting which was remarkably persistent. But freedom was growing. The skirt trailing behind a yard or so, which had to be held up with one hand when out of doors, was out. Skirts were shortened just to clear the ground, and the bustle slowly diminished to allow the rear to show its natural curve. The artificial exoskeleton, at least for those whose hard youth had not softened to flow point, was gradually expanding to a 'natural' girdle. The emancipation was recognised and welcomed by both César and Auguste. They were to make it their central marketing theme and in this they would be working, so to speak, with the grain.[50]

The women's fashion and lifestyle magazine, *Women's World* proclaimed that: 'Now, women dress for dinner in as many different ways as the meal is served. Low gowns, half high gowns, or tea gowns which are akin to dressing gowns, or tea gowns that closely resemble the revised court bodice, inspired by the modes of mediaeval times—all these are popular!'[51]

Women's dress began to respond more specifically to women's activities, which meant not just how they looked, but what they did. Significant among these roles was that of the different teas, lunches, dinners and suppers that formed the circuit of the day of any woman of means and leisure. In concert with the changes in women's dress, dining had become more versatile, allowed for different variations, which had a lot to do with the changes in classes, the ways in which people behaved, and the spaces they inhabited. As Ritz and Escoffier helped to shape it, the restaurant was more and more a recreational space in which food, while a central factor, was an integer in the spaces of social interaction and personal display. In the spirit of service and efficiency, the hotel even had 'theatre phones' installed in the lobby to listen to performances held in the Savoy theatre next door (sixpence per five minutes),[52] an innovation of which Proust was also fond. But unlike the reclusive Proust, when one wasn't drinking or dining one could still be seen to be participating in the spectacle, and for that one also had to dress the part. As Barr affirms, '[a]t the Savoy, everyone dressed the part'.[53]

When Ritz arrived at the Savoy to work in 1890, he and his loyal adherents did more than order a new set of clothes in the latest style, he set about rearranging the interior decorations, much to the consternation of Helen D'Oyly Carte, the proprietor's wife, who had been largely responsible for it. As Barr recounts, she had followed a British private club-house style that was tilted to the masculine and the heavy. It was in a busy, Victorian style with an abundance of wallpaper pattern and generous amount of thick drapery. There were 'imposing armoires and in-set mirrors. And all the drapery and wallpaper everywhere (Japanese designs, tapestries) – it was overwhelming. The lighting, meanwhile, was too bright, unflattering to the ladies in their evening-gowns.'[54] Ritz softened the light, and reduced the density of design and an extravagant abundance of flowers (weighing heavily on the budget). After the renovations, much of this apparatus was replaced with a more airy, subdued splendour that was more complimentary to women's complexions and their clothing. Barr continues: 'Guests entered from the lobby with a white-and-gold papered anteroom in which there were two fireplaces, comfortable terracotta-coloured armchairs, and numerous palm trees in large pots—a place where gentlemen might wait for their dinner guests.'[55] The dining room followed the same aesthetic.

It is hard to overstress the interrelationship between the theatre and the hotel as it lay well beyond logistics, such as having the obvious place of articulation before and after performances, as well as accommodating travelling audiences and the celebrity actors and actresses of each season. They were also united by the premium given to drama and spectacle, something for which Ritz had a rare and intuitive gift, seizing upon the multitude of options suddenly open to him now that gaslight had been abandoned for electric lighting. In her eye-opening (enlightening?) account of the changes to lighting in theatres of the nineteenth century, Gabriela Cruz describes how dramaturges and opera composer altered the content, staging and drama in accordance with the new range of opportunities available to them. This came first with the transition from dim and cumbersome candlelight, requiring countless candles and constant attention, to gaslight, which instantly enabled a greater modulation of light that in turn opened a wider dramatic spectrum. Such advances also influenced the choices in the subjects of opera. Cruz argues that works such as Meyerbeer's *Robert the Devil* (1831) or Wagner's *Flying Dutchman* (1843), with their brooding, sombre themes, were conceived as a result of the new possibilities provided by better and more varied lighting. When the Savoy opened with its much-vaunted electric lighting, its modernity would already have been seen against (in light of) what had been a decades-long, but still relatively new, tradition of staging, whose new saturation of light or dark was matched by saturation of drama. The new modulations of light available to the shows inevitably spilled to the kinds of shows that the audiences and clientele made as well. By the time that the Savoy opened its theatrical and its gastronomic doors, the women were already attuned to the new possibilities available to them to make the most favourable impression. This affected the kinds of chiaroscuro afforded by the clothing to the choice of colours sympathetic to being viewed from a distance while capable of managing both high and low-key illumination. Cruz demonstrates how the evolution of lighting is not only a factor in the history of the technicalities of staging but was also a governing factor in the ways in which music and theatre conceived of itself.[56] The broader range of 'light and shade' in musical terms cannot be divorced from the greater range of light and shade in physical terms. No less, we can carry these notions over to the dramaturgy of the restaurant, its design and how people (in this case mostly women) sought to be seen within it.

Escoffier had famously said of food, *faites simple*, keep it simple, and Ritz had instinctively done the same. In neither case was what they meant equivalent to the reductive minimalism of contemporary taste, it was rather in contrast to what had been before them, which was copiousness, decorative bombast, an amassing of elements that were no longer in keeping with the modern way of life, the increasingly indefinite class lines, the modern woman and the superabundance of display available to a greater range of people. The active life, the *vita activa*, saw changes in food and fashion, both large and small.

4
TASTEMAKERS: THE FIRST CELEBRITY COOK AND THE FIRST CELEBRITY DRESSMAKER

The title for this chapter sounds a little like a nursery rhyme or a fable with the word 'celebrity' thrown in. The elevation of activities such as cooking and making clothes to a status rivalling that of an art form occurs in the late eighteenth century with a new, industrial economy and the opening of free markets. The conferral of tastemaker status to an individual has a dual status that benefits both giver and receiver, for to be able to command the attention and the fruits of a celebrity producer-provider is itself a status-elevating privilege. It adds to the codex of discernment and marks the consumer out as belonging to an elite. 'The greater the display of one's knowledge and social connections', believes Rachel Matthews 'the more readily one's personal opinions are transformed into a judgement of taste.'[1] The chef and fashion designer so named makes the leap from service provider – cook, tailor or dressmaker – to a coveted arbiter of consumption. While it may be said that the first celebrity chef was quicker to emerge from the Enlightenment than the couturier, there were already signs within the fashion industry of a particular hierarchy that went well beyond subjective preference and the recognition of conscientiousness and skill. Couturiers, associated with the rich and influential, were beginning to be recognized as authorial names, notably Rose Bertin, chief dressmaker to Marie Antoinette, whose boutique carried the alluringly Orientalist name 'Le Grand Mogul', and who was called the unofficial 'French Minister of Fashion'. Her contemporary and culinary counterpart was Marie-Antoine Carême. However, even though Bertin had a stranglehold over fashion in her time, it would take Charles Frederick Worth, around twenty years after Carême's death, to elevate fashion to a level rivalling art. This had as much to do with a far more open market of vying contenders for celebrity status and for making claims for what constituted a high-end luxury activity. Worth was fortunate enough to have the support of the extravagant Princess Metternich, and crucially, of Empress Eugénie whose patronage elevated Worth's status to that of royal tastemaker and celebrity couturier.

Seen broadly, the elevation of Carême and Worth to figures beyond the venerable status of servility is the result of competitiveness amongst producers and consumers, and the widening availability of objects of taste. Writings of taste as a metaphor for aesthetic judgement were bound with ideas of beauty that gained prominence in philosophy in the eighteenth century, (although theories of taste stretch back to Aristotle and Plato, taste was thought to relate to the appetite rather than to rational judgement). David Hume understood taste as a subjective feeling that was to be found within the beholder, Alexander Gerard considered taste an act of the imagination and Immanuel Kant believed that although taste was subjective, beautiful objects contained universal appeal, while Edmund Burke attempted to uncover the ambiguities surrounding taste by uncovering the principles of pleasure and pain. By the nineteenth century thinkers moved away from the idea of an aesthetic taste to that of an aesthetic attitude (or *contemplation*) found in the work of Arthur Schopenhauer. Taste was more about the ideas that was embedded in a particular object and when viewed with the correct aesthetic attitude, became beautiful to a person's perception, rather than the appreciation of or taste in food.

Although Voltaire and Hume underlined the correlations between the metaphorical and literal meaning of taste, it was not until John Dewey's essay *Art as Experience* (1934) that gustatory taste took precedent over the senses. A pragmatist philosopher whose work is not usually associated with foods, his writing is peppered with references to gastronomical experiences and the belief that cooking, and sharing could be integrated into learning. He exemplifies the aesthetic experience by using as an example (amongst others) of a dinner at a Parisian restaurant that 'stands out as an enduring memorial of what food may be'.[2] Dewey presents the food connoisseur as one who has the experience and expertise to appreciate excellence in food. 'Even the pleasure of the palette is different in quality to an epicure than in one who merely "likes" [their] food as [they] eat it,'[3] and he notes that,

> the difference is not of mere intensity. The epicure is conscious of much more than the taste of food. Rather, they enter taste as directly experienced qualities that depend upon reference to its source and its manner of production in connection with criteria of excellence.[4]

Dewey is dealing with taste as the learned ability to discriminate aesthetically between dishes, ingredients and cuisines. In other words, gustatory taste can be altered according to education or experience, what Pierre Bourdieu later would define as *habitus*. Taste is learned and not innate. It is a marker of social difference, or social distinction to reinforce social division.[5] Mary Douglas was probably right when she wrote that 'each individual, by cultural training, enters a sensory world that is pre-segmented and prejudged for [them].'[6]

Tastemakers are influential people who set standards and lay the rules of what constitutes good or legitimate taste, influences the practices of producers and the buying power of consumers. By balancing commercial goals with creative innovations, tastemakers create an aesthetic trend that has symbolic affects and material implications for the cultural field. Restaurant guides like the *Gault et Millau* and the *Michelin Guide*, cookbooks and lifestyle and fashion magazines are influential tastemakers that wield material and symbolic power.[7] Their role as arbiters of fine taste is to judge aesthetic values and to educate people on superior food and fashionable dressing. Although gastronomy and haute couture belong to the elite who are wealthy enough to indulge in them, the gastronome and the fashion designer sets standards and shape tastes. As their work is disseminated outside of their exclusive circles they are 'fundamental players in the cultural game'.[8] 'A gastronome', notes Stephen Mennell,

> . . . is generally understood to be a person who not only cultivates [their] own refined taste for the pleasure of the table, but also by writing about it, helps to cultivate other people's too. The gastronome is more than a gourmet -[they] are also a theorist and a propagandist about culinary taste.[9]

Carême

While there had been influential cooks and culinary tastemakers such as Bonnefons and La Chapelle, there is no disagreement whatsoever amongst historians of gastronomy as to who the first celebrity chef was. One of the underlying motifs of this book has been the extent to which social and economic forces have shaped the possibility of the restaurant and cook together with the growing circuits of fashion, criticism and opinion. Since the Middle Ages, chief cooks were called a series of titles describing their leadership over the culinary household, culminating in *chef de cuisine*, which is now abridged to *chef*, but until the late eighteenth century, these titles and status was conferred first and foremost by the patron. This is not to say that the patron was far from unaware that his or her own status was shaped by the quality of the court, of which the quality at the table was a crucial element; it was not until after the Revolution that cooks had a level of mobility in France that was unthinkable only decades before, since popularity was a matter of a more open market as opposed to regulated at the hands of a few. Carême took advantage of the period when overstepping boundaries was possible, and expected, and where the growing cult of celebrity was required to secure a comfortable living.

As a result, we might consider the epithets of 'King of Chefs' and the 'Inventor of French Cuisine' at more than face value, and as markers of the age of hyperbole and celebrity as well of his own talent, which included, as with all celebrity chefs to this day, that of unrepentant self-promotion. Credited as the foremost pioneer of grande cuisine and as the inventor of French Cuisine, Carême is perhaps better described as the inventor if the French *style* of cuisine. Whilst never static, the French style is built around a set of principles and techniques that form the basis of what counts for – symbolically, materially, or both – the highest standards of food consumption. It is in food and fashion consumption that is built around conduct and appearances.

Carême's life (1784–1833) straddles what we can in retrospect define as the most critical period in the evolution of restaurants and gastronomy as they have evolved to the present day. Certain biographical details are worth glossing as they illustrate the nature of the new kind of culinary individual, and there are numerous analogies in the fashion industry of the rise from humble origins to a higher if yet ill-defined social order, if not to celebrity status. Of lowly origins, Carême began as a menial in a restaurant and transitioned at fifteen to one of the foremost patisseries of Paris, Bailly's on the rue Vivienne, which was frequented by several notable people, including Charles-Maurice de Talleyrand, who was then Foreign Minister. From early on Carême proved himself to be the consummate showman, producing sumptuously intricate decorative confections, receiving attention from passers-by including eventually Napoleon himself, who regularly called upon Bailly for the equivalent of what today is known as catering services. The catering for banquets and balls was then referred as *Extraordinaires*, shortened to *extras*. The kinds of show required of these events was exploited by Carême who made the most of the attention-grabbing extravaganzas.

Whilst still under Bailly's employ, Carême had been allowed by his *patron* to make periodic visits to the Bibliothèque Royale, subsequently called the Bibliothèque Nationale (National Library), situated on the same street as the restaurant. It was here that Carême amassed a considerable amount of knowledge that he would later synthesize for his own ends. Apparently in the early days of study, while still acclimatizing to the mass of cookery texts, his first response was to the illustrations, which he copied (the former location of the Bibliothèque Nationale near the Paris Stock Exchange now exclusively holds the vast collection of prints and engravings from which Carême drew his inspiration). He also sketched the outside environs such as buildings, which would become the basis for his lavish food designs, his *pieces montées*.[10] Ultimately Carême's literacy developed from the study of cookery books, and it was cookery books that were his lens to the world. What is worth emphasizing is that his sensibility grew with the written, the visual and the practical almost in tandem.

This was a time of enormous social shifts in France, owing to the then expanding Napoleonic Empire, and the rising fortunes of a new ruling class. The new and glamorous Marshallate and the various other members of the establishment, a good many of them from humble origins and keen to compensate, snaffled up many of the cooks abandoned by the aristocratic households of the *ancien régime* and who had not turned their mind to private enterprise in restaurants, a popular but still precarious business. After leaving Bailly, Carême, cherishing his freedom, worked as an organizer of *extras*, most frequently for Talleyrand, and some for Marshal Joachim Murat. Murat, known informally as 'the Dandy King', was an ambitious and hot-headed man with an unabashed inclination for ostentation in the parties he threw and in the extremes to which he would go in his military dress, examples of which are recorded in numerous portraits and paintings of military campaigns of the period (Figure 4.1). (It is often conjectured that Napoleon's adoption of the austere grey frock coat or his redeployment of the green uniform from when he was colonel of the grenadiers was a reaction to the extravagance of many of his generals, showing him to be a modest *honnêt homme*, or man of virtue.)

Figure 4.1 Fragment of portrait of Joachim Murat, Prince d'Empire, Grand Duke of Clèves and of Berg, King of Naples under the name of Napoleon in 1808 (1767–1815), Marshal of France in 1804. (Wikipedia Commons, Public Domain.)

In these years Carême worked under a small coterie of experienced and recognized culinary eminences, including Laguipière (to whom he would later dedicate *Le Cuisiner parisien*) and Robert, who had been chef for the Prince de Condé before the Revolution (bringing with him his skilled culinary retinue), and it was from them that Carême expanded his culinary repertoire. Unlike his counterparts in restaurants catering for the middle classes, or lower, those in charge of *extras* had oversight over a sizeable staff and an equally sizeable budget, with the patron calling for ever greater feats of culinary mastery for the sake of the event and for the sake of himself. Carême referred to the extras as the 'grande école' (great school) the cooks equivalent to the more officiated Grands Écoles established by the Revolution and under Napoleon.[11] It was their lavish scale that necessitated a broad division of labour, from cold courses to warm dishes and sauces to pastry, a division that was only incipient but would be instituted in restaurants by Escoffier at the end of the century.

While Talleyrand was his regular patron, under who he worked for longer periods on and off for some twelve years, it was still in a relatively independent capacity as opposed to a house chef. Sources remain conflicted, however, of the exact role of Carême for Talleyrand, but his support of Carême remained the mainstay of his career. So much so that, in his *Cuisiner Parisienne*, in his complaint against Grimod, where Carême defends the development of French cuisine to practice over theory, he singles out Talleyrand as a supporter of the new art of cuisine. In this passage we see several things, including Carême's consciousness of the many changes wrought from the collapse of the *ancien régime*, and the ushering in of a new élite and, in turn, the cultivation of a new specialized and commensurably élite workforce. The increase, with such rapidity and in such a small period is thanks both to the support of the new classes after the Revolution and of the specialists that responded to it. The increase in culinary quality

> is thanks to the genius of our contemporary cooks at to extraordinary causes, such as the grand celebrations given on the occasion of our victories, above all those given at the City Hall (*Hôtel-de-Ville*) of Paris, which were the most magnificent; the creation of a new nobility, and finally the establishment of numerous, well organized, houses of government: the marshals of France, the ministers and the ambassadors. The men of talent that ran them competed with a new-found zeal to the end that cuisine of the great houses was on was on par with its their prestige. But, I repeat again, it was at the grand dinners given by the Prince de Talleyrand, then Foreign Minister, and by the celebrated Robert, that resulted in the expansion (*accroiseement*) of French cuisine, not because of the author of the *Almanach des gourmands*.[12]

There are several things at stake in this passage, which included the argument for the stakes that Carême was making for himself as the introducer of the new art of cuisine. He does so by signalling first the hands of others. In this respect his social attitudes would lay the template for the chef and the couturier to come to the service of the high classes while also de facto identifying with them. As we will see later in this book, celebrity chefs rely on the media, while Carême's authority was boosted, if not soldered through his claims to culinary scholarship (and hence his need to take on Grimod). This meant that, as Parkhurst Ferguson remarks, he always 'straddled two worlds. The dual allegiances sustained an unprecedented culinary authority, both for his contemporaries, sensitive to the prestige of his traditional elite associations, and for his successors, who routinized a profession on his culinary innovations.'[13] He used the legacy of the Revolution as well as the new authority of the Napoleonic regime to his advantage. He was something of a free agent while prospering from the support of the highest echelons of the establishment.

Toward the end of the Empire, Carême opened his own patisserie on the rue de la Paix, better known today as close to the Opera, but, for our own purposes, not far from where, about fifty years later, Worth and Otto Gustave Bobergh would set up the first house of haute couture at 7 rue de la Paix. In Carême's time the street was called rue Napoleon since its opening in 1806 – changing after 1814 – and, leading off the Place Vendôme, has been since its inception the location of all forms of desirable goods, including fashion and jewellery (Cartier opened his first shop on the street in 1898). During these years of relative independence, Carême assiduously maintained, within what was a punishing working regimen, his visits to the library, publishing his first book, *Hitoire de la table romaine* (History of the Roman Table).

Upon the fall of Napoleon and the Restoration in 1814, Carême monopolized on the influx of foreign dignitaries who competed to have him cook for them, and it was during this period that he also found time to publish in 1815 two related books on pastry, *Le Patissier pittoresque* (Picturesque Pastry) and *Le Patissier royal parisien* (Royal Parisian Pastry). Of the two, the former was the richer in illustration, including designs for his *pieces montées* composed during the Empire years. The latter was in two volumes and composed of recipes. In 1816 he agreed to head the kitchen of the Prince Regent in London, where he stayed for two years, beginning an international peregrination that would secure him as the celebrated cook of his age, an age when reputation was far more at the behest of competing opinion than ever before. After his eight-month stint with the future George IV he moved to Vienna for Lord Stewart, England's ambassador to Austria. When Stewart was summoned back to England, Carême followed, but this did not eventuate whereupon he found himself back in Paris. He agreed to travel to St Petersburg but found the conditions not to his liking so endured an arduous journey back to Paris where he was quickly taken up by Princess Ekaterina Bagration. After a few false starts and waiting in vain for Lord Stewart again and for Prince Esterhazy, Carême finally wound up with the Baron de

Rothschild, spending the last years of his life until 1833 with him in Paris and on his estate at Ferrières. Carême died in his Paris home on the Rue Neuve Saint Roche aged forty-eight, from complications, it is agreed, incurred from decades inhaling the fumes of coal-fired ovens, one of several brutal conditions that assured the limited longevity of any hardened cook.

His ill-fated trip to St Petersburg had mixed results. He appraised Russian produce with a foreigner's bias and produced a series of plans for actual architectural monuments to be installed throughout the city. An equally telling anecdote about the importance of show came earlier in March 1814, after the fall of Napoleon, when Carême was employed again by Talleyrand to do an *extra* to celebrate the re-entry of Louis XVIII and to welcome the victors, including Tsar Alexander I who arrived at the end of the month. In his arrangements for a dedicatory dinner for the Tsar, Talleyrand found that there was not a suitable number of French senators willing to make an appearance, lest they appear to be turncoats, or partaking in a feast following a military humiliation. Talleyrand's solution was to hire forty actors to dress up and play a gathering of senators. They all toasted Louis XVIII volubly over the meal devised by Carême, and the Tsar was none the wiser, or at least dissembled as such. Talleyrand promptly installed the Tsar at the Elysée Palace, soon after which Carême was called upon to serve the Russian Emperor. Given that the kitchens had been graced by Laguipière and knowing the extent to which Alexander aimed at delivering the most splendid feasts, he happily obliged. As Darra Goldstein concludes, 'Carême's labour heightened Alexander I's prestige; at the same time, his own position was strengthened by their association.'[14]

Of all of Carême's books, it is *le Cuisiner parisien, ou l'art de la cuisine française au dix-neuvième siècle* (revised edition, 1828) that is the best known and celebrated. After a lengthy dedication to Laguipière which is also a meditation on his perishing (in Vilna in 1812, on campaign as chef to Joachim Murat) in Napoleon's Russian campaign, Carême mounts a firm case of the incontestable superiority of French cuisine, especially as it had evolved after 1793, a date that places himself at the epicentre of this climax. Naming numerous contemporaries, most of whom have now fallen from documentary view, he doffs his hat several times to La Chapelle, but states that the food that is now prepared is one of singular refinement on the old, urging the good reader to compare the cuisine of his time with the century before. He claims that 'the superiority of modern cuisine is immense; simplicity and elegance conjoin with sumptuousness, characterizing it honourably.' The menus to follow, he assures the reader, present 'incontestable proof' of this.[15] As to be expected, Carême makes a surreptitious but unmissable conflation between the newly introduced universal of 'modern cuisine' and the cuisine that he describes and presents. It is his solemn duty to do this as, he states, that he has travelled extensively, and the greatest houses of Europe are dominated by French chefs and by French cuisine: 'I've seen England, Russia, Germany, and Italy and everywhere I met cooks holding the prime positions in foreign courts.'[16]

Carême was the ultimate arbiter of French cooking, in which French cooking would be the arbiter of his own success. Moreover, his appeal for simplicity in cooking was multivalent and not to be taken at face value. On the one hand, it was in generic compliance with the post-Revolutionary legacy, which had become more rhetorical by then than real, for eschewing complications (as especially seen in dress), and on the other it was simplicity when compared to the *ancien régime*. As Parkhurst Ferguson continues: 'Simplicity implied a host of other qualities—harmony, elegance, and above all, that notoriously slippery attribute, good taste.'[17] The call to fashionable newness and to good taste was a powerful one, as it implied social opprobrium for those ignorant or unwilling to entertain it. Whereas earlier writers had at times stressed the integrity of ingredients, Carême did this in the interests of cooking as well as undercrossing a break with the past, which since the beginnings of the spice trade in the fifteenth century, had loaded and obscured flavours with spices. Like Worth fifty years later, who lifted liberally from master paintings for his 'inspiration', Carême was a master synthesizer. We might also compare the famous photograph of Worth in his beret and scarf, posing as the consummate artist, with the best-known likeness of Carême (by Pierre-François-Léonard Fontaine) in which he poses as scholar and poet. Instead of being accompanied by the tools of his trade, which was common to the pictorial conventions of the last few centuries, he is depicted with a Byronic open shirt and loose cravat, next to a quill at the end of a row of books (Figure 4.2).

But it would take longer for couturiers to reach the heights that Carême had secured for chefs. Metzner affirms: 'Eventually, in the twentieth century, French clothing designers would become as celebrated as French chefs. And the prestige of the latter would not decline.'[18] In the wake of Carême, chefs would occasionally receive the award of the Legion d'Honneur, a national honorific started by Napoleon. Couturiers and designers would only be honoured in this way much later on.

Seen against the backdrop of his time, Carême is someone very much under the spell of Napoleon: child of the Revolution, who for the good of his country became confederator and facilitator. As Parkhurst Ferguson observes: 'Even if Carême did not invent all the dishes that he explicated, he named a good many of them, conferring an identity that stamped this cuisine as indelibly French'[19] and further, as himself as the prime facilitator. For just as Worth was not the only person to precipitate haute couture at the time, he is still seen as the prime catalyst because of his personality and bombast. He was not without competition: Alexandre Viard's *Cuisiner imperial* (The Imperial Chef) (1806) ran to thirty editions and was arguably the most turned-to work by a cook in the nineteenth century. So too, Antoine Beauvilliers published *L'Art du cuisine* (The Art of Cooking) in 1814, a work that also received widespread attention, except that his book sounded a valedictory point to French cuisine, not a new beginning and the heralding of a brilliant future as Carême did with such magisterial flourish. Carême was hailed by Balzac as synonymous with gastronomic excellence, 'just as it was Carême', Ferguson continues, 'not

Figure 4.2 Marie-Antoine Carême, 8 June 1784–1833, Fontaine, Pierre-François-Léonard – Bibliothèque Sainte-Geneviève. (Wikipedia Commons, Public Domain.)

Viard or Beauvilliers, whom Dumas characterized as the "apostle of gastronomes," the only chef honoured with a full entry in his encyclopaedic *Grande Dictionnaire de cuisine*'.[20] This was an age as Metzner puts it, 'of expansive visions and commensurate creations: the Grandes Écoles, Napoleon's Grande Armée, Carême's grande cuisine, and Balzac's *Comédie humaine*'.[21]

While Carême achieved fame in his own lifetime, unprecedented for what then was only described as a cook, his reputation was soldered by several people who worked for him, who also rivalled their master in the art of self-promotion. One salient figure was Charles Elmé Francatelli, who, after working with Carême in Paris, became Queen Victoria's chief cook and maître d'hôtel. True to style, he sedimented his reputation with a series of books, intended for the middle-class imagination. Francatelli kept to the standards and traditions of French cooking but was able to vary it to suit English tastes. In the banquet to celebrate the Great Exhibition of 1851, for instance, the Lord Mayor of London decided that English food need not be adhered to, and instead much of the food derived from Francatelli's most influential and well-known book, *The Modern Cook,* which would reach its third edition in 1877.[22]

Worth

For a brief time in the Second Empire, fashion would make up for lost time in its grandeur, but by the end of the nineteenth century, in both food and fashion, grandeur became more of an idea, an historical rallying-point that would need to be tempered. The excesses of grande cuisine, as with the elaborate bustles, lace, frills and paraphernalia of the reign of Napoleon III and Eugénie, became harder to sustain and to justify. Social life now partook in shared public spaces of the cabaret, the restaurant and the bar, where it became easier to pretend or conceal one's class and identity, a tendency begun around a hundred years before. The convergence of fashion and food would prove to be the essential factor, the glue, in the social interactions of modernity into the early twentieth century in which the old social classes existed more as a token and a dream.

Little is known about Worth's early life; he did not keep a journal, or write any personal letters, and if he did, these no longer exist and may have been destroyed for whatever reason. What we know of Worth is from secondary accounts written by journalists and observers, which tended to be scathing, or from his clients who were wealthy doyennes and full of adulation.[23] What we do know of Worth is that he was born in England in 1825 in the small market town of Bourne during the Georgian period and grew up in a relatively modest home, until his father, a solicitor, squandered his finances leaving the family destitute. As a youth of thirteen, he was apprenticed to textile merchants in London and at the age of twenty moved to Paris where he gained employment as a clerk at Maison Gagelin (1854) the fashionable clothier that supplied Princess Eugénie's trousseau on her marriage to Napoleon III. It was at Gagelin's that he met his wife Marie Vernet, who would become his first house model, and where he got his 'big break' after submitting his prize-winning dress design on behalf of Maison Gagelin to the *Universal Exhibition* in Paris (1855).

Worth spent a great deal of his free time combing through artists' portfolios, attending exhibitions and galleries and spending hours on end in bookshops refining his taste and sharpening his aesthetic senses.[24] It is of note that Worth was born into a professional family, was well educated, and had access to cultural capital. His employment in the textile trade gave him a vast amount of knowledge of expensive fabrics, such as cashmere and silks that were imported from the colonies and were only the province of the connoisseurs and wealthy clients. We know that he rigorously studied the paintings of a range of artists because their stylistic references rendered in taffetas and silks were executed in the designs of his gowns. A knowledge of art provided a plethora of imagery which Worth was able to access and use to visualize clothing.

It was common for society women to have their portraits painted by leading artists, which acted as an early form of fashion editorial and a record of the tastes of the period. As Aileen Ribeiro remarks 'artists provide invaluable testimony to the culture, the manners, and the vision of their times'.[25] Worth's gowns are immortalized in the paintings of Franz Xaver Winterhalter of affluent society women and court ladies, most notably his patrons the Austrian socialite Princess Pauline von Metternich-Pauline von Metternich and the Spanish Contessa Eugénie de Montijo who became empress of France (Figure 4.3) after her marriage to Napoleon III. In the small-scale oil portrait, the Empress Eugénie is wearing a gown of taffeta, silk and lace with ribbons designed by Worth. Her auburn hair is powdered and accessorized with ribbons, plumes and flowers. Her Spanish complexion is lightened to resemble Marie Antoinette who was known for her exquisite taste in ornate clothing and whom Eugénie emulated to appease the French populace and acquire their allegiance. 'By manipulating the signs of fashion,' writes Teresa Dolan, 'she (mis)construed her own image as a monarch.'[26]

> Eugénie's adaptation of a *style Marie Antoinette* in dress and décor reflected her effort to link her imperial reign with the court of Louis XVI; she wished to connect her personal image with what she perceived to be the political astuteness and personal courage of a beheaded queen.[27]

Worth used his vast knowledge of fabrics and relied on engraving, mezzotints and portraits of Marie Antoinette to create Eugénie's gowns. You could say that for the first time a milliner had become a stylist, creating a complete 'look', a *toute ensemble*, as opposed to merely a gown which was the practice of dressmakers and milliners at the time. Soon enough, Worth, now aged only thirty, had begun to gain a reputation for exquisite taste amongst the society women that visited Maison Gagelin (Figure 4.4).

Feeling bored and creatively stifled, Worth convinced the wealthy businessman Otto Bobergh to give him the financial backing to start a dressmaking business. Soon after, he left his job and opened his own couture house on the exclusive Rue de la Paix. Success came quickly for Worth, thanks to the support of the extravagant Princess von Metternich, the wife of the Austrian Ambassador to the court of Napoleon III. The princess had a reputation for having discerning taste. Her excessive spending on clothes had secured the attention of her jealous adversaries who nicknamed her *le singe à la mode* (the fashionable monkey).[28] The princess was impressed by Worth's designs and ordered a gown to wear to the next ball at the Tuileries where she was seen by the most fashionable women in Paris, including the Empress Eugénie. The princess soon became what in

Figure 4.3 The Empress Eugénie (Eugénie de Montijo, 1826–1920, Condesa de Teba). Franz Xavier Winterhalter (German, Menzenschwand 1805–1873 Frankfurt), 1854. Oil on Canvas. Dimension 36 1/2 × 29 in. (92.7 × 73.7 cm.) Purchase, Mr and Mrs Claus von Bülow Gift, 1978, Metropolitan Museum of Modern Art, New York.

contemporary fashion is known as a brand ambassador for the House of Worth. Soon enough, appointments for fittings and gowns began coming in thick and fast. Worth began designing the art that became known as haute couture and in the process reinvented himself as an artist, in dress, manner and deportment.

When Monsieur Griffiths was commissioned by *The Strand Magazine* (1894) to write an article on Paris Dressmakers he decided to 'call upon the Oracles of

Figure 4.4 Illustration to 'Paris Dressmakers' by M. Griffith, published in *The Strand Magazine* no. 48, Vol. VIII, July to December 1894. (Wikipedia Commons, Public Domain.)

Paris Fashions'[29] beginning with the House of Worth, where he found the designer 'deep in consultation with an elderly lady, a pretty young one and a very bored looking young man.'[30]

> M. Worth was dressed in a dark, loose dressing-gown, relieved with touches of blue, and the right-hand side bottom corner was lifted up and drawn through a buttonhole a little above the waist; on his head he wore a mitre-shaped hat of black velvet, sometimes his gown is richly trimmed with fur (Figure 4.5).[31]

When Monsieur Griffiths asked Worth 'what is really the origin of a fashion?,'[32] Worth replied:

> Well, it is difficult to enter into all the details which influence changes of style; but briefly I may say that, when a manufacturer invents any special fabric or design, he sends me a pattern, asking if I can make use of it. That fabric may require a severe style of dress, or if light and soft is adapted for draperies,

> puffings etc. If the material pleases me, I order a large quantity, to be specially made for me, and design my dresses accordingly . . . the style it is best suited to becomes the fashion.[33]

Worth's self-invention as an artist, together with his entrepreneurial prowess and his control of taste made him a tastemaker and arbiter of style during the Second Empire. The visibility of his work was bolstered by the aristocratic women that he clothed which placed his designs in demand and at a high premium. When the Empress Eugénie noticed Princess von Metternich's gown on the night of the state ball at the Tuileries, she swiftly appointed Worth as her primary clothier. Even though from the beginning of her reign, the Empress was known as a trendsetter and a tastemaker, Worth – as the first man-milliner – executed a great amount of power over the Empress' choice of gowns and her overall style. At times he even became quite dictatorial, imposing his will that she wore several of his gowns in a day and by no means was she to wear the same gown too

Figure 4.5 Charles Frederick Worth, 1826–1895. English Fashion Designer. From *The Strand Magazine* published in 1894. (Photo by: Universal History Archive/Universal Images Group via Getty Images.)

often. Fashion journals chronicled her every taste in colour and contour and when she decided to ditch the crinoline, Worth designed a new silhouette for a skirt. Together they made a formidable team, Eugénie with her bloated display of wealth and good taste and Worth with his creative inspiration and style. Eugénie introduced Worth to influential aristocrats throughout Europe and in turn, he was thoroughly devoted to her making her his muse.

The rest, as we say, is history: The House of Worth and his rise to fame is well known amongst scholars of fashion. Before Worth came onto to the fashion scene, wealthy women gave their couturiers instructions when commissioning garments; instead, Worth dictated trends to his clients by designing collections of 'looks' rather than following their suggestions. According to Amy de la Haye and Valerie Mendes, rigorous control over taste-making was among his notable 'firsts'. This was

> the role [that] Worth created for himself as a dictatorial couturier, who designed and determined the styles of dress his clients were to wear. His business provided all the necessary accoutrements for a complete wardrobe of fashionable and ceremonial dress, together with the requisite accessories.[34]

Worth created an alternative social order where the customer made her choice of garment from live models rather than fashion dolls, which was then adapted to the client's measurements and tastes. A label containing Worth's *griffe* would then be sewn onto to the lapel lining of the gown, elevating the garment to the status of an original artwork and the dressmaker to that of an artist (Figure 4.6).

In *Notes in Paris* (1867) the critic Hippolyte Taine describes Worth as a domineering and affected milliner, 'who looks like a dwarf . . . receives [clients] in his loose velvet coat. Proudly stretched out on his divan, a cigar in his mouth. He says to them: walk, turn around; well; come back in a week. I will compose you a suitable toilette.'[35] Worth insisted that his clients were introduced to him before he designed a gown for them and many of his wealthy clients would consult with him before attending a ball, even tolerating his rudeness for the sake of a dress. 'If any seem surprised by his acid rancour he replies, "I am a great artist; I have Delacroix's feeling for colour, and I compose. A toilette is worth a picture any day".'[36] Taine portrays Worth as a lazy, self-obsessed artist and as an excessive perfectionist who placed the same aesthetic value on dressmaking as on an artwork. He possessed 'all the whims of an artist . . . his waywardness, his abrupt changes of manner, his tumultuous outpourings of new inspiration'[37] were not only endured by his clientele, but 'indeed they formed part of the attraction of the setting.'[38] The countess de Mercy-Argenteau remembers that Worth 'was very amusing, and his vogue came quite as much from his personality as from his talent as a dressmaker.'[39]

Figure 4.6 House of Worth label, 1900. Silk taffeta, lace, satin by Charles Frederick Worth. Bertha Palmer (nee Honore, 1849–1918) was an American socialite and businesswoman and was the first wife of businessman Potter Palmer. (Photo by Chicago History Museum/Getty Images.)

> When I wanted an important toilette for a Court ball . . . I had to call several times. He would first look at me for a long time without speaking; then in an inspired and faraway voice [he would say]; 'Light gauze . . . light grey. . . . Roses and leaves . . . a trail of lace' . . . and he would disappear . . . If he decided that I was to wear blue or green, I had to do as I was told. He was a tyrant, but we all adored him.[40]

The countess's encounter with Worth was experienced by most Worth clients. It was a mutually beneficial relationship whose foundations were based on the promotion of the 'celebrity designer together with his celebrity client'.[41] As Abigail Joseph believes, Worth's relationship with his clients was one of 'command, support, promotion, and in all its complex vicissitudes, the identification between a high-fashion designer and the women affiliated with him as models, muses and customers.'[42]

By 1868, the House of Worth had become the epicentre of fashion and good taste that attracted a large clientele (Figure 4.7). When customers arrived at Worth's atelier they were greeted by two doormen dressed in frock-coats and guided up a staircase covered by a thick red carpet and lined with exotic plants, past a series of drawing rooms that led to a mirrored show room containing gowns displayed on wooden mannequins where the floor was covered with grey

Figure 4.7 The House of Worth, 7 rue de la Paix, Paris. Unknown author – Illustration to 'Paris Dressmakers' by M. Griffith, published in The Strand Magazine no. 48, Vol. VIII, July to December 1894. Public Domain.

carpet and imitation tiger-skin print. The drawing rooms were furnished with plush fabrics, colourful silks and glass cabinets that contained Worth's collection of curios, fans and snuff boxes.[43] In Émile Zola's novel *La Curée* (The Kill, 1871–72), the reader is presented with the character Worms (an alliteration of Worth), a 'couturier of genius to whom the great ladies of the Second Empire bowed down.'[44] His description of Worth's showroom is worth quoting in its entirety because it paints an image of the couturier's extravagant tastes and his venerated status among the nouveau riche of Haussmann's Paris.

> The great man's showroom was huge and square and furnished with enormous divans . . . dresses undoubtedly have a perfume of their own; silk, satin, velvet and lace had mingled their faint aromas with those of hair and of amber-scented shoulders; and the atmosphere of the room had a sweet smelling warmth, the fragrance of flesh and luxury, that transformed the apartment into a chapel consecrated to some secret divinity.[45]

The Maison provided a place for women to meet and socialize and they were served tea, biscuits, plates of cakes and glasses of Madeira whilst they waited their turn to meet with the illustrious couturier. The salon also contained a kitchen that served meals to Worth's numerous employees and a studio where all the models were photographed wearing his latest creations , that were then sent to clients in America.[46] 'The seductive salon at Maison Worth' writes Jess Berry 'conveyed dramatic opulence [and] . . . enhanced the appearance of the couturier's fashions to glamourous and lavish effects.'[47]

While it is a commonplace to say that any figure is a product of their time, it is harder to speculate to what extent this was made possible by others or by dint of personal gifts. True enough, Carême and Worth were children of a widening market economy and a larger class-base thirsty for conspicuous consumption; they had unmistakable gifts in synthesizing influence, were in control and had a mastery over branding in which their 'creations' were made to seem seamless, with them as geniuses. Self-made men, they are still the cultural bench-marks for the 'top-down' approach of restaurants and fashion houses, the idea that to be a consumer of them is to enter into, to participate in an entirely new world, a parallel universe of privilege in which things were no longer just perfectible but perfected.

5

CUISINE AND COUTURE CULTURE: THE BOUTIQUE AS A SPACE OF CONSUMPTION

The installation of a dedicated food space in a shopping environment is nothing new since department stores and shopping malls have been serving food to consumers since the early twentieth century. What has changed is the way in which fashion brands have established and used restaurants as a way of advancing and entrenching the kind of sensibility, and the kind of customer it wants to both attract and reflect. Central to fashion is the co-mingling of those who are suited to a *look* and a lifestyle and those who aspire to it. Although altogether porous, brands pretend to have circumscribed values that are the product of countless representations, bringing associations to ways of life, to historical paradigms, social mores, linguistic codes. As Finkelstein notes in her study of fashion and manners, the social relations of dining out in restaurants and the way that food is consumed is a technique that individuals use to signify their fashionable tastes and sophistication. 'A meal [at a restaurant] has more to do with styles of sociality than with the basic matter of bodily maintenance.'[1] The restaurant transfers the banal act of eating for bodily nourishment into a complex social system. In retrospect, the trend of fashion houses to open restaurants in their boutiques or adjacent is only logical, as these provide spaces where people can continue their consumption of the fashion brand beyond buying accessories and clothing and wearing them. In the brand restaurant consumers can literally imbibe the fashion, as if partaking in their own specially sanctioned consumerist ritual.

We may consider the restaurant founded by the fashion brand as a transition from early department store tea rooms and restaurants, or it may be better characterized as simply expanding the possibilities of the imaginative experience central to fashion itself. The restaurant is yet another place to partake in ephemera, where desires are briefly satisfied. A signal example of the way a fashion brand has smoothly adapted to the restaurant space is Ralph Lauren's Polo Bar on 1 East 55th Street in Manhattan, New York, just off 5th Avenue. Just as Lauren's Polo brand is a liberal and seemingly never-ending pastiche of the Ascot set and Ivy-League aristocracy, the bar is encoded with all the trappings of an exclusive English Men's club, except that it is free of cigar smoke and is not exclusive to men. It is rich in wood and leather and the walls, which are covered with tasteful equestrian artworks, are a deep British racing green. The food is in keeping with club-style, that is, it is replete with favourites and classics, but which are executed at a high level of quality. Dishes include shrimp cocktail, mushroom soup, Caesar salad, BLT salad, a hot dog (Sauerkraut Sweet Relish on a Toasted Brioche Bun),[2] a corned beef sandwich, together with Veal Milanese. There are of course steaks and burgers as well as sides of mashed potatoes and creamed spinach. It is fare consonant with the success of the Ralph Lauren Polo brand, which is an assurance that there are classics and constants in capitalism, and that to be fashionable one only need to follow a few simple rules; provenance, quality and exclusivity. The concept behind retail restaurants is quite simple: people eat out more often than they shop for, say, a pair of shoes. What began as a way to make a brand more accessible and encourage consumers to stay in stores for longer has now created lifestyle destinations where people meet, eat and shop: come in for a burger, leave with a pair of jeans. For the sake of clarity, let us call these eating establishments 'designer restaurants' or 'designer cafés' and let us look at the ways in which branding, and aesthetics converge with consumption and taste regimes to offer a fashionable consumption experience.

It is worth pausing for a moment to look closely at the kind of food, or food design of these establishments, because there is a clear communality among them that is oriented around classics, which is to say mainstays of Western and Western-eclectic food. While the marriage between gastronomy and fashion is one that is never to be taken for granted, we may also ask the extent to which it is a fair and equitable marriage. For the trend seems to be that the food is there as a supplement to the business of fashion comsumption. Its purpose is to allow the consumer to linger in the warm glow of a designer's ambit of taste, with the gustatory playing the role of enhancing the experience. The other dimension to the relative regularity of gustatory design is that it confirms that what is being offered is reliable and enduring. To return to Simmel's famous dictum again, fashion is a paradoxical balance of difference and belonging. The restaurants' fare in these boutiques are all about reliability but always the implication of a small twist: after all no two Caesar salads are the same. The idea is to offer a 3-star experience of everyday fare – such as a brioche bun as opposed to a plain one. To defy any sense of too much derivation, some dishes will be given special names (à la Escoffier) or even bear the badge of the designer or firm that auspices the restaurant. In short, there is nothing to compete with the imaginative world of the fashion boutique, the restaurant is there to bolster and perpetuate the illusion of plenty.

Department store tea rooms

The concept of the designer restaurant has its early beginnings in the glamorous tea rooms of the nineteenth-century department store that catered exclusively to women, where they could shop and dine unchaperoned.[3] 'Some establishments did not serve women at all,' writes Paul Freedman, while other restaurants permitted women to dine under certain arrangements and in separate areas than men.[4] Such circumstances included women travelling alone, groups of women dining together, or female office workers and salesclerks wanting to dine for lunch.[5] Public life was deemed as masculine, and men were considered the citizen producers whilst women were locked inside the home as wives and bearers of children. Industrialization brought along a variety of merchandize that became more readily available to consumers, like mass-produced clothing, perfume, petticoats, linen and gloves. As William Leach observes, stores marketed 'out of season flowers and in their petshops sold anything from rare birds to marmoset monkeys'.'[6] The increased availability of products resulted in the need to create new markets and so woman were targeted. The logic behind the new consumer economy was that if women were given a 'safe' place to eat and shop that was socially acceptable, then 'they could partake [in] the luxury and the theatrical behaviour of the rich'.[7]

By the early twentieth century many women had entered the workforce in service-oriented consumer industries such as retail and office work. Working women were able to enjoy the emancipating impact that consumer culture offered by the power of spending as well as gaining access to a public social life. Department stores were one of the few spaces where women could move around without the 'protection' of men. Ice-cream parlours and food stalls in urban districts served women, but by the closing decade of the nineteenth century these eating establishments were supplemented by department store tea rooms and restaurants. 'Although not formally defined for women only,' notes Freedman, 'these genteel restaurants eschewed alcohol and provided food conforming (or supposedly conforming) to women's tastes: a somewhat consistent repertoire of light food (such as salads) and sweet, childish treats (ice cream).'[8] Not only did the menu reflect gendered tastes, but the interior dining spaces were designed to cater to either men or women.

In 1904 the Dayton department store in Minneapolis advertised its tearoom The Dinette as 'cheerful with many frosted windows and a colour scheme of chartreuse and gold tones, specializing in salads, light lunches.'[9] Like most department stores, Dayton's offered a segregated dining space called the 'Men's

Grill' where men could conduct their business affairs and 'eat alone, undisturbed by the presence of the more attractive sex.'[10] In an advertisement announcing the refurbishment of the Dayton tea rooms, 'The men's grill with [its] masculine atmosphere of oak panelling and red leather serves a menu suited to masculine tastes.'[11] Men were served hearty meals like steak au poivre, or corned beef and hash while women's choice of 'light' meals were chicken salad or mayonnaise chicken, sweetbreads or oysters and creamy deserts.[12] Just as there were partitions for menswear and womenswear as above, the same ordering but more by implication was carried out on the menu.

The interiors of department stores were designed to increase consumer spending by flaming material desires. This was achieved by using various sales techniques including advertising, merchandising and store layout. In her book, *Temptations: Sex, Selling, and the Department Store* (1993), Gail Reekie remarks that department store space was planned to maximize spending, which included segregating men's and women's departments, a feature of early drapery stores that became even more pronounced in the early twentieth century. Next to the Reading Room at the Bon Marché was a buffet that offered 'cakes and biscuits, along with cups of hot chocolate or glasses of Madeira and claret served with napkins and brilliant glasses of filtered ice-water.'[13] Much like the Men's Grill, the Reading Room was a space where men were supplied with the daily newspaper and other amusements as they waited for their wives to finish their shopping. Department stores were places where consumers were entertained by commodities, where 'selling [was] mingled with amusement', to purchase items.[14] These 'particular items' or 'models of desire'[15] as René Girard describes them in a different context were women's fashion and accessories.

Many tea rooms were strategically placed near womenswear departments, which included cosmetics, fine fragrance, lingerie and accessories. Women could shop and then take light refreshments in the adjoining tearooms with their female companions enabling shopping to become a leisure activity. 'By presenting itself as a home of leisure' comments Susan Porter Benson,

> the department store sought to elevate its agenda beyond commerce, to distinguish itself as a purveyor of middleclass taste. Expanding its range of activities with its lines of goods the institution [department store] offered to entertain the public while educating them in the latest trends in art, dress, and home furnishings.[16]

Department stores were a destination where women shopped, dined and socialized in an exclusively designed environment where the latest fashionable goods were displayed and could be purchased. In his study of women and department stores, William Leach locates the first fashion parade to have been staged in a department store in 1903 by the Ehrich Brothers in New York, but was later eclipsed by Wanamaker's '*promenade des toilettes*' at Gimbels which contained ramps and stages and the first live female models.[17] Leach believes that the department store did more than any other institution in bringing fashion to the American masses because it was associated with the 'glamour of Paris, of aristocracy and nobility, and the aura of theatre and the movie screen.'[18] Its comprehensive architecture meant that it could curate environments of desire, and many of them, featured in large rooms, sweeping spaces and cavernously high ceilings. These were the new cathedrals of consumption which presented an ideal world in miniature, which also meant, after all, eating and drinking.

Department store tearooms hosted special events and fundraisers, including fashion parades displaying the latest ready-to-wear fashions. The practice of combining food and tea with fashion parades came from Worth who served light refreshments to clients in his Parisian salon (est. 1858) as they waited to be fitted into gowns. The practice was then adopted by the Bon Marché department store who offered a banquet of cakes and biscuits accompanied with hot chocolate or glasses of Madeira and claret. Other department stores followed suit such as Galleries Lafayette and Samaritaine in Paris.[19]

Women would often compare what they were wearing with the catwalk models and with each other. Although 'everyone could "look equally",' not everyone could 'buy equality' and the tearoom fashion parade became an arena of class division.[20] Finkelstein writes that the tearoom fashion parade functioned like a theatre, 'the individual can gaze at length at others and have them recognise that they are being looked at without their being any disturbing sense that a social norm has been violated. The gaze is part of the event, as are the clothes, coiffure, companions, and styles of conversations.[21] Department store tearooms became places where that reinforced fine taste and class aspirations and where 'new ideas and practices would gain social currency.'[22] They were spaces that combined interior design with femininity, fashion, food, and contemporary manners and 'knowing how to hold one's cup, pour tea and eat a cake using a cake fork'[23] separated the *beau monde* from the *nouveaux riches.*

In the boom decades following the gold rush (1851–1914) Australian department stores offered extravagant in-house dining experiences. Anthony Hordern and Sons (established in 1823 after Harding, Howell and Company's Grand Fashionable Magazine in London, 1796) had its Tudor Tea Rooms and The Rainbow Room and David Jones, who began trading in 1838, had the Great Restaurant with silver service and damask tableware. The following year Farmers (later, Grace Bros. and now Myer) opened its Roof Garden Restaurant featuring a goldfish pool, caverns, and a water fountain that catered solely for women and children (Figure 5.1). Tea rooms were a popular venue for children's parties with special menus created for them based on themes. Some department store tearooms hired staff to plan parties, send invitations, hire entertainers and wrap

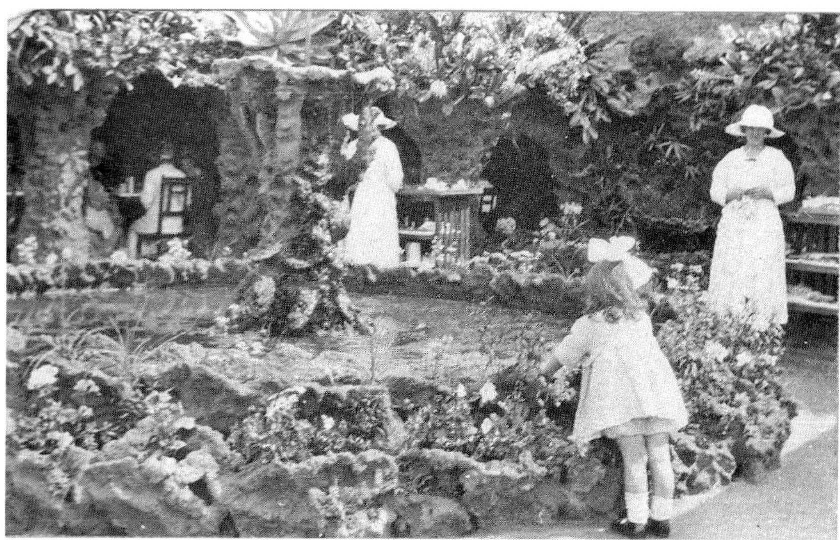

Figure 5.1 Farmers Tea Garden, Sydney. NSW, *c.* 1919. Joyce Turner (in foreground), photographer Ernest Turner. State Library of New South Wales.

gifts, whilst others planned food around themes.[24] Jan Whitaker writes that restaurants were established on roof gardens before air conditioning was made available. Au Printemps placed tables and chairs on their rooftop terrace every spring and summer so that consumers could enjoy a view of Paris. Whitaker notes that in 1916 Feline's in Boston had a rooftop restaurant, and in 1954 it installed a zoo with a lion and tiger.[25]

The roof gardens at the former Derry and Toms department store on Kensington High Street in London, already described as 'one of the most fashionable and popular promenades in London',[26] (Figure 5.2) contained a tearoom where customers could seek respite from their shopping. Pioneered by Selfridges department store, roof gardens had been popular in England since the Edwardian period and were influenced by early American skyscraper architecture. Derry and Toms' roof gardens were designed by the Welsh landscape artist Ralph Handcock in 1933 and was opened to the public in 1938. Considered to be the largest roof garden in the world at the time (today it is the largest in Europe), it was divided into the English Woodland Garden, the Tudor Court, the Spanish Garden and the Sun Pavilion which contained the tearooms. The Sun Pavilion was accessed by customers from the lower retail floors via two lifts and was oriented facing south to enjoy a panoramic view of the city. The tearooms contained a service area counter and a soda fountain against the rear wall with an open rotunda providing access to the garden. In 1971, Derry and Toms was sold to Barbara Hulanicki and her husband Stephen Fitz-Simon (known as Fitz) but the department store continued trading until 1973 when it was transformed into the boutique giant Big Biba.

Figure 5.2 The roof gardens at Derry and Toms in Kensington High Street, London. The gardens, 1 3/4 acres in extent, are very popular with tourists and residents, as well as shoppers. Before he retired, a local vicar visited there every day for thirteen years to write his sermons, 12 September 1965. (Photo by Bill Rowntree/Mirrorpix/Getty Images.)

From department stores to boutique restaurants. Mary Quants' Bazaar

Department stores restaurants were popular venues for fashion parades up until the 1950s when stores often presented frequent, if not daily fashion shows to diners (Figure 5.3). By the late 1950s the popularity of the department store began to wane as people moved out of the city centres to the suburbs. Discount stores began dominating the market and the formal-looking restaurant with its chandeliers and plush settings became outdated and was viewed as a 'place where old ladies went to shop, dine and watch a fashion show.'[27] Boutiques had come to replace the department store experience as a place to shop and be seen.

In November 1955, former art students Mary Quant, her flamboyant boyfriend (and later husband) Alexander Plunket Greene (APG) and their friend, photographer Archie McNair, opened a club-like boutique called Bazaar (with an inheritance from APG) on Kings Road in the centre of London's 'Swinging Chelsea' (Figure 5.4). The shop was exclusive and catered in the main to wealthy young women. Quant, Plunket Greene and McNair were part of the middle-class

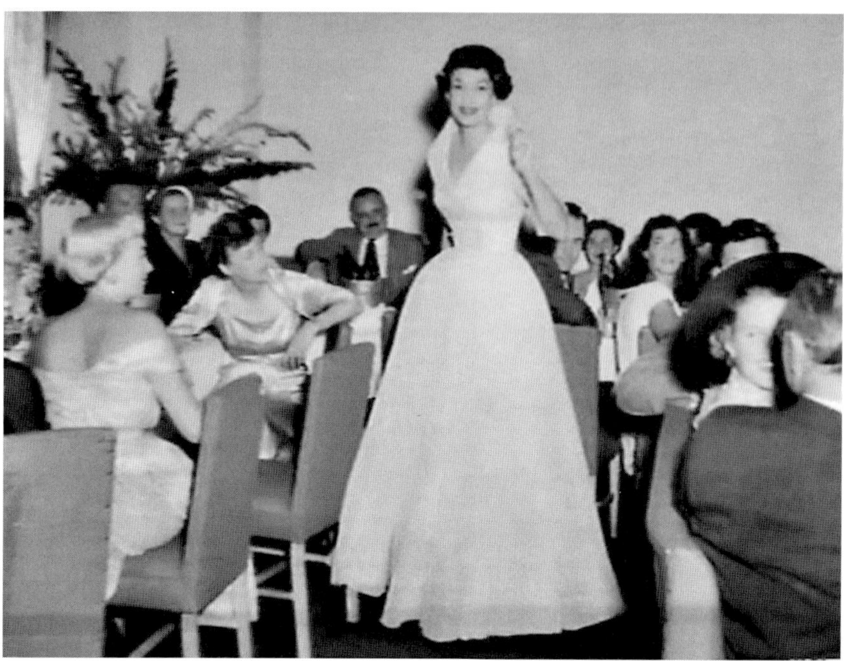

Figure 5.3 Fashion model in a ball gown at a fashion parade in the restaurant of David Jones' department store in Sydney, Australia. Australian Photographic Agency. Mitchell Library, State Library of New South Wales.

Figure 5.4 British fashion designer Mary Quant's shop, Bazaar, on King's Road, Chelsea, London, UK, 25 August 1966. The entrance to Alexanders basement restaurant is on the left. (Photo by Keystone/Hulton Archive/Getty Images.)

Chelsea Set, the earliest of the London youth style tribes, described by Quant as a 'bohemian world of painters, photographers, architects, writers, socialites, actors, con-men, and superior tarts.'[28] 'We were bored and frustrated,' said Quant, '[we were] uninterested in science and politics – which, in our view, merely led to war – [so] we poured in our thousands into art schools.'[29] Quant (like Vivienne Westwood) was a self-taught designer who used masculine suiting fabric and mixed them with feminine textures like chiffon, satin crepe and georgette. She designed trench coats, tunics and knickerbockers, and dresses with cowl-like or Peter Pan collars that sat at the hip then flared out in pleats. For her first Paris fashion show in 1963, Quant designed the 'Wet Collection', a series of PVC dresses and raincoats in bright colours.

Bazaars' interior was designed by Terence Conran and sold a mixture of Quant's waistless androgynous designs and bespoke accessories made by their art school friends. The window displays were wildly eccentric with mannequins adopting quirky poses like hanging from the ceiling and motorbikes were used as visual merchandize. At one time, Quant had a mannequin walk a real lobster on a gold chain, even though the lobster was dead. Jess Berry believes that Hulanicki's Biba and Quant's Bazaar were innovators of new visual merchandising techniques. Biba's stylized black and gold Art Nouveau style interior decorated with household furnishing created the casual environment that reflected the clothes of the era and Quant's boutique windows entertained and shocked people with their narrative tableaux scenes.[30] Customers were served drinks as they browsed through the boutique, or they could dine at Alexanders, the basement restaurant, which became the meeting place for the in-crowd: Brigitte Bardot, Leslie Caron, Princess Margaret and her husband Tony Snowdon, photographers Richard Avedon and David Bailey. In the same way that department stores provided restaurants and meals as part of the shopping experience, 'Bazaar took fashion boutiques from being about the transaction to being experiential . . . the constantly changing stock, the flashy windows, the restaurant, the drinks. It was a cultural hub, a place to be seen.'[31] One night Prince Rainier and Grace Kelly were sitting at a table sharing a bowl of tagliatelle pasta and flirting outrageously with each other whilst Audrey Hepburn sat at a nearby table with a *Vogue* magazine fashion editor chatting and ordering food from the menu.[32] Hepburn was in London filming the British romantic comedy drama *Two for the Road* (1967, Stanley Donan, UK) and had spent the afternoon in Bazaar trying on a number of off-the-rack garments for the film. In the 1960s actress Julie Christie shopped at Biba where she chose some of her onscreen garments for her Oscar-winning role from the shops stock for the film *Darling* (1965) directed by John Schlesinger.

What initially started as a successful mail order business called Biba's Postal Boutique, soon relocated to a small shop on Abingdon Road in an unfashionable part of Kensington just as London began swinging in 1964. The Biba brand maintained enormous cross-class appeal and catered for a particular type of girl drawn in Hulanicki's catalogues as 'young, skinny, and pale'. This 'Biba Girl' was described by Hulanicki as 'a postwar baby who had been deprived of nourishing protein in childhood and so grew up into a beautiful skinny person. It didn't take much for them to look outstanding.'[33] Young girls were able to afford of the moment young fashion in often pioneering designs for the first time – feather boas, floppy felt hats, triangular scarves and zipped canvas knee-length boots and gimmicky accessories. Nine years later when Hulanicki and Fitz took possession over the seven-storied Derry and Tom department store building on High Street Kensington, Biba became Big Biba, a superstore boutique with a very different customer following and more upmarket.

The roof gardens, the tearooms and the adjoining restaurant and fashion theatre (on the lower floor) became The Rainbow Room which was known for its legendary parties. At the Big Biba Roof Garden launch party held in spring 1974, fire eaters and tight-rope walkers mingled amongst the penguins and the flamingos while the crowd sipped green crème de menthe cocktails whilst being entertained by a string-quartet.[34] 'It was like a strange Disneyland, like walking into Narnia, like stepping in off the cold reality of the street into fairyland.'[35] Described by *The Sunday Times* newspaper as 'the most beautiful store in the world.'[36] 'Big Biba' was more than a London boutique, it was a lifestyle destination. It sold more than clothes and cosmetics, it offered furniture, soap powder, food and even pet food for the fashionista's fluffy companion. Called 'the Willy Wonka of fashion'[37] Big Biba was extravagant with each floor containing its own decadent theme and particular design. 'Walk into Big Biba', wrote *The Evening News*, 'and you'll feel as if you stepped inside a dream machine.'[38] The children's floor contained a storybook village with a castle, a carousel and a children's café that served ice cream. The lingerie department, called The Mistress Room, was designed as a boudoir with a bed, a nightstand and wardrobe. The communal changerooms were Egyptian-themed with gigantic mirrors and the music department contained a giant record player that played music whilst consumers shopped. The biggest attraction by far was The Rainbow Room restaurant, located on the fifth floor of the building with its rainbow-covered ceiling lights and art deco interior. There were mirrors everywhere and the colour scheme was made up of pinks, peaches and beiges that were echoed in the furniture and tablecloths (Figure 5.5).

The Rainbow Room was open until 2.00 am every morning (except for Sunday's when it closed at midnight) and doubled as a venue for rock concerts with performances by The New York Dolls, David Bowie and Bryan Ferry's Roxy Music. Liberace held a private banquet for members of his British fan club and The Pointer Sisters made an appearance in the adjoining room, which was once the fashion theatre, but was now reserved for book and album launches. Big Biba was decadence writ large.

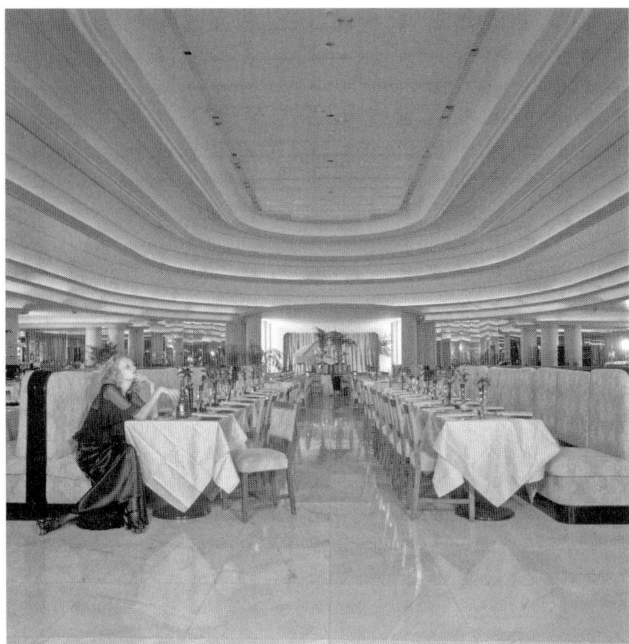

Figure 5.5 Biba Boutique. English model Twiggy sits alone in The Rainbow Room of Biba's Kensington store, 1971. (Photo by Justin de Villeneuve/Getty Images.)

Figure 5.6 British fashion model Twiggy wearing a black dress with a black hat and pink suede high heels in Biba's Kensington store, 1971. (Photo by Justin de Villeneuve/Getty Images.)

Fashion illustrator Kasia Charko, who designed the black and gold Biba logo, remembers having dinner at the restaurant and ordering *crudités* for starters not knowing that it was a plate full of vegetables.[39] Food was served on black and gold trimmed plates and was considered adventurous, combining cosmopolitan tastes with traditional English cuisine. A typical menu included biriani with yogurt, mackerel patè, fish soup and Chinese noodles as well as herb frittata as entrées. Main courses were a choice of roast beef with three vegetables, ham with pease pudding, or Turkey and Walnut pie. There were also a variety of deserts such as pudding, Ginger syllabub and the signature Biba Rainbow cake. Biba house wine was available in a carafe or bottled as well as sparkling wines and champagnes.[40] 'In those days the fashion in food was for it to be smothered in heavy sauces,' writes Hulanicki in her autobiography, 'we wanted a style of cooking that was much simpler, letting the natural flavours do the work . . . the standard of both the ingredients and the cooking has to be far higher when there is no spicy sludge to disguise it.'[41] Hulanicki was a convert of the nouvelle cuisine style of cooking that had dispensed with the heavy sauces of traditional French cuisine in favour of a lighter meal containing delicate flavours that was becoming fashionable in Paris during the early 1970s. The Rainbow Room was not too dissimilar in size and architectural style to the enormous art deco dining room at the legendary Parisian brasserie La Coupole (the Dome). Although La Coupole was constructed in 1927, six years earlier than the Derry and Toms building, they both contained long elliptical skylines with concealed lighting (Figure 5.7).

Figure 5.7 Parisian restaurant La Coupole reopens after renovations. (Photo by Sergio Gaudenti/Sygma via Getty Images.)

La Coupole was a magnet for the literary and artistic avant-garde that flocked into Montparnasse during the Jazz Age. Even its Bar Américain (American-style bar) was synonymous with its clientele of American expatriates and Parisian intelligentsia who frequented the brasserie. Hemingway was a habitué, and there are several photographs of Samuel Beckett sitting at one of the outside tables. *La Coupole* keeps its ties to its bohemian roots alive by hosting a variety of artistic interventions. For example, in 2013 the interior was arrayed in panels from graffiti and streets artists, another concrete example of the intergration of the spontaneous and everyday into chic.

Although The Rainbow Room possessed all the scale and grandeur worthy of a five-star restaurant, Hulanicki wanted the restaurant to mimic the popularity and cosmopolitanism of *La Coupole.* 'For over a hundred years *La Coupole* had been *the* meeting place for everybody'[42] and it was open all day and night which is why it was such a trendy spot for the *bon vivant*.[43] One night when Hulanicki was dining at the brasserie, she introduced herself to the maître d' and explained her plans for The Rainbow Room; 'he immediately agreed to show [her] round the scenes, to see how his whole operation worked.'[44] Soon enough, The Rainbow Room became a carbon copy of *La Coupole* in every way, the legendary parties only adding to the seduction and glamour of the Biba myth. Reflecting back to Biba's glory years, Hulanicki recalls that 'for far too long English girls have had to hide in clothes chosen by their mothers. Now, at last they are free.'[45]

Breakfast at Tiffany's and the Blue Box Café

Audrey Hepburn became a fashion muse for designer Hubert de Givenchy in the 1950s, when – already an Oscar-winner – she asked him to design the screen wardrobe for her leading role in *Sabrina* (1954, Billy Wilder, US). They became great friends and from then on she invariably wore his clothes, not only in her films, but in her private life. Givenchy designed the legendary black evening dress that Hepburn wore in the opening minutes of *Breakfast at Tiffany's* (1961, Blake Edwards, US). The film was the cinematic interpretation of Truman Capote's 1958 novella of the same name, and catapulted the jewellery store to fame. In 2021, it was carefully referenced in a Tiffany & Co.'s advertisement 'About Love' starring married couple and music artists Jay Z (styled as the artist Basquiat) and Beyoncé who wears a similar floor-length black sheath evening dress and sings the ballad 'Moon River' (Henry Mancini and John Mercer) just as Hepburn did in the film, fifty years earlier. *Breakfast at Tiffany's* was very successful both at the box office and with the critics – the film was nominated for five Oscars. Certain aspects of the film are worrying today, notably Mickey Rooney's casting as a Japanese photographer and his crass performance – but it has nevertheless created indelible images of style. The Givenchy dress became iconic – as did the film's poster, which remains a favourite.

Breakfast at Tiffany's constructs a narrative about food, fashion and class that has been etched into the popular imagination. So much so, that in 2017 Tiffany & Co opened its first eatery, the Blue Box Café, (named after its blue eggshell packaging) in its New York flagship store on 5th Avenue. This, of course, is where Hepburn's character, Holly Golightly, arrives in the early hours of the morning , accessorizing her black evening dress with matching gloves, high-piled hair, oversized sunglasses and several strands of pearls. She steps out of a taxicab carrying a paper bag and walks up to the store window display, opens the bag, removes a disposable cup of coffee and a pastry , and consumes both while gazing longingly through the window at the rows of diamond necklaces (Figure 5.8). This scene gives the film its title and serves to introduce the protagonist as a country 'hillbilly' (Lula Mae Barnes) who 'stole milk and turkey eggs' to stay alive and ran away to become a New York café society girl. Holly's transformation is a narrative about female social mobility and the prestige associated with the power of consumption. The diamond necklace in the window display acts as a metaphor for class aspiration that Holly strives to attain through conspicuous consumption. The cheap takeaway coffee and pastry, her arrival at Tiffany's on

Figure 5.8 The movie *Breakfast at Tiffany's*, directed by Blake Edwards and based on the novel by Truman Capote. Seen here, Audrey Hepburn as Holly Golightly during the opening sequence, pausing in front of Tiffany's jewellery store in New York City. Initial theatrical release 5 October 1961. Screen capture. Paramount Pictures. (Photo by CBS via Getty Images.)

5th Avenue ('Millionaires Row') when the steel door of the stone façade is closed, the act of window shopping itself – all serve to highlight Holly's outsider, working-class status. Regardless of her expensive attire, Capote (and director Edwards) remind the post-war audience that the only way up for a girl is hanging on the arm of a man. In Capote's novel, of course, Holly is in fact a call girl – this aspect of her relationship with rich men was carefully sanitized for the film.

Move forward to 2017 and breakfast at Tiffany's has changed dramatically with the opening of its Blue Box Café. Seating only forty diners, the café has become just as desirable as any Tiffany product. Situated on the fourth floor next to the accessories department, the interior space is robin's egg blue from the walls to the chairs and the booths - even the staff wear egg blue ties and aprons. Upscale menu items all serve to appeal to the brand's affluent clientele. Breakfast is a *prix fixe* that is served all day and includes tea or coffee; miniature croissants with honey, sour cranberry jam and chocolate Nutella spread, avocado toast, seasonal fruit and your choice of a selection of entrées, truffled eggs with bacon, buttermilk waffles or smoked salmon on a deconstructed bagel. Or diners may order 'The Ten Carat Breakfast' consisting of Siberian osetra caviar (30 g) over buttermilk waffle with lemon crème fraiche. Lunch is a choice of black bass crudo or mushroom soup, a 'Tiffany sandwich' or a 'Fifth Avenue Salad' with Maine lobster and grapefruit. The waitlist for a table at the Blue Box Café is 30 days, regardless of the level of foot traffic in the store, indicating that 'breakfast at Tiffany's' is more about the consumer acting out their Audrey Hepburn fantasies, rather than craving a Tiffany product.

Experiential eating: Boutique restaurants

As we noted at the beginning of this chapter, the installation of a dedicated food space has its beginnings in the tea rooms of department stores, which developed as a way to keep customers in the store longer and spend more; now the strategy is to attract customers into the store by offering them exclusive experiences. As e-commerce and the coronavirus continue to impact on people's shopping practices, retail outlets are going to greater lengths to attract more footfall. Whilst the internet delivers the fast and stress-free purchase of goods, it cannot (at this time) replicate real world experience. Along with editorial content and in-store installations, boutiques have added dining experiences to their offerings. This can often entail fashion retailers opening more than one restaurant in the same building for different purposes.

Forty Five Ten, is a luxury full service experience boutique in Dallas Texas which merges fashion, art and design. The four boutique spaces are unified by a glass-brick storefront and its interior is embellished with fine art. The women's store features brands including Marc Jacobs, Rosie Assouline and Marni, and contains a Jose Dávila sculpture. The men's store is stocked with Thom Brown, Jill Sander and Visvim. The third boutique, anchored by a Lars Fiske installation, specializes in vintage garments and is curated by a group of 'collectors' with pieces including a Halston leopard slip dress, an Yves St Laurent black taffeta ball skirt, Chanel quilted bags and John Galliano (for Christian Dior) *bijoux*. The fourth space, 4510/SIX, is a concept store that sells garments by emerging designers from Simon Porte Jacquemus and Molly Goddard to Sandy Liang and others. Besides the specificity of the brand mix, Forty Five Ten offers its customers two eating experiences. The No Aloha coffee shop on the ground floor sells artbooks, stationary and small ceramics to attract people walking past and first-time shoppers. In contrast, the fine dining restaurant, the Mirador, located on the top floor attracts existing customers, business crowds, socialites and guests staying at the store's niche hotel, The Joule. More of an 'anti-café' than a café, No Aloha is rather like an art space with a commissioned site-specific mural installed by Brooklyn-based Katherine Bernhardt instead of natural wood or tiles. The adjacent patio leads to a The Eye sculpture created by Tony Tasset, in a grassy yard. The menu matches the creative venue with chia seed artichoke and goats' cheese tart on a bed of microgreens with carrot and radish slivers or a purple endive and rutabaga raclette tart. The Mirador is a different experience altogether that caters for its affluent loyal clientele. Personal shoppers bringing their clients for lunch are met by prominently displayed mannequins wearing designer collections that rotate and change every two weeks. The interior speaks of serious money with floor-to-ceiling windows and a wrap-around terrace that overlooks Tasset's installation. The menu is just as extravagant and expensive with devilled eggs and caviar, beef tartare or tuna crudo for starters and chicken paillard with green lemon and sunchoke puree as a main.

Loyal customers who associate favourable experiences with a brand will increase the likelihood of repeat purchases with a retail outlet. Chanel's two-star Michelin restaurant, Beige, designed by Karl Lagerfeld and helmed by chef Alain Ducasse, is located on top floor of the brand's ten-story Ginza building in Tokyo. Named after Chanel's favourite colour, the restaurant fosters good will to its loyal customers who are gifted with a voucher or invited to lunch or a special event dinner. The interior design of the restaurant and its menu act as an extension of Chanel's brand aesthetic. Praline chocolate biscuits are topped with chocolate mousse shaped into the brand's signature camelia and the lounge club chairs are upholstered in Chanel tweed. At the end of their meal customers are gifted with a take-home box of macaroons embossed with the Chanel logo. Fine dining experience also makes for good social media moments, which increase a brands popularity.

Concept store eateries

Perhaps the first mainstream usage of 'concept' within art and culture occurs with pop music, with the first concept album arguably that of the Beatles' *Sergeant Pepper* album (1967) , and culminating with Pink Floyd's *The Wall* (1979). As opposed to just a collection of songs composed at a certain time, here all the songs follow an overarching idea or narrative. Similarly, a concept fashion store is more than the sum of its parts but is built upon a guiding impetus behind the clothes. In many ways it is the inversion of a tailor or a dressmaker whose shop is there to service the whim of the customer, for concept stores in effect tell the customer what to wear and what taste to follow. Concept stores are a natural offshoot of the concept album, with design and product having a suggestive and mostly a posterior relationship to the kind of style and narrative it is intended to complement. They sell a variety of diverse products ranging from clothes to ceramics and even gadgets that are carefully curated and connected to an overarching theme that targets a particular audience. The stores are about discovery and experience, so the products and design of the interior space of the store change regularly to keep telling the same story.

Several concept stores build a community around the lifestyle they embody by offering experiential elements such as an events or exhibition space, or a café. Take 10 Corsa Como (founded by Italian *Vogue* editor Carla Sozzani) in Milan that offers a boutique, an art gallery and bookshop, a small hotel containing only three rooms and a café. El Fresco contains an outdoor terrace with garden furniture and colonnades of gas burners that are illuminated in the evening by fairy lights, and there is a garden where produce is grown, cooked and served in the restaurant. The menu serves a variety of classic Italian and Mediterranean dishes, like fresh garganelli pasta with ricotta cheese and Sicilian cherry tomatoes, and includes an extensive cocktail list.

Another notable example in the lineage of concept boutiques was the fashionably famous Colette Boutique in Paris (which closed in 2017) established by Colette Rousseaux on the rue Saint-Honoré. Described by *Forbes* magazine as 'the trendiest store in the world,'[46] Colette maintained close relations with high-end houses such as Balenciaga, Chanel and Hermès and was a magnet for the fashion crowd, especially buyers and magazine editors during the show seasons. Beyond clothing, Colette extended its many accessories with a carefully curated mix of music, zany art gadgets and exclusive pieces like Balenciaga lighters and coffee mugs. Moreover, it was conceived – much as Westwood's shop had been in its heyday a melting pot for anyone from Chrissie Hynde to Bryan Ferry – as a meeting place for the fashion savvy and those into cultural well-being, launching not only fashion products but also books and music. Colette encouraged designers to do the same: in 2017 a collaboration with Balenciaga resulted in Demna Gvasalia staging numerous events over six weeks, which included mixed-media installations and an art exhibition. Thom Browne, during a month-long residency, transformed the second floor into a simulation of his American office furnished in a nostalgic-chic mid-twentieth-century style. At the same time, a tattoo artist offered Thom Browne brand tattoos. Colette's was very much a hybrid boutique that claimed to offer everything for the discerning pursuer of the good life, including a library and an art gallery that hosted regular exhibitions. The restaurant was in the basement. Unlike wine bars or bars with countless wines and cocktails on its list, this was a water bar with a curated number of mineral and still waters numbering close to a hundred imported from all over the world. In an interview with *Women's Wear Daily* (WWD), supermodel Kate Moss said, to much controversy, 'that nothing tastes as good as skinny feels.'[47]Although Moss was accused of encouraging eating disorders, water has become chic amongst the fashion crowd because it contains no calories, and you can drink as much as you like. The *menu du jour* at Colette's Café was fashionably light and fashionably French with *Quiche au fromage de chèvre et basilic de Loradisa* or *Blanc de poulette et salade*. Desert may be a choice between *Salade de fruits* or Cheesecake Mazaltov, made with a very light cheese containing zero fat baked by Parisian *pâtissier* Jean-Paul Hévin, washed down with a glass of imported water.

Dover Street Market, established by Rei Kawakubo and her partner Adrian Joffe, opened in the former Burberry Building in 2004 in the heart of Mayfair in London. Dating from 1912, the grand building would also house the prestigious Institute of Contemporary Art (ICA). When the concept boutique moved premises to the Haymarket in 2016, several others had opened in Tokyo, New York, Singapore and Beijing, all at high-end addresses, all carrying the name of its founding address, or just 'DSM' for short. What marks these stories apart is that they are a hybrid of gallery and fashion boutique, in which Kawakubo literally curates the collections much as a curator would curates works of art. Far from being limited to her own designs, the stories are stocked by blue-chip labels such as YSL, Prada and Gucci and also more renegade designs, such as those by Gosha Rubchinsky and Vetements. Not only do these stores have a classy eatery but they offer gimmicks such as a Balenciaga customized T-shirt printing service. One could say that such stores were constructed as a complex of commercially driven art installation and ongoing performances and performative events in which the customer was encouraged to participate. While fashion is always a matter of participation, this took it up a notch – the contrived and curated utopias of high-end capitalism. They are the dreamlands that Walter Benjamin saw in the Parisian arcades , but no longer as boxed-in or as plural , but rather a lavish synthesis that meant that one has not so much visited a boutique but experienced it for a greater length of time. Like 10 Corso Como and Colette, the Rose Bakery at DSM London was created by Rose Carrarini and husband Jean Charles and modelled after their Rose Bakery in Paris. The cafés interior is stark with simple plywood tables and Alvar Alto-designed chairs that reflects the cafés rustic and humble menu. 'We wanted a place where people felt at home,' said Carrarini, 'somewhere where people came back to often and the quality of the food shone.'[48] Artisan teas and cakes sit on the menu alongside dishes like Crab Benedict and Cod in a white wine reduction or Wild Garlic Pappardelle with Morel Mushrooms.

The film *Elysium* (2013, Neill Blomkamp, US) as the title suggests, tells of a future world that consists of two tiers, in which the rich and powerful live in Elysium while the rest of the overpopulated world grind their lives out below. The concept stores with their galleries, art exhibitions and associated restaurants are very much products of high-end capitalism and the increasing divisions of wealth. They offer consumption not only as experience but as sanctuary. Whereas in the age of imperialism the wealthy, when not in their homes, could gather in country and city clubs, the concept store is the logical offshoot, except the price of admission is free – for now.

6

HIPPY TO COUTURE: SLOW FOOD FASHION AND FAST FOOD FASHION

In the early years of the new millennium there appeared an important article that changed the way in which we think about fashion and food, and the ways in which fashion and is produced and consumed. In 2007, environmentalist and textile academic Kate Fletcher wrote an article for the online zine *Ecologist* calling for fashion to slow down and reassess its effect on ecosystems, communities and workers. 'Fast fashion isn't about speed but greed',[1] urged Fletcher, it is about 'selling more [clothes and] making more money'.[2] Perhaps too little too late, but Fletcher was one of a growing chorus of activists and critics who drew attention to the inconvenient truths, suppressed by the mainstream fashion industry, about mass production of clothing and its connection to human exploitation and environmental devastation. Coined by the *New York Times* in the 1990s, 'fast fashion' describes the business model developed by super boutique Zara (and later H&M) in which designs travelled from concept to finished product in fifteen days, increasing demand and production and waste products. In short, the call was for no more 'it bags', no more 'must-haves'. Instead, Fletcher warned that fashion had to slow down, to become ethical, to start taking into consideration the processes and resources required to make clothing. She argued for better made garments that lasted longer according to practices of manufacture that respected people, animals and the planet. In other words, her plea was to reduce consumption and production which was blowing out of control and increasing pollution, toxifying waterways, and creating millions of tons of landfill. Although it may seem that fast food and fashion are ideological adversaries and diametrically opposed, the two have much more in common than one might first believe. Fast food is egalitarian, cheap and freely available, fast fashion uses inferior materials, are low-priced and disposable, in contrast to haute couture which relies on superlative craftmanship, fine materials, is expensive and elitist and comparable to fine dining at a Michelin-starred restaurant. In this chapter we look at the ways that 'slow food fashion' and 'fast food fashion' come together as forms of activism and protest.

Slow food fashion

Slow, or sustainable fashion derives its philosophy and initiatives from the slow food movement, established in 1986 when journalist Carlo Petrini and a group of activists gathered at the Spanish Steps in Rome to protest the opening of a McDonald's fast food restaurant. Drawing on the traditions of the social movements of the 1960s and 1970s, slow food rejects factory farming, the production of genetically modified organisms (GMOs), industrial-grade insecticides, large-scale industrial (intensive) production that relies on substantial quantities of fossil fuels for the transportation of produce, and energy-sapping mass storage. Instead, slow food promotes quality locally grown sustainable products that are seasonal, gown with sensitivity to the soil and with natural vermin-repellants. In other words, buy local or grow your own.

The year following Fletcher's article, trend forecaster Li Edelcoort was interviewed by the online zine ICON. She was asked what her thoughts were concerning the world's future. 'The future will be the emerging of the cottage industries,' replied Edelcoort,

> human scale enterprises that are service-driven, design-driven, and bring production back to our areas. They will become bigger and act as a sort of mattress – a second economy to absorb the shocks of the big one. Soon we'll be governed by one bank, one airline. The bigger we can grow this mattress, the better. Who knows – maybe we will have two economies at one point.[3]

A few years later, Edelcoort predicted that people would retreat to nature and to a subsistence living on farms. Cycling would replace gym workouts and as a result, bodies will become leaner. People, she suggested, will focus on the pleasures of food and community, grow their own fodder, and make their own clothes with the resources available to them. 'Many young people [will leave] cities because of [the high] cost [of living] and pollution,' Edelcoort said, 'there [will be] this "re-farm" movement where people have either [a] little farm, just taking care of their own needs, or they work [on a] a bigger farm or they rent [a] farm, [or] they want to be near a farm.'[4] The farmer, the gastronome and the couturier will be venerated.

It was also about this time that restaurants in the cities began growing their own produce on terraces, roof tops and community gardens, which are considered to have the least environmental impact. Solar energy was embraced, and 'homesteader' entered the vernacular to describe an identity category. People began to see themselves as an integral part of the ecological cycle, as equal to animals and nature. Concepts like 'nose to tail' eating, where the whole animal is consumed and 'paddock to plate' principles that ensures sustainable practices in the growing, sourcing and transporting of fresh and unprocessed food, became the norm rather than the trend.

In 2002 William McDonough and Michael Braungart integrated the concepts of nature and design to provide a framework in rethinking the way society uses resources in a circular economy to eliminate waste. McDonough and Braungart

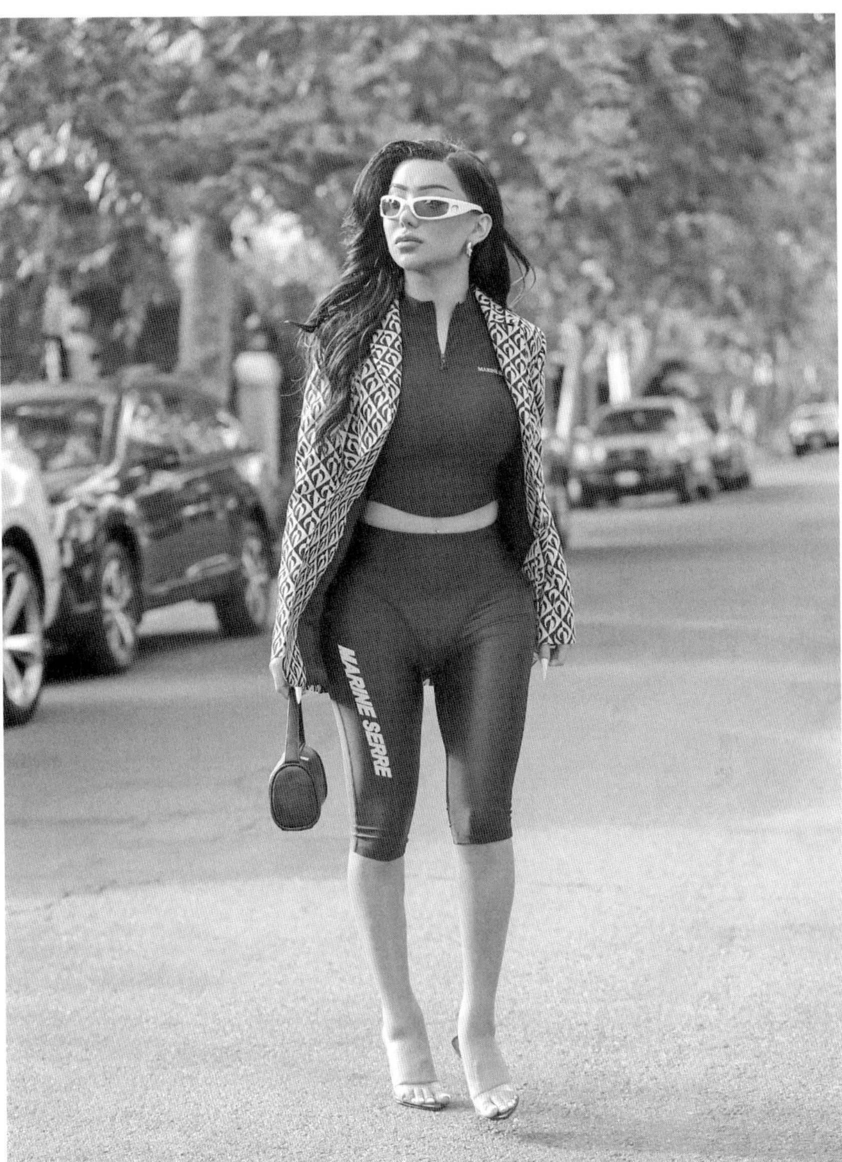

Figure 6.1 Celebrity Nikita Dragun is seen on 29 June 2021, in Los Angeles, California wearing Marine Serre Spring–Summer 2021. (Photo by Bellocqimages/Bauer-Griffin/GC Images.)

observed that in nature the waste of one system became the food of another. Everything can be disassembled and returned to the soil as *biological nutrients* (composting) or re-used as quality materials for new products as *technical nutrients* (recycling). They called this concept 'cradle to cradle', or regenerative design.[5] Unlike regenerative design which is about *reducing waste* using knowledge obtained from nature, biomimicry *mimics* the design and production of nature, natural materials and systems. Examples of biomimicry (also known as 'smart fabrics') include using bacteria to create fabric dyes that do not fade over time or growing fabric from algae using only sun and water, reducing energy consumption and pollution.

Salvatore Ferragamo's *Orange Fibre*, (2017) a citrus capsule collection, launched to coincide with Earth Day, was made entirely of citrus juice bioproducts and Stella McCartney designed the 'Falabela' handbag, using leather created from mushrooms. McCartney is an environmental activist who uses Econyl, a fabric made from recycled plastic bottles, regenerative cashmere, and faux furs. Words like 'hacking' used to describe hand-made clothing and handiwork once considered the domain of 'thrifty housewives' has become a sign of self-sufficiency and liberation from fashion trends.[6] 'Open source' patterns are available to download from the internet and DIY clothing and 'swap-o-ramas' are being conducted online. Creative re-use or 'upcycling' clothing has become an initiative adopted by many young designers as a method of repurposing garments and found objects. Marine Serre's Spring–Summer 2021 Ready to Wear 'Amor Fati' (Love of Fate) collection was made entirely of recycled yarns and materials. Repurposed suiting fabrics – in a jacquard weave with her signature moon print – were used for single-breasted suits and carpet was created into tassel-edged skirts, tops and half-zip anoraks. Serre designed the collection during lockdown and had been thinking about the rise of bike usage and used biodegradable nylon for functional skin-tight garments (Figure 6.1).

Whole foods and fashionable brands

On 31 December 2019, the first cases of the coronavirus COVID-19 were reported in Wuhan China; soon after, people began to flee overpopulated cities. Some moved to rural centres, others returned home from abroad and countries went into lockdown for months on end. State sanctioned 'social distancing' enforced as a measure against the spread of the virus, forced restaurants, bars and cafes to shut down. Supermarkets (deemed an essential service) became one of the few establishments where people could shop for food and at the same time be seen.

The following year government-run global vaccination schemes came into place allowing people vaccinated against the virus to resume and participate in

Figure 6.2 An employee wearing a mask, walks out of an Erewhon store in the Pacific Palisades amid the coronavirus pandemic on 24 April 2021, in Los Angeles, California. Los Angeles County moved into COVID-19 orange tier restrictions on 5 April allowing increased capacity at restaurants, movie theatres and museums. (Photo by Alexi Rosenfeld/Getty Images.)

everyday social activities by displaying an 'app pass'. Those who chose to forgo the vaccination programme, which they considered a form of state control and an infringement of civil liberties, were banned from participation.

In Hollywood Los Angeles, masked customers waited patiently in line to enter Erewhon, a thriving organic local supermarket chain where celebrities shop amongst the locals (Figure 6.2). During the 2021 pandemic lockdown, its outdoor dining areas became the unofficial meeting place for the young, beautiful and bored. Like a moth to a nontoxic flame, the store drew Instagram *flâneurs* in droves.'[7] Akin to the Water-Bar once operated by the cult-Parisian retailer Collette (see Chapter 7), Erewhon's Tonic and Juice Bar serves costly fermented tea drinks, bone broth shots, hydrogen infused water and mushroom extract tonics all served with a choice of locally grown raw organic cocoa truffles. Max Bellinger believes that the grocery store is 'tailor-made' for today's influencer culture, where 'fastidiously curated assortments [of] food [are] lit like fashion editorials.' The supermarket has partnered with clothing label Agolde to design and manufacture organic and sustainable-grown cotton jeans. Made from recycled yarn and non-genetically modified cotton the jeans are curated next to the collagen sparkling tea and cotton hoodies (priced at $300 US), sweatpants and face masks.

Where once health food stores were the domain of hippies and feminists wearing tie-dyed T-shirts and Birkenstock sandals, Birkenstocks are now seen on the catwalk, including its various Comme des Garçons, and Yohji Yamamoto iterations. Erewhon is more than a haven for the body and health-conscious customer, or a one-stop shop place for the rich and famous, for the millennial generation Erewhon represents a marker of self and an association with place.

> 'With my millennial generation it's the embodiment of what people think of L.A,' said one social influencer, its 'your coffee shop, your supermarket, the neighbourhood you live in, they all become these badges. This is me, I'm a West Hollywood, Alfred coffee shop, Erewhon girl.'[8]

Established in Boston in 1966 by whole-foods pioneers, Michio and Aveline Kushi, Erewhon (an anagram for nowhere) was once a small health food store that catered to the counterculture generation. It was named after a satirical novel written by English author Samuel Butler of the same name and based on his own experience as a sheep farmer at Mesopotamia Station, on the remote South Island of New Zealand in the 1860s. Influenced by Charles Darwin's *Origin of the Species* (1859), which was misleadingly interpreted by European Imperial powers as a justification for colonization (Social Darwinism). Set in a mythical place, the novel tells the story of a young man who sets off to make his own fortunes and stumbles upon an idyllic faraway land in the middle of nowhere that was populated by beautiful people, a lost civilization living in nature without any machines. A satire of Victorian society written in a gendered exploratory mode, the novel exemplifies a corollary of the utopian imagination of liberation from poverty and the harsh conditions of nineteenth-century industrial society. Healthy food was the answer to world peace for Michio Kushi who came across Butler's novel at Columbia University library where he was studying political science after migrating to America from Japan in 1949. The novel's utopian theme appealed to Kushi who had experienced the devastation of the hydrogen bomb and detrimental effects of military weapons on people. He believed that 'if people ate better, they would be healthy and being healthy meant that they could think better. Thinking better they would realize that war made no sense.'[9]

Although the supermarket chain is a family-owned local grocer, it has now been channelled into what Warren Balasco calls the 'commodified dissent of cool marketers such as fashion brand Gap, Time-Warner, and Whole Foods [owned by Amazon].'[10] The cuisine that the counterculture ate was part of the second natural food movement in the mid-1960s. The first movement began in 1953 and was led by physicians and academics whose mission was to raise awareness of the pesticides and new agricultural chemicals that were poisoning the natural environment and the food system. The second movement which continues today, began with the idea of changing the existing food system into something different that was natural and wholesome. The counterculture wanted to grow foods naturally that were good for the body and good for the environment. They embraced whole foods and legumes; soy foods like tofu and tempeh, organic, fresh vegetables and nutrition boosters like wheat germ and sprouted grain.[11] They rejected Western values and looked towards Eastern mysticism and philosophies as well as alternative cooking methods and food systems.

Driven by utopian ideals, hippies were suspicious of government authority and rejected commercialism. They shopped at flea markets and thrift stores for jeans, T-shirts, kaftans, peasant blouses, flowing skirts and leather sandals. They adopted the peace sign as their unofficial logo, which was often sewn on surplus army jackets or worn as a badge or an amulet. The look was anti-fashion, an organized, self-conscious stance against the prevailing mainstream fashions of the time. It was in the 1960s that the health food movement and the hippie subculture became part of the countercultural insurgency that introduced vegetarian, organic and macrobiotic food as a form of counter-cuisine. 'Revolutionizing' individual and collective eating practices could transform economic institutions and the conservative processes that controlled the food system.

Protest food and dress

Food, like dress, is both an empty and an overdetermined signifier that makes sense and meaning of social and cultural life. For instance, what we eat, where we eat, or where we buy our food is influenced by various factors, including gender, class, age and so forth. As David Bell and Gill Valentine observe, 'every mouthful, every meal can tell us something about ourselves, and about our place in the world.'[12] The same can be said of clothing, what clothes we wear, when we wear them and how we choose to wear them signifies participation in a social group whose choices are influenced by gender, class, sexuality and so forth. Food such as caviar, oysters, smoked salmon, prosciutto, spatchcock or quail have come to signify cosmopolitanism, whereas hamburgers and fries signify the opposite. A three-piece suit is classified as conservative, a ripped T-shirt and jeans is associated with rebellion. Food and dress practices mark ideological moments. The Black Panthers wore leather jackets and berets to signify their deputization as a counter police force during the 1960s civil rights movement. The Panthers also instigated the Free Breakfast for Children program to address food injustices. Women's 'power suits' with their A-line silhouette and padded shoulders sublimated the triumph of Reaganite corporatism in the 1980s. The choice of what to eat or what not to eat, or what to wear or not what to wear can be about protest and community as well as a cosmology of subjectivity. The choice not to consume meat, or to maintain a vegetarian, biodynamic, free-range, or organic diet is as much about the refusal to participate in the capitalist food system of factory farming and environmental destruction as it about exercising a sense of self by controlling ingestion.

Like fashion, the value of food is bound up with changing tastes, relations of economic production and social status. In his study of the eating choices of the Black Cat collective, a group of American punks who frequented the Black Cat vegetarian café in Seattle during the 1990s, Dylan Clark noted that many punks associated the production of food with the human domination of nature and with white, male, corporate supremacy and imperialism. Punks rejected processed food that was 'milled, refined, butchered, baked, packaged, branded and advertised.'[13] They likened mainstream food production to colonialism; the logging of rainforest for cash cropping, the effects of cancer-causing pesticides on workers, chemical contamination of water supplies and the practice of large-scale stock raising of domestic animals by agribusinesses. Punks rejected commodified food opting for brandless bulk chow that was home-grown, produced on farms, stolen from upscale natural food stores, or retrieved from garbage bins.[14] The military style clothing worn by 'hardcore' American punks was a style of protest and revolt that reflected disruption, destruction and anti-establishment values. It was a very different style of punk than its British counterpart designed primarily by Vivienne Westwood with its dyed mohawk hairstyles, safety pins, graffiti T-shirts, fetish and bondage gear that signified chaos at every level. American punks wore their hair as crew cuts, combat boots, camouflage pants or black jeans, bullet belts, hoodies and T-shirts. This deconstructed military style of clothing once a sign of nationalism and hegemonic power becomes a means of subcultural revolt as music, the natural whole food movement, and subcultural style are channelled into dissent.

Farm-to-table and farm-to-closet

It was at the height of the Free Speech Movement and campus uprisings in the mid-1960s, that activist and (professionally untrained) chef Alice Waters, then a student studying French cultural theory at the University of California, Berkley became involved in the counterculture movement. She travelled to France where she discovered fresh market produce and simple cooking. Like most Americans at the time, Waters grew up eating frozen peas and fish sticks for dinner and canned fruit salad for desert so her trip to France was an awakening. As Waters reminisces, 'It was like I had never eaten before.' Clarkson Potter goes on to state that

> she vividly recalls tasting her first warm baguette with apricot jam, Brittany oysters fresh from the Atlantic, pungent cheeses and the discovery of mesclun, the tasty, tender mixed greens that made her enjoy salad for the first time.[15]

When Waters returned to the United States from Paris in 1971, all that she wanted to do was live and eat like the French, so she bought a copy of Elizabeth David's *French Country Cooking* (see Chapter 9). Like Waters, David had lived in France and was influenced by market living. Waters began cooking for her circle of bohemian friends before deciding without any formal training as a chef to open a French-style bistro in Berkeley called Chez Panisse. The affordable *prix fixe* menu was made using fresh organic ingredients and seasonal produce. Waters brought back mesclun seeds on a return trip to France and planted them in her back yard to serve as salad to Chez Panisse diners. As the bistro grew in popularity and numbers, Waters developed a network of local farmers and artisans to source fresh organic ingredients, establishing the beginnings of the farm-to-table movement in America which led to the slow food movement that spread across the world. Like Jamie Oliver who changed the school lunch program for British children, Alice Waters set up the Edible Schoolyard Program with the aim of promoting environmental and social well-being. The organic garden and kitchen programme teaches children how to grow, harvest and prepare their food from the garden and to learn the value of healthy eating.

Thirty years later, Rebecca Burgess a trained weaver and dyer, began a project to create a wardrobe from environmentally friendly, locally sourced and produced natural yarns and fibres. The project led to the establishment of Fibreshed, a not-for-profit community-based organization that connects grassroots producers from soil-to-skin. The value of organic, local and traceable products of the farm-to-table movement was incorporated into the farm-to-closet concept. The eco-fashion label Christy Dawn known for its use of dead stock fabrics, began exploring regenerative cotton for its 2019 Winter–Fall collection by working alongside a network of farmers and spinning and weaving artisans on ten acres of land in Erode, India using traditional agricultural practices. The California-based label has set up The Land Stewardship programme to connect its customers to the land and to the farmers and artisans who produce their garments. Although the farm-to-closet concept is still a niche market, conglomerates such as Kering, owners of fashion brands Gucci and Alexander McQueen, have launched the Regenerative Fund for Nature with Conservation International and are investing in farmers and land to produce regenerative materials to make the fashion supply chain more sustainable.

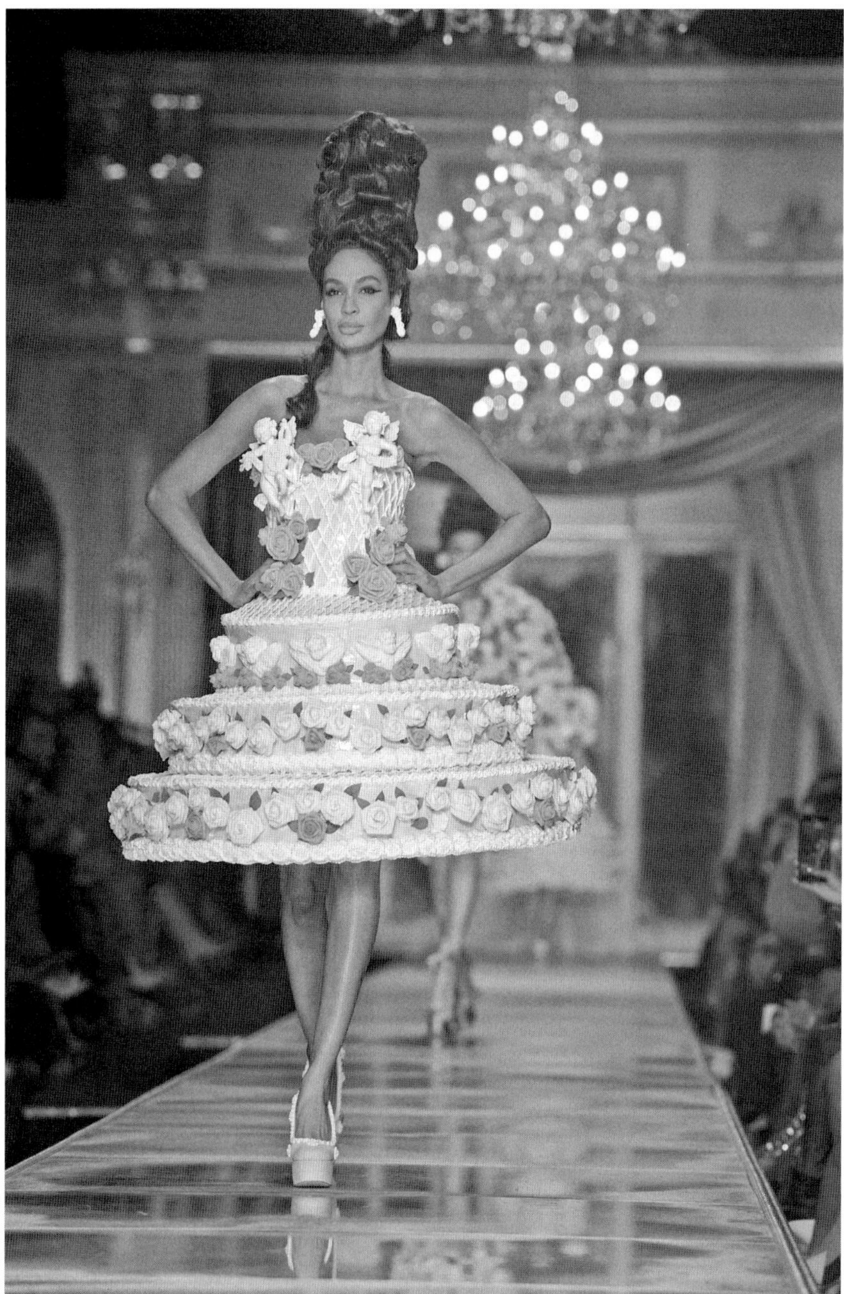

Figure 6.3 Joan Smalls walks the runway during the Moschino fashion show as part of Milan Fashion Week Fall/Winter 2020–2021 on 20 February 2020, in Milan, Italy. (Photo by Daniele Venturelll/Daniele Venturelli/Getty Images.)

Fast food fashion

Food as protest and fashion come together in Moschino's Fall–Winter 2020–2021 collection, in which designer Jeremy Scott dressed models in *pannier* skirts resembling multi-layered cakes and *petits fours* with latex 124444 frosting and towering *pouffe* wigs (Figure 6.3). It was the style of wig worn by Marie Antoinette at the coronation of her husband, Louis XVI, that triggered a fashion trend amongst French noblewomen. The collection was intended to draw attention to decadence, excess and the inequalities of class by referencing Marie Antoinette's (apocryphally attributed) legendary words, '*Qu'ils mangent de la brioche*' (let them eat cake), to indicate her contempt for the starving populace when they were facing a bread shortage. Although it is questionable as to whether she really did make this comment, the anecdote has often been cited as an expression of the obliviousness of the wealthy ruling class to the living conditions of ordinary people. As the runway show notes stated, 'the confectionary cocktail dresses stand as a sly comment on the denseness of certain people in power.'[16] Let them eat Big Mac.

This was not the first time that Scott has used fast food visual imagery as motifs for his collections to make a comment about the exploitation of the working class by wealthy elites. His Winter–Fall 2006–2007 collection 'Eat the Rich' was loosely based on the 1987 British slapstick comedy of the same name directed by Peter Richardson. Alex (played by Lanah Pellay, previously known as Alan Pellay) is employed as a waiter at Bastards, the very expensive London restaurant. Alex is fired for being rude to the diners after being the subject of daily abuse by wealthy customers, including Beatles icon Paul McCartney who appears in a cameo role as a banquet guest. Alex robs the social benefits office after witnessing a terrorist attack on an embassy and goes on the run with his friend. He returns to the restaurant with a team of terrorists and guns down the staff and diners in revenge. They overtake the restaurant, aptly rename it Eat the Rich and serve up their bodies for consumption. The anti-establishment and class conscious film addresses the social inequalities of minority groups who siege wealth and power from the upper class in a revolutionary act of revenge.

Included in Scott's collection were sweatshirts with frowning boxes of fries and dresses covered in cubist French fries. A dress printed with a Snickers chocolate bar wrapper was reimagined with Scott's name 'Jeremy' replacing the word Snickers and the word 'hungry' running parallel to the text. The double 'y' is intended as a cry of hunger by placing emphasis on the 'y', pronounced phonetically as 'huhng-gree'. Scott would return to the theme of the chocolate wrapper dress for his Winter–Fall 2014 collection, except this time it was a simulated Hershey chocolate bar with a bar code and nutritional information table along with a 25 cent price tag. Tropes of capitalism are twisted, and their original meanings perverted as food brand logos are dismantled and given a new context in the collection. By pastiching corporate logos Scott effectively inserts a ghost or spectre into the clothing suggesting that the garment or logo is haunted with a previous life. The garment is no longer an original but a copy, a residual form of something past.

Writing about Franco Moschino's dripping chocolate tote bag released in 1996 (and released again in 2003), Patrizia Calefato remarks that the bag (and the same can be said for the dresses) was 'a simulation of a delicious ingredient which symbolically represents luxury and lust.'[17] The excesses between food, luxury and fashion, argues Calefato, can be read as 'a litmus-test of the gap between wealth and poverty.'[18]

In contemporary Western society, food like fashion has come to represent social stratification and class distinction. Cheap, readily available processed food with its excessive sugar content, saturated fats and high calories has been historically associated with the working class and linked to obesity. Whereas the upper class has access to healthy (and expensive) produce that has come to signify exclusivity. As Bourdieu argues food consumed by the upper classes reflects 'tastes of refinement' and value in society evidenced in patterns of spending.[19] Affluent consumers are empowered to determine what is good food, or good taste as much as what are fashionable clothes. Or not, so thought Franco Moschino when he designed a T-shirt which read '*il buon gusto non esiste*' (good taste doesn't exist) matched with a skirt made from shredded garbage food bin bags as part of his Spring–Summer 1984 collection.

Just as much as fast food is cheap, so too is fast fashion with its low cost fabrics and collections that comes with the exploitation of labour somewhere along the supply chain. The hourly wage for flipping burgers at McDonald's is comparable to the hourly wage paid to a garment worker living in a third-world country for the cost of making a shirt. The harm on worker's health is just as comparable, so too are the environmental costs in the production and manufacturing of a garment. The increased cost of food and living and the demand for cheaper, faster clothing has created unsustainable consumption practices. Scott's collection was all too familiar with its red and yellow colour palette and trade-mark Golden Arches. Curved into a heart shaped 'M for Moschino' the motif was designed by the labels founder Franco Moschino, known as couture's junk culture aficionado. The collection received criticism from health campaigners and journalists decried the hypocrisy of fashions celebration of fast food whilst columnists compared restaurant workers paltry wages to the prices of the collection.[20] Like all fast fashion, the collection was made available to purchase online after the show. 'The McDonald's-themed show riffed on "fast fashion",' notes Lizzie Widdicombe, 'the phenomenon, popularized by [labels] Zara and H&M, of consumers churning through knocked-off runway trends.'[21]

Franco Moschino, had attracted a reputation as a subversive designer who was known for his quirky creations, irony and visual puns and who mined popular culture of its signs of excess and commodity consumption. His 'Dinner Dress and Jacket' paraded as part of his Winter–Autumn 1989 collection contained knives, forks and spoons on the bolero jacket in place of buttons was intended as a visual pun on the waiters uniform dress code (Figure 6.4).

The concept of food had been a favourite theme in Moschino's oeuvre and he often claimed that he was not a designer, 'but a restaurant trying to provide those well-cooked traditional dishes which were invented by unknown cooks.'[22] Employing the surrealist strategy of displacement Moschino designed a shirt printed with floating fried eggs (1989) and a quilted black denim mini skirt with plastic fried eggs decorating the hemline. The egg's hard exterior and soft interior with its intrauterine meaning was a reoccurring theme of Salvador Dalí's work. *Eggs on a Plate* (1932) is from one of Dalí's most recognizable artwork and in *The Persistence of Memory* (1931) in which a melting time-piece simulates a fried egg.

Scott used Moschino's familiar tactics of hybridizing fast food packaging, motifs and logo's in his collections. Such as McDonald's, Budweiser beer, Kelloggs Fruit Loops, Gummy Bears and the animated character Spongebob Squarepants created by Steven Hillenburg. As Sarah Tinoco writes, 'Scott imitates the branding of other companies on a grand scale to express an innovative point'[23] . . . by printing different food labels 'on his garments, he was contradicting fashions ongoing obsession with dietary concerns and having fun with it.' In his Fall–Winter 2014 collection the McDonald's boxed 'Happy Meal' for children was transformed into quilted leather clutch purses and handbags suspiciously resembling the Classic Chanel bag with its chained yellow shoulder strap interlaced with red leather. The bag was served on a tray by a model wearing a dress that simulated a McDonald's workers uniform including cap, except that it had all the trimmings of a couture label. This was not the first time that the House of Moschino was taking a poke at the House of Chanel, in 1991 Franco Moschino parodied the black Chanel suit by embroidering in gold thread the words 'This is a Waist of Money' where the traditional gold chain with black leather trimming belt would have been. When Moschino was interviewed by Holly Brubach for *The New Yorker* on his variation of the Chanel suit, Moschino replied, 'I have been making fun of Chanel with deep respect,'[24] Moschino was later sued by Chanel for his irreverence. Which brings us back to Chanel and Scott's 'Fast Food' collection. A model wore a Chanel-copy jacket made of red boucle wool and contrasting yellow trim, the same Chanel jacket (but in pink) that was worn by Jacqueline Kennedy when President John F. Kennedy was assassinated in Dallas Texas in 1963 which became 'emblematic of the ending of [America's] innocence.'[25].

Days after JFK's assassination and funeral, Jackie invited *Life* magazine journalist Theodore H. White to the Kennedy family compound at Hyannis, Massachusetts where she crafted a fairy tale story about the 1,000 days that JFK spent in the White House. 'Don't let it be forgot, that for one brief, shining

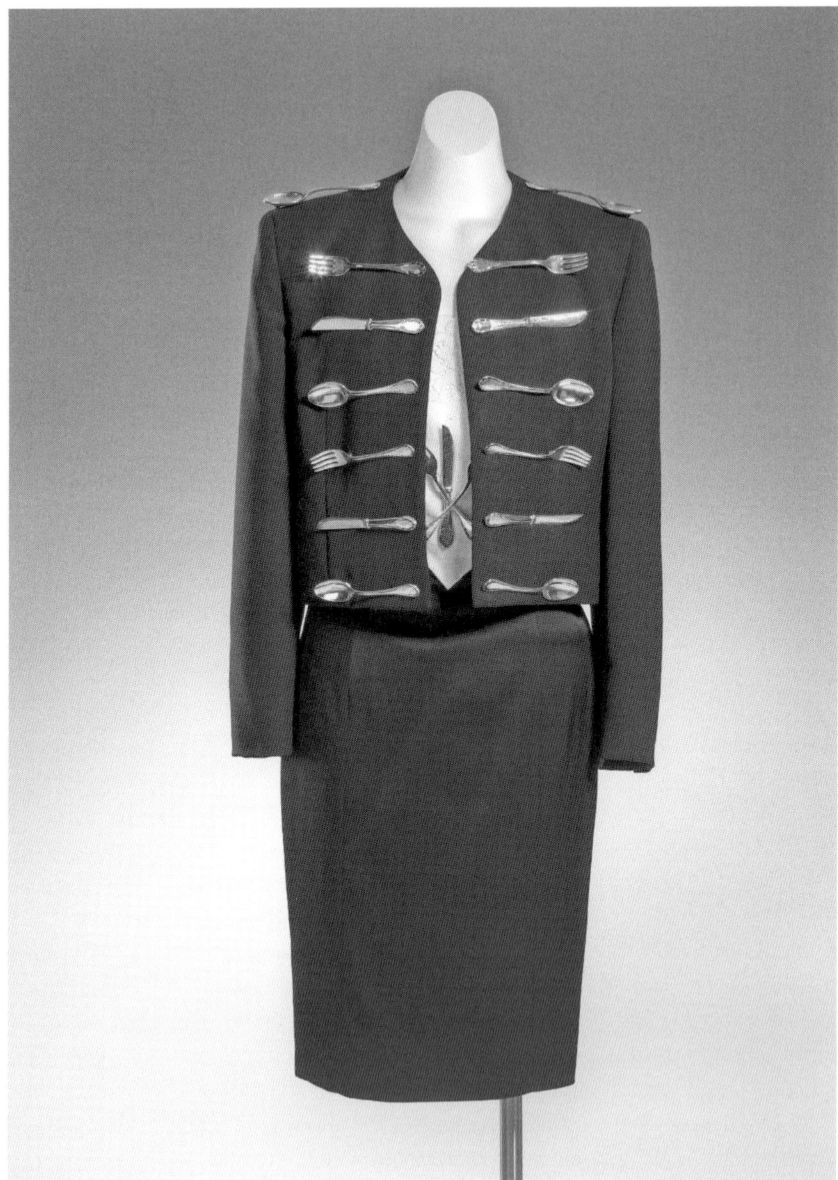

Figure 6.4 Dinner jacket and dress. Autumn–Winter collection 1989–1990. Wool, acetate, rayon, metal and linen. Gift of Virginia Cable through the Australian Government's Cultural Gifts Program, 2009. National Gallery of Victoria, Melbourne.

moment there was Camelot,'[26] said Jackie to White, referring to her favourite Broadway musical of the same name. With a circulation of seven million and a readership of more than thirty million, the myth and image of Camelot 'as a place of noble acts and youthful idealism'[27] immediately took hold. Like that moment in cinema when the image of Greta Garbo's face 'a kind of absolute state of the flesh . . . that plunged audiences into the deepest ecstasy,'[28] or, the face of Rudolf Valentino 'that caused suicides,'[29] the face of Jackie is marked by a sad poetic elegance that reconciles awe and charm. It is this mass-produced image that Andy Warhol chose to incorporate into his famed pop art silk screen portraits, *Sixteen Jackies* (1964, acrylic and enamel on canvas) using bold red and gold colours. The same image that Scott channelled for his collection in McDonald's red and yellow.

It was almost ironic when Scott presented his Moschino Winter-Fall 2014 collection at Milan Fashion Week in Italy. Nowhere else could the reference to McDonald's seem to appear so out of place than in a country that prides itself in its national cuisine that triggered the slow food movement (a point that we made earlier in this chapter). Fearing the 'Americanization of Italy',[30] Italian activists, politicians and celebrities began giving away plates of cooked spaghetti at the protest to remind themselves of their culinary heritage. Even the Italian fashion designer Valentino began legal action to close down the restaurant (which backed onto his office) because it created a 'significant and constant noise and an unbearable smell of fried food fouling the air.'[31]

Spaghetti is the alimentary sign of Italianness and steak and *frîtes* are the alimentary signs of Frenchness, so believes Barthes. 'It is a food which unites . . . Being part of a nation it follows the index of patriotic values [and] helps them to rise in wartime. . . Steak communicates [French] national glamour.'[32] To share a plate of spaghetti is to share in national identity. Spaghetti is simple. It is a combination of flour, eggs and water. It need not be dressed up with extravagant sauces and complex methods of cooking. It is a symbol of heritage of tradition, of home, of a people and of history. On the one hand, the opening of a McDonald's franchise in Rome signalled an imperial act of American colonization and occupation, and on the other hand, it signified the corporatization of Italian food. 'American fast food, with its suggestion of speed, standardization, and the homogenization of taste,'[33] notes Arie Sover and Orna Ben-Meir, 'represents the very opposite of Italian gastronomic practices.'[34] By sublimating American junk food in his collection, Scott was 'declaring cultural and sartorial hegemony.'[35]

Italian fashion, food and heritage

In his cultural history of Italian cooking, John Mariano writes that the 1970 edition of the French culinary bible, *Larousse Gastronomique* almost entirely ignored

Italian cooking. Except for one dish: *spagetti à l'italienne*, which instructs the reader to boil *nouilles* (noodles) and pour a *sauce tomate aux herbes* (tomato sauce with herbs).[36] French cuisine, Jack Goody points out, was established by building on Italian foundations through supply, preparation, cooking, serving and the consumption of food that set apart high cuisine from low cuisine.[37] 'There was no Italian food before there *was* an Italy insists Mariano, There was Tuscan food and Ligurian food and Sicilian food and Sardinian food, but for two thousand years there was no Italian food.'[38] That is until 1861, when the regions were unified under the auspices of King Victor Emmanuelle II. Fresh pasta made with expensive ingredients like cheese, cream and eggs was created in the wealthy northern Italian cities, like Bologna, Italy's gastronomic capital, and dry pasta which was suitable for storing and transporting was developed in the poorer regions of Naples and Sicily in southern Italy.[39] In *Italian Identity in the Kitchen, or Food and Nation* (2013), Massimo Montanari writes that at the time of the unification of Italy, pasta was associated with Naples. By the Middle Ages the importance of pasta was already established in the alimentary system of Italy, however by the seventeenth century when Naples was under Spanish rule, problems with the availability of fresh produce, primarily meat and cabbage which were the principle ingredient in the Neapolitan popular diet, were replaced by bread and pasta. The greater availability of the muller and the invention of the mechanical press reduced the cost of production and pasta was promoted as a basic food of the people that became synonymous with Naples and with the meaning of 'Italianness'.[40] Montanari observes that to eat pasta

> suggests sharing a culture, thereby transforming the symbol of Naples (and by extension the entire south) into a symbol of the nation. The 'national revolution,' insofar as it signifies 'the acquisition of the south by the north,' was also a revolution of the gastronomic image in which macaroni is an essential part.'

Culinary and sartorial histories are building blocks for the assertion of a national identity, or as Sneja Gunew rightfully argued, when Australia introduced its multicultural policy in the 1970s, it was the celebration of custom, costume and cooking that was employed as a way of defining Australian culture, albeit pluralistic.[41] Just as Italian cuisine consists of regional variations, so too is Italian fashion made up of regional producers – such as 'Como silks, wools from Bielle, Prato carded wool, embroidery from Assisi [or] Brenta shoes.'[42] Whilst Italy's regional culinary identity was firmly established by the 1950s, Italy began to assert its identity in the field of fashion between the 1970s and 1980s with the establishment of the *stilisti*, the Italian prêt-à-porter designers, of which Franco Moschino was one launching his Cheap and Chic line in 1988.[43] As Simona Segre Reinach notes, the basic ingredients of Italian fashion were defined in

1981 in a special issue dedicated to fashion in *Domus*, the famed architectural and design journal as clear shapes, sharp cuts, refined craftmanship and precious fabrics.[44]

It was about this time in the mid-1980s that the 'Made in Italy' campaign was well-advanced as part of the boom in the Italian manufacturing and production industry. In short, the marketing slogan was used to promote traditional Italian industries known as the Four 'A's, *Abbigliamento* (clothes) *Agroalimentare* (food) *Arredamento* (furniture) and *Automobili* (automobiles) and their specialness as Italian brands to the international market. As Sover and Ben-Meir explain,

> Italian fashion reinvented itself by relying on an adherence to the markings of a rich cultural heritage. This was reflected . . . in tributes to the luxury of the Italian Renaissance, an instinctive progression toward the globalisation of fashion via various modernist aesthetics, and an ability to reinvent image ideals through advertising and promotion.[45]

Good food, good wine, expensive cars and fashion became synonymous with Italian heritage, luxury and affluence. Large roadside billboards displayed images of the *le beau monde* eating Barilla pasta, sipping Campari and dressed in Armani and Missoni whilst they zipped around on Vespas or Alfa Romeos. Italo-American pop star Madonna wore her 'Italianness' on her T-shirt (Figure 6.5) and in Hollywood actor Sylvester Stallone starred as the champion boxer Rocky Balboa, nicknamed the Italian Stallion for his prowess in the ring.

Pasta, Moschino and kitsch

Italian fashion became more accessible in the 1980s as designers created diffusion lines, like Armani Jeans or Trussardi wallets or by licensing their name on products from perfume to cigarettes and sunglasses. Milan became the worlds fashion capital and everything Italian was sexy, including pasta which became a national signifier. Franco Moschino responded to the campaign with his usual paradoxical approach to couture fashion with parody and humour and designed a simple black dress with high neckline and long sleeves with the addition of a white apron with the words 'Maid in Italy' embroidered in the front with a small red love heart. Moschino deploys symbolic systems from Italian culture, in this case gastronomy, as a subversive device to highlight the corporatization (and manufacture) of Italian heritage and culture for a mass market. Moschino was always suspicious of mass culture, especially mass fashion, which he believed duped people into false consciousness. He ridiculed the fashion industry's hierarchies by parodying symbols and signs of high culture and crafting them with cheap materials such as denim or adorning them with real

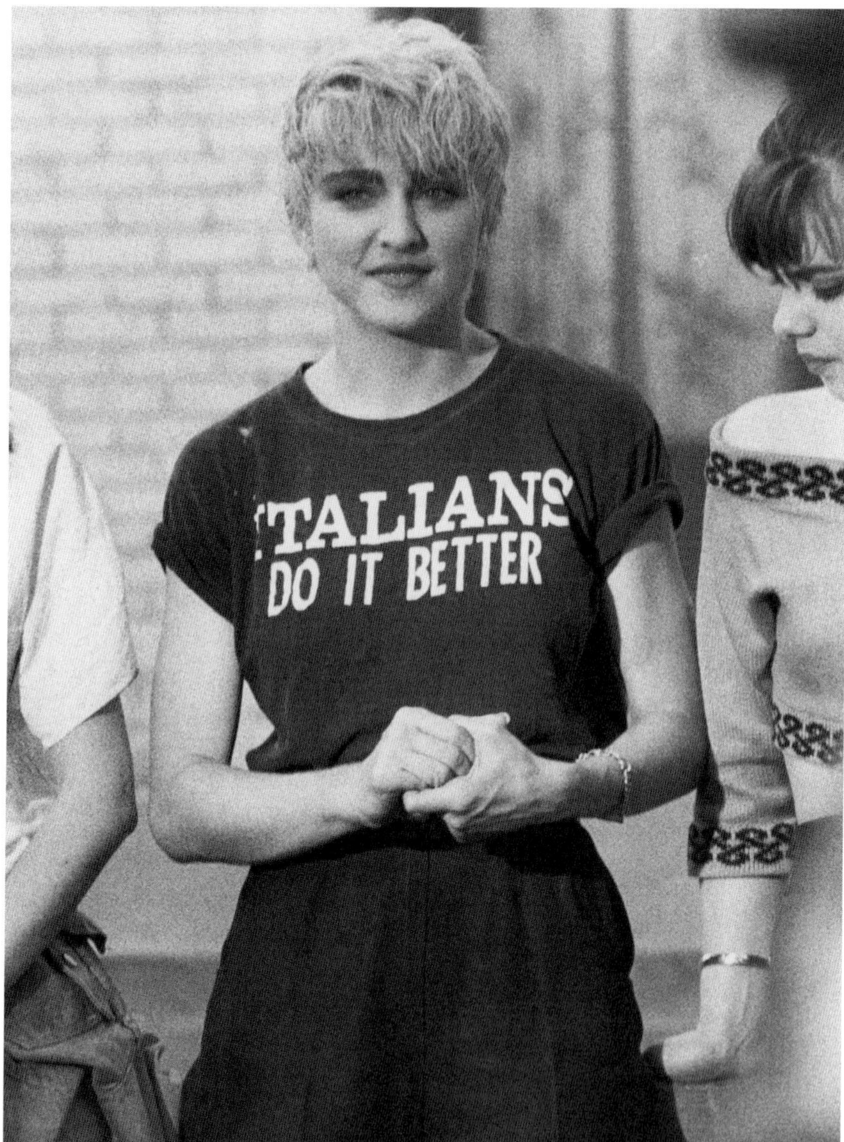

Figure 6.5 American singer and actress Madonna filming the video for her song 'Papa Don't Preach' in New York City, 1986. The video is being directed by James Foley. Madonna is wearing a T-shirt with the slogan 'Italians Do It Better'. Actress Debi Mazar is on the right. (Photo by Vinnie Zuffante/Michael Ochs Archives/Getty Images.)

Figure 6.6 Lily McMenamy, Jeremy Scott and Rita Ora attend Moschino Dinner during the Milan Fashion Week Womenswear Autumn–Winter 2014 at Giacomo Arengario Restaurant on 20 February 2014 in Milan, Italy. (Photo by Venturelli/Getty Images.)

silver wear, like the knives, spoons and forks on his Dinner Suit or real pasta as buttons on a garment. His crusades against the fashion system were not only aimed at Chanel, but included heritage brands, Yves St Laurent and Louis Vuitton, whom he often appropriated to underscore the complexities of creative authorship and the mass market. On the one hand Moschino's 'Maid in Italy' was deployed as a quip at Chanel by appropriating her 'little black dress' and on the second hand, as a visual pun to emphasize the hegemony of the fashion system and consumers obsession (or enslavement) by it. 'I copy and desecrated other designers,' said Moschino, '[to] recount what happens by trying to understand the motivations of people.'[46] Moschino cultivated the persona of the court jester of fashion as a mechanism of speaking out and exposing the fashion system and would often be photographed winking at the camera, which became his signature look.

In the early 1990s, Franco Moschino designed a vest with six bowtie pasta (*farfalle*) buttons (a spare farfalle button was sewn into the vest's label) with a splat of spaghetti and red sauce which was intended to look like a spill, with the phrase 'Sorry I'm Italian' embroidered on the back. The vest was made of natural fibres and dyes and was part of Moschino's 'Nature Friendly Garment' (1994) collection. The excessive and artificial play havoc with the serious and the elated. In the hands of Moschino, good taste becomes a by-word for a form of suppressed reductivism and opprobrium levelled at audacity. 'The Moschino oeuvre is an attempt to reconcile the natural with the artificial, arranging the apparent opposites to show their continuity.'[47] Moschino was committed to environmental issues and much of his work was anti-fashion, anti-consumption and anti-commercialism embroidering his garments with cult captions like 'Bullchic' and 'Fashion off', 'Stop the Fashion System' and 'nature is better than couture'. He used ecological furs in his collections instead of animal skins and introduced a green line called Ecocouture. Moschino considered himself as a commentator rather than a designer whose task was to repurpose, remake and re-interpret the workings of fashion rather than design garments.[48] So when Jeremy Scott appeared on stage at the end of his Fall–Winter 2014 collection at Milan Fashion Week wearing a T-shirt printed with the words 'I don't speak Italian, but I do speak Moschino', (Figure 6.6) Scott was following Moschino's anarchic philosophical mantra that from chaos comes ideas.

7
IDEAL BODIES AND THE CULT OF SLENDERNESS

While the rest of the world was still experiencing COVID-19 lockdown restrictions and closed borders, Sydney launched its Afterpay Australian Fashion Week which ran from 31 May to 4 June 2021. The various 'maskless' designer shows were scattered across the city's historical sites and included a diversity of models, indigenous, Asian, Black, genderfluid, thin and plump, young and old. Oversized silhouettes and an abundance of layering dominated the catwalk. On the one hand, this was Covid-era comfort dressing reflecting the months of baking and snacking that came with people's lack of social interaction, frustration and boredom during lockdown. On the other hand, the patterns and styles replicated a fashion industry that was responding to pressure from political groups to dismantle, decolonize and change. Beauty ideals were recalibrated as clothes designed for gendered body types began disappearing and formerly conventional body shapes and sizes were being called into question. The Trans* liberation movement with its call for gender diversity, 'Black Lives Matter' (BLM) for race equality and the #MeToo movement against sexism highlighted all the faults with the current fashion system. The upside of the pandemic crisis was that it presented the opportunity to design a new world. Two years before the pandemic, *Vogue* announced: 'Fashion is broken from the inside out and like an ouroboros the snake is eating its own tail.'[1] 'The industry keeps revisiting the many problems [of] the ready-to-wear system.'[2] Unlike haute couture or made to measure, which fits the garment onto the body, in the ready-to-wear system, which applies a sizing system in the manufacture of clothing, the body needs to fit into the garment.

Fashion, like cinema and photography, is a child of modernity whose foundations lie in the colonial enterprise and Western hegemonic discourses of imperialism. Writing in 2020, Toby Slade and Angela M. Jansen observe that '[t]he exploitation of the environment, the exploitation of people and labour, and the exploitation of cultures are all interrelated, without the logic of coloniality, extended in globalisation and national capitalism, and their embedded hierarchies, fashion as it recently operates will be impossible.'[3] There is no escaping or denying fashion's role in the act of fashioning ideal beauty and body types that are embedded in constructions of whiteness and bourgeois values and taste regimes. Food and ingredients (or lack thereof), ways of cooking (nouvelle cuisine) and fad diets (Atkins, Paleo, Keto) have perpetuated the ability to achieve goals of calorie loss achievable. But the deprivation of food that comes hand in hand with maintaining unachievable body size has created eating disorders such as bulimia and anorexia, that have plagued the modelling and fashion industry for some time despite the protest of portraying a single body type as optimal.

The concept of the ideal body has been dogging fashion for quite a while now. Although these ideals have changed over time, they have essentially remained the same and have been incorporated into the habits and routines of allied industries that legitimize the practice of fashion, such as fitness, health and beauty. Let us use the phrase 'the cult of slenderness' for this network of industry sectors, including the media and modelling agencies, that support and promote what Paolo Velonté calls 'the tyranny of thinness.'[4] As Velonté notes, there have been instances in which mainstream fashion has explored the 'curvy' world, in special issues of *Vogue Italia* (June 2010) or *Elle* (April 2010) magazines, or by designers using plus-sized testimonials (Kim Kardashian for Pierre Balmain since 2014) or plus size catwalk models (Beth Ditto for Jean Paul Gaultier, Spring–Summer 2011).[5] However, as Velonté cautions, these 'explorations have been restricted to the sphere of communication and have not affected the system of fashion production, distribution and consumption.'[6] In other words, the slender body is nonetheless the standard of beauty that dominates the Western fashion industry and nowhere is it more prominent and disciplined than in the modelling industry where the weight, shape and size of models set ideal standards of beauty.

Food and women's body ideals

Although it is generally accepted that concepts of the ideal body have shifted over time, a thread can be drawn between food, diets and cooking methods, linking the size and shape of the ideal body with the consumption of fashion. In any case, the connections between food, the body and the fashion world are more than evident and can be traced together with trends in the food and fashion industry. One example might be the plump body of the nineteenth and early twentieth centuries. The availability and consumption of food during the Industrial Revolution varied according to class. As Susanne Daly and Ross G. Forman claim, 'food is a benign marker of social position, but it gestures at the grimmer reality that social status often determines who lives and who dies.'[7] Laura Frazer remarks that the outbreak of tuberculosis in Europe during the late eighteenth and early nineteenth centuries affected people's attitudes towards body sizes. She writes that many artists, including John Keats and Emily Brontë among others, suffered at some time or another from tuberculosis, which made them look thin, pale and sickly. 'Members of the upper classes,'[8] Frazer writes, 'believed that having tuberculosis, and being slender itself, were signs that one possessed a delicate, intellectual and superior nature . . . It was glamorous to look sickly.'[9] She notes that Lord Byron, who was five foot six inches who at his most weighed over two hundred pounds (91 kilos or 14.5 stones), embarked on a series of obsessive diets to lose weight and become thin. His diet consisted of nothing more than drinking water with vinegar and eating biscuits and potatoes.

Slum-dwellers, who lived in miserable conditions ate mainly bread, gruel and broth whilst factory workers and labourers spent approximately 58 per cent of their income on food and 40 per cent of this expenditure was on bread.[10] According to Emma Griffiths, a great proportion on their income was spent on cheap energy-dense food, including some (salted) meat scraps, usually bacon. The remaining income was spent on sugar, yeast, tea, salt, butter and cheese. Rice, eggs, currants and raisins were often bought in small quantities for puddings.[11] A study conducted by Paul Clayton and Judith Rowbotham on 'How the Mid-Victorians Worked, Ate and Died' records that wealthy Victorians enjoyed a great variety of foods including oily fish such as herrings, haddock and cod as well as grains, potatoes and shellfish such as oysters, cockles and mussels. The bourgeoise enjoyed large quantities of wine along with meat including goose, ham, turkey and beef which were generously seasoned with expensive spices imported from India.[12] A typical breakfast might consist of cold meats, stone-ground bread with lard and cheese washed down with beer. This extravagant spending on food was matched only by their expenditure on luxury goods, including clothes and accessories which became indicators of class aspirations.

Although Thorstein Veblen did not write about food and dining per se, he did write about upper-class behaviour and conspicuous consumption as an ideology as well as a social strategy. In his *Theory of the Leisure Class* (1899) Veblen argues that clothing and fashion were an important way in which the leisure class could compete among themselves for status and prestige as well as a way of displaying their superiority of their class, in short, *conspicuous consumption* and *conspicuous leisure*. The ownership of quality clothing or access made by time-consuming methods and expensive materials added to the prestigious reputation of the wearer granting them social status. The appearance in public of current up-to-date clothing and the latest fashions becomes a sign of pecuniary strength.[13] The same analysis may be applied to the consumption of food and especially to restaurant dining which disciplined food and eating. 'Dining more than ever,' notes Pricilla Parkhurst Ferguson, 'became a matter of savoir-faire . . . and flaunting one's savoir-faire signified power.'[14] Writing many years after Veblen, Bourdieu notes that the food that was consumed by the upper classes reflected 'tastes of refinement' and their perceived value in society.[15] Historically exclusive food items, such as curry powder, were marked high demand and low supply. In 1849, the Victorian 'celebrity' chef Alexis Soya, who always kept a supply of curry sauce made up in his larder, lamented that the high price of curry powder 'was one of those stimulating condiments which would be invaluable to the poor.'[16]

The abundance of food that was available to the upper classes because of the trade routes of the colonial enterprise was reflected in the lavishness of cloth, embroidery and styles in fashion throughout Europe. Women's physical silhouette narrowed as new fashions and styles placed a great emphasis on women's corseted waists. In *The Feminine Ideal*, Marianne Thessander writes that in and around the 1900s the most expensive corsets were to be found in Paris and were made of embroidered white silk. Others were made of white satin with embroidered butterflies as well as corsets made of brightly coloured silks and lace embroidery.[17] According to Thessander, the corset had become a fashionable item of dress and a symbol of aristocracy, self-discipline and physical control. 'The women's corseted figure and expensive and impractical dress demonstrated her own and her husband's social position.'[18]

The corset eventually gave way to the long and slender body represented in Paul Poiret's new style of women's wear that drew its focus away from the waist, hips and bust and instead focused on accentuated curves and toned-down lines. In other words, the fashion for corsets (and plumpness) changed as aristocratic tastes shifted with the changing economy. The move from an agricultural to an industrial economy affected the manufacture and distribution of food products. The introduction of refrigeration and canning made food more accessible as companies began to process food products and distribute then via the railways. Food became cheaper, and more abundant to the working classes and so plumpness was no longer a sign of prestige. Slenderness soon became a symbol of class distinction and finer sensibilities and fashion soon followed suit. When Coco Chanel introduced skinny *mannequins* to model her collections in the 1920s this was certainly also the case, although it is now generally agreed that she chose them simply as extensions of her own petite proportions. Jean Patou launched a new range of women's clothing that violated the binary between formal and informal wear by introducing sport, play and physical activities as concepts in fashion. His boutique *Le Coin du sport* ('Sports Corner') at 7 rue Saint-Florentin in Paris became a popular shopping destination for the 'New Woman' whose pastime was engaging in athletic activities.

As men returned from the Second World War and women were pushed back into the home and the domestic interior, women were encouraged to be 'domestic goddesses' as family dinners, cocktail parties and home entertaining took precedent for the middle class. The ideal female body at this time was not athletic, but curvier and more fecund. The full-figured silhouette with narrow waist, extenuated hips and enhanced breast size that accompanied Christian Dior's 'New Look' in 1947 was indicative of the prosperity that followed the economic boom after the Second World War (Figure 7.1). This 'New Look' promoted the traditional hour-glass shape of femininity that was nostalgic and harkened back to the Hellenic body ideal. The look extenuated the breasts and hips and narrowed the waist, a style that could only be achieved through corsetry and brasserie. Many styles of corsets and high waist girdles were available which, with the help of darts and boning, created a slender waist that eroticized and enhanced parts of women's bodies. The Hollywood star system also promoted this 'new' curvaceous body that was made fashionable by film stars Marylin Monroe and Jayne Mansfield. It was a body ideal that would remain fashionable for the next ten years.

In America the rise in manufacturing and technology resulted in new 'convenience' food ranging from canned food and evaporated milk to boxed cake mixes. Food began to be packaged in clear cellophane wrapping and the self-service grocery store made way for the supermarket chain. Although fast food outlets with their highly mechanized and systematic food preparations were already established in America since the 1920s, food was still being rationed in

Figure 7.1 Fashion couturier Christian Dior (1905–1957), designer of the 'New Look' and the 'A-line', with six of his models after a fashion parade at the Savoy Hotel, London, 25 April 1950. (Photo by Fred Ramage/Keystone/Getty Images.)

Britain until 1954. The bistro with its simple interior, hearty food and its rustic presentation became a popular eating venue in France.

Nouvelle cuisine, skinny cooking and skinny models

When thinness is made too much of as a standard, as it did in the 1960s with the waif-thin body of British model Twiggy who wore the revolutionary designs of Mary Quant in London and André Courrèges in Paris, the ideal body in fashion began to shift to one that was thin and girlish and very similar to the lanky boyish body of the 1920s (Figure 7.2). 'Young women rebelled against the perpetuation of the ideal of overblown femininity [of the 1950s], which they believed contributed to sex discrimination, and instead cultivated a desexualized, pubescent ideal.'[19] Quant played a major role in this shift not just in fashion with her fun clothes that appealed to the burgeoning youth market, but to a new physical expression which was no longer curvaceous and voluptuous but childlike. Quant's pinafore dress made references to British school girl's uniforms whilst her tight 'skinny-ribbed' sweater was influenced by her experience of wearing an eight-year-old boy's sweater 'for fun . . . and was enchanted by the result.'[20] The appeal of the heavy-lidded false eyelashes further enhanced this childlike look. Fashion designer and founder of the London Boutique Biba, Hulanicki comments in her autobiography that the ideal woman was 'was very pretty and young. She had an upturned nose, rosy cheeks and long asparagus legs with tiny feet.'[21] It was a look that soon became known as the 'dolly bird' and was widely circulated by the British media. In an essay charting the way in which the image of the 1960s 'dolly bird' was exploited within the media, Pamela Church Gibson notes that 'to a modern feminist ear, the phrase is disturbing , for by combining two colloquial terms meaning 'young girl' into one phrase, the demeaning effect of both is intensified.' [22] Writing about the realities of this new look Elizabeth Wilson comments:

> When girls – for all women were girls in those days – wore skirts that rose to the crotch and curtains of hair that descended to meet it, when they exposed nipples in see-through crocheted tank tops that never met hipster pants, they were looking . . . like children . . . The sixties preferred a decadent Lolita image. As personified by the newly famous models of the period, it was the decade of the rag doll, of the waif, of the pre-pubertal Twiggy who shot to fame before she reached the age of consent.[23]

The 'mini-skirt' was all the rage producing a straight silhouette without waist or hips. The body became a set of geometric shapes that drew attention away

Figure 7.2 English model Twiggy in a mini-dress, London, 6 August 1966. (Photo by Popperfoto via Getty Images/Getty Images.)

from the body to the legs. Skinny became the new *de rigueur* and food soon followed suit.

Margaret Visser writes that the marriage of food and slender bodies is simply enough: 'The recent fashion for nouvelle cuisine is a social expression of the modern ideal that successful people ought to continue to be not only very rich but also very thin.'[24] As we have seen already, since at least the eighteenth century with La Chapelle, there are several competing historical claims to nouvelle cuisine, which has been invoked periodically to signify a food-trend's break with the past. Escoffier's style was simplified in relation to the architectural-operatic feats excelled at by Carême. Menon also used the term in his *Nouveau traité* (New Treatise). In today's terms it refers to the style and approach to food that began to be made in the 1960s when the food critics Henri Gault and Christian Millau invoked the term yet again to designate a much lighter and more sparing approach to cooking where the emphasis lay more on subtle flavours and sympathetic combinations than on filling the belly. This food was lighter, eschewing heavy sauces or what were seen as unnecessary and archaic complications. Wanting to distinguish their new style of cooking, Henri Gault and Christian Millau announced with much gusto in 1973:

> Down with the old-fashioned image of the typical *bon vivant*, that puffy personage with his napkin tucked under his chin, his lips dripping veal stock . . . no more of those terrible brown sauces and white sauces, those *espagnoles*, those *périgueux* with truffles, those *béchamels* and *mornays* that have assassinated as many livers as they have covered indifferent foods. They are forbidden!'[25]

In short, Gault and Millau's aim was to strip French cooking of its fatty ingredients and focus on its simplicity. Much like fashionable body ideals that tapered the plump full-breasted feminine ideal of the 1950s to the slim, flat-chested, elongated bodies of models like Twiggy or Jean Shrimpton. And like fashion with its emphasis on stylization and aesthetics, nouvelle cuisine emphasized the importance of plating and presentation. Gone were the flambéing and carving performances of haute cuisine as dishes became streamlined (like fashion) and carefully arranged on a plate. Although at the time, plenty of people liked to laugh at the fussiness of the presentation and complained that the portions were too small.[26] Soon enough Gault and Millau established the *Gault et Millau* (1969), a food rating system that awarded restaurants a score out of twenty, twenty being the highest accolade. Much like the *Guide Michelin* that awards restaurants up to three stars for culinary excellence, the *Gault et Millau* uses up to four *toques* or chefs hats, as a signifier of gastronomic distinction.

Much like Barthes' analysis of the fashion system that creates desire by selling the *meaning* of fashion rather than the material object, or *mere* clothing, the Michelin star and the *Gault et Millau* hat are signifiers in a system of communication that indicates the *value* of food (ingredients, products, techniques, display) rather than *mere* food for gestation purposes. 'This is true for clothing; it is also true for food,' he states in his essay 'Towards a Psychosociology of Contemporary Food Consumption' (1961). By this he means that 'not only the elements of display in food, such as foods involved in rites of hospitality, but all foods serve as a sign among the members of a given society.'[27] Once food is 'satisfied by standardized production, preparation and consumption . . . it takes on the characteristics of an institution.'[28] The star and hat ratings become a *unit* in a system of differences in signification in the communication of food. As an example, the transformational analysis of a cow's tongue to *langue de boeuf aux cornichons* (Beef Tongue with Gherkins) involves a difference to what is signified: the former signifies everyday life, the biological and the living, the latter the extravagant presentation and cooking methods of an haute cuisine meal. Similarly, fish eggs (or roe) are transformed to caviar in the process of production, preparation and consumption. French chef Eric Rupier, who has his own eponymous caviar product, advises to 'simply dollop caviar on the back of the hand with a bone or mother-of-pearl spoon – metal utensils are to be avoided as they may oxidize caviar – or pile the roe high atop a warm blini along with a smattering of crème fraiche.'[29] Similarly, Two-Michelin star chef Jean Georges Vongerichten serves the otherwise mundane *croque monsieur* (cheese and ham toasted sandwiches) embellished with caviar and beef wagyu at his restaurant. The changeover from fish eggs to caviar signifies a change in social class as caviar is transformed to a sign of wealth and refinement. The same can be said of the 'little black dress'. This simple, calf-length black dress with a straight silhouette was that which was transformed (in the hands of Chanel) from a garment of mourning for the aristocracy in the nineteenth century, to one of elegance for women of all social classes to fit the ideal figure in the 1920s. Through alterations in design, (technique, fabric, pattern) and advertising, the dress is converted to a sign of modernity. *Vogue* magazine called the dress 'Chanel's Ford' like the Model T Ford automobile that was exclusive and fashionable at the time.

Specialists and sticklers are inclined to distinguish nouvelle cuisine from *cuisine minceur*, or 'thin cooking' (the translation does not much work), which was a coinage of Michel Guérard as a food for spas and gastric recuperation. Whatever the differences may be, the rejection and break of the nouvelle cuisine of the twentieth century was that of the once ubiquitous tradition established (through refinement and adoption as much as his own invention) by Escoffier. It was in acknowledgement of a far more body-conscious world, cosmetically and biologically. Where plumpness and obesity once belonged to the body of material means – the reverse had come to be the case. Obesity is the sign of a cheap starchy diet replete in processed fats and addictive sugars, that is, foods that are cheap and mass produced. Slender bodies are equated with control whereas the overweight body is now associated with a body that has no time, nor inclination of education, to care for itself. In addition to connotations bound to class and lifestyle, it carries with it moral opprobrium related to discipline and self-respect, notions that were also revived in the 1960s with the fashion for methods of self-improvement. In short, the body, and body type, has long been a battleground for status and moral judgement.

Yet it is also the overly thin body, which began to be seen in female models since the 1990s, that has courted a similar controversy with 'Heroin Chic' a style that gained precedent in fashion media with images of models that were thin and dishevelled posed in urban settings in various positions mimicking drug withdrawal. Thinness became associated with the body's rejection of food and the model's refusal to eat, as Mary Rizzo cautions, '[t]his is a body made of denial – denial of nourishment, denial of an adult figure, and a denial of female sexuality, associated with hips and breasts. This body refuses to become what society expects of it.'[30] The anorectic body of Heroin Chic found its place in the childlike image of supermodel Kate Moss (then eighteen years old) for Calvin Klein's perfume advertising campaign 'Obsession' (as well as other Klein campaigns) launched in 1993 and photographed by Mario Sorrenti. The rise of Grunge music with bands Alice in Chains and Kurt Cobain's Nirvana and their candid omissions of heroin drug use significantly influenced the popularity of the style, especially amongst teenagers and young consumers. Fashion photographer Corrine Day, (one of the first to photograph Kate Moss) was instrumental in pushing fashion images away from the curvaceous and glamourous image represented by the 1980s supermodels, Claudia Schiffer, Cindy Crawford, Linda Evangelista and Elle Macpherson. Rebecca Arnold notes that Day used 'unconventional-looking models and urban settings to reflect what she thought were truer influences of young nineties life.'[31]

Certainly, a more muscular body ideal exemplified by broad shoulders emerged in the 1980s with the fitness and body image boom. Gyms became commercial institutions with a definable culture of protein shakes and diets as well as exercise regimes like weight-lifting and high-intensity interval training. The film industry made exceptional bodies the norm with films such as *Blue Lagoon* (1980, Randel Kleiser) staring Calvin Klein supermodel Brooke Shields and *The Woman in Red* (1984, Gene Wilder) starring Christian Dior model Kelly LeBrock who became one of the most highly sought-after models associated with the Ford modelling agency. Gym culture gave rise to a new form of dress style – work out or aerobics fashion – with popular items including leotards in bright neon colours that covered the torso and sometimes the arms and were worn with leggings or tights. Accessories and gadgets were marketed to appeal to the fitness conscious consumer such as the Walkman which Sony launched in 1979, the portable media player that allowed people to insert a cassette and listen to music of their choice while on the move – ubiquitous today, but a novelty then. Although broad shoulders found their way into shoulder pads and power suits became the defining fashion statement, the fashion industry made skinny a mandate and brought it to unconscionable extremes.

Sizing and ready-to-wear

Food has been in the ambit of the fashion industry more broadly, but nowhere has it been more telling than on the bodies of models. The nexus to it all has been the perceptions and fallacies related to what constitutes a healthy body. As Susan Bordo writes, ideal standards of beauty and weight can be 'self-punishing and have expanded the repertoire of eating problems from starvation diets and the dream of a body that is curvaceous but rigorously toned.'[32] The 'size zero' aesthetic has claimed its store of casualties, both figuratively and literally speaking and prompted a widespread backlash, including a reaction that seeks to embrace 'plus size' body types, albeit the success of this has always been small relative to the regnant mainstream. Joanne Entwistle and Elizabeth Wissinger cite an important turning point in recent times, that of a twenty-two-year-old model who died during fashion week in Montevideo in South America in 2006 which prompted a backlash in the media about inappropriate and unrealistic ideals of what women should be and the suffering it caused. Fashion week organizations across the globe set about with measures of addressing the trend of emaciated models such Madrid Fashion Week stipulating a minimum height-to-weight ratio, or a Body Mass Index (BMI) of 18. Milan then drew up a code of conduct, and Britain staged two 'body image summits'. They concluded that,

> as these examples demonstrate, images and stories of fashion models consist of moral dramas that focus attention on their bodies as in some way excessive, abject, as well as desirable. These fixations have produced their wave of 'moral panics' about models' 'effects,' from fears about their supposed influence on the rise in eating disorders among young women, to concerns as to the possible promotion of a hedonistic, drug-taking lifestyle.[33]

The following year, the Council of Fashion Designers of America (CFDA) with the support of *Vogue* magazine and its editor Anna Wintour announced the CFDA Health Initiative (2007). The initiative encouraged the fashion industry (photographers, editors, casting directors and modelling agents) to share responsibility in fostering an industry that promoted healthy bodies and eating. The initiative specified guidelines for a healthy diet, minimum age requirements for models and the supply of nutritional food during photo shoots. Parallel to this, nutritional diets, superfoods and supplements would assist without forfeiting on nutrients or lifestyle choices.

Where the close association of the model and slenderness historically derives is easy to locate, for it lies in the transition to mass production post Second World War, the ready-to-wear industry and the introduction of the clothing sizing system. haute couture as it rose from Worth in the closing decades of the nineteenth century was always about serving the élite, as was haute cuisine – this was capitalism on display, they were about plenty accessible to the few. In haute couture the garment was designed to fit a particular body, regardless of size, measurements were taken of the body then the garment was adjusted to fit in the making process. In prêt-à-porter, also known as 'ready-to-wear', or 'off the rack', garment sizes were standardized to affect speedy production and to rationalize fabric use and minimize waste. The sizing system also allowed changes to the original pattern by either grading the size up or down which provided considerable economic advantages. In short, size 4–6 (US) or 8–10 (Australia and UK) became the standard size for women and 'fit' and runway models adapted to the size. As sample sizes from runway collections became smaller, model's diet to remain on top of the game. French fashion labels began using size 32 models, (size 0 in the US) for female models and size 44 for male models, which is internationally labelled XXS, creating unrealistic demands and promoting an unhealthy image. According to Australian *Vogue* editor Kirstie Clements, a model who cannot fit into a sample size at a casting session because she has gained a little weight will be reprimanded by her agency. The model begins to diet, loses weight, and is praised by her peers. Rather than maintaining her weight through exercise and responsible dieting the model continues to lose weight believing that thinner is more desirable. Models who are unable to lose weight have breast reduction surgery or implants to enhance the size of their breasts.[34] Lip sculpting and refinement, injectables (Botox and fillers), rhinoplasty and skin resurfacing are all common procedures in the glamour industry.

In 2015 the French government passed a bill (effective in 2017), prohibiting the use of underage and size zero models that promote unhealthy and unattainable beauty ideals. Models are now required to provide a doctor's certificate, valid for two years, attesting that their health is compatible with their work. Employers who violate the rule face six months imprisonment and a 75,000 Euro fine. A second law was passed that same year requiring all digitally enhanced photographs to be labelled '*photographie retouchée*' (retouched photographs).[35] The French luxury groups Moët Hennessy Louis Vuitton (LVMH) and Kering who own fashion labels Gucci, Louis Vuitton, YSL and Christian Dior have ceased to require models to work from 11.00 pm and 6.00 am. Models aged between sixteen and eighteen who are required to stay away from home must be accompanied by a parent or chaperone.

The kinds of furore that the fashion industry has incited over the size of women's bodies has caused the industry to retort by suggesting that it is being unfairly singled-out and that the celebrity and the film industry must also bear responsibility for the trend. In the wake of the 2006 outcry and the subsequent rules imposed on a model's BMI, Karl Lagerfeld protested that such strictures were 'politically correct fascism'.[36] He added, perhaps with the developed world only in mind: 'There are more fat people in the world than skinny ones, and the fat ones have big, big problems. Nobody cares they are not glamorous.'[37] Lagerfeld did not deny the problems but laid the responsibility on the parents and doctors of the models not fashion designers. Priority, he contended, goes to the 'look' which is not dependent on a prescribed body type.[38] Instead as Entwistle and Don Slater note, the 'look' is the amalgamation of a variety of actions and the assemblages of elements from a diverse group of actors (models, photographers) in the production and consumption of fashion in any given time.[39]

Fad diets and Diet Coke

> I only like what I'm allowed to like. I'm beyond temptation. There is no weakness. When I see tons of food in the studio . . . for me, it's as if this stuff was made out of plastic. The idea doesn't even enter my mind that a human being could put that into their mouth. I'm like the animals in the forest. They don't touch what they cannot eat.[40]

The above passage taken from an interview with Karl Lagerfeld aptly encapsulates how achieving an ideal body size is about having control of your body and what you eat. Fad diets are like fashion trends that come in and out of style, this is because celebrities endorse a diet as much as they endorse a designer by wearing their garments in public, say to the Oscars for example. The Atkins Diet that restricts carbohydrates and promotes the consumption of proteins and fats, was developed in the 1960s by cardiologist Robert C. Atkins and was the first fad diet to gain a large following by celebrities. Then Oprah Winfrey lost 67 pounds (4.7 stone or 30 kilos) in the 1980s by following a liquid diet made up of a high protein, vitamin-packed nutrient powder mixed with water or Diet Coke. Intermittent dieting which restricts eating to certain times during the day and plant-based diets such as Keto have also been popular with celebrities. In her Netflix film *Homecoming* (2019, Beyoncé Knowles, US) American musical performer Beyoncé Knowles revealed her 'diet secrets' of how she lost 218 pounds (15.4 stones or 98 kilos) after the birth of her twins to prepare for the 2018 Coachella Valley Music and Arts Festival, 'In order for me to meet my goals,' said Beyoncé, 'I'm limiting myself to no bread, no carbs, no sugar, no dairy, no meat, no fish, no alcohol.'[41]

In November 2000 Karl Lagerfeld decided that he was no longer satisfied with his body which was considered plump for the day's standards and decided to lose weight. It was not that he had endured ill health – unlike Christian Dior who had suffered two heart attacks and a massive stroke – he simply wanted to dress differently and change his appearance. It was all to do with vanity and aesthetics and in any case, Lagerfeld said he was bored with the way that he looked. He had been wearing diaphanous jackets with a large wooden fan hung around his neck for far too long and it was time for a change. He was also craving to wear clothes designed by Heidi Slimane which were made to be worn by young skinny men with streamlined silhouettes, certainly not for Lagerfeld who was not only overweight, but he had just celebrated his sixty-eighth birthday. So, he sought the professional services of Dr Jean-Claude Houdret who specializes in herbal medicine, homeopathy and nutrition. Dr Houdret placed Lagerfeld on a strict diet. After a punishing thirteen months Lagerfeld had lost 91 pounds (6.5 stone or 41 kilos) transforming his body into a pencil-thin shape. 'Fashion is the healthiest motivation for losing weight,' declared a triumphant Lagerfeld when he was interviewed by the media.[42]

The secret to Lagerfeld's weight loss was in a well-balanced diet, low in calories with no red meat or sugar, no white flour, let alone any processed foods. Lagerfeld decided to share his weight loss program and write a book with Dr Houdret called *The Karl Lagerfeld Diet* (2005). The book contains several essays on cosmetic surgery and skin care, an interview with Lagerfield on dieting, an essay on being a contemporary dandy and several recipes and diets consisting of a combination of protein powders and raw vegetables. Winter breakfast is an egg, either poached or boiled, a slice of toast (no butter), juice and low-fat yogurt. Summer breakfast is just fruit and yogurt eliminating the egg and toast altogether. Lunch and dinner dishes include salmon and Brussels sprouts, veal with plums, quail flambé, fish soufflé and lobster. Lagerfeld even included his favourite recipe of stuffed peppers and tomatoes. A glass or two of red wine a day is also permitted, 'but only red [because] it has natural chemical products that are good for the brain and circulation.'[43] Dr Houdret also encouraged the liberal use of artificial sweeteners and diet sodas and discouraged exercise because it 'runs the risk of making you hungry.'[44] So Lagerfeld became addicted to Diet Coke consuming up to ten bottles a day. 'I drink Diet Coke from the minute I get up to the minute I go to bed,' he told *Harper's Bazaar* magazine, 'I can even drink it in the middle of the night and I can sleep. I don't drink coffee, I don't drink tea, I don't drink anything else.'[45] Shortly after, online media, magazines and newspapers were saturated with images of the 'Kaiser's' new look. He wore a tailored black pin striped jacket over a crisp white shirt with a detachable high collar tucked into a pair of skinny jeans over his Cuban heel boots. Fingerless gloves and dark black Ray Ban sunglasses completed his new style (Figure 7.3). He looked almost like a vampire with his snow-white hair and pale skin, yet elegant and sophisticated.

Figure 7.3 Designer Karl Lagerfeld poses for a photograph at the Fendi Party celebrating the Loris Cecchini 'Empty Walls: Just Doors' exhibition at the Palais Du Tokyo on 10 January 2006 in Paris, France. (Photo by Chris Jackson/Getty Images.)

In 2010 Lagerfeld attracted the attention of the soft drink giant Coca-Cola who featured him dressed in a black silhouette form (including signature ponytail) on a limited edition bottle of Coca-Cola Light. The previous year *Coca-Cola* had invited Italian labels and designers Donatella Versace, Roberto Cavali, Angela Missoni, Consuelo Castiglioni, Alberto Ferreti, Moschino and Etro to place their logo on bottles of Coca-Cola Light to raise money for the survivors of the Abruzzo earthquake in Italy donating nearly 40 million US dollars to the Italian Red Cross. Then in 2011 Lagerfeld designed three limited edition bottles (featuring his signature ponytail silhouette) for Diet Coke's 'Love it Light' campaign. Each bottle was individually sold and packaged in prism-shaped collectors' boxes.

The 'Love it Light' campaign was targeted to the fashion-conscious consumer distributing free fashion magazines and Assos clothes to kick off the drinks launch. Special subscription rates to *Grazia, Heat* and *Closer* magazines was offered with every purchase of the special promotional 2-litre bottles and fridge pack, as well as a fashion make-over to coincide with London Fashion week. Diet Coke saturated the market, sponsoring fashion events with barrels of Diet Coke on ice and fashion models and celebrities were photographed clutching a can of Diet Coke in their hand. (Figure 7.4). A Yahoo website called 'Style it Light' was formed in partnership with *Marie Claire* and *InStyle* magazines and the explosion of celebrity and paparazzi culture in the 1990s delivered Diet Coke into every home. 'Who would have guessed,' asked the *Guardian*, 'that a cloyingly sweet, mass produced, calorie free drink would become the most stylish drink in the world?'[46] Even Lady Gaga wore Diet Coke cans as hair rollers in her *Telephone* (2010) music video with Beyoncé. Diet Coke had become firmly entrenched as the elixir of the beau monde. 'The supermodel diet of Marlboro Lights and Diet Coke may not have topped the bestsellers chart alongside the Atkins [diet],'[47] states Christa de Souza, but 'Diet Coke became the ultimate accessible fashion accessory.' Cheaper than an 'it-bag', more obvious than a perfume, and available in every corner shop.[48]

Diet Coke then enlisted the services of Puppet Heap, a design and production company that specializes in puppet fabrication for film, television and theatre to create a new 'Love it Light' campaign. Working in collaboration with media corporations Legs Media and Mother (London), Puppet Heap created three puppet friends, Eleanor, Bernadette and Irene who work together at a fashion magazine. 'They take a spontaneous and light attitude to whatever life throws at them and [do] not take things too seriously – just like a real life Diet Coke girl.'[49] The description of the marionettes as embodiments of fashion-conscious young women who are extolled for their superficiality renders the doll and women as frivolous and interchangeable. The marionette's association with women, fashion and glamour raises questions about the representation of women as shallow and

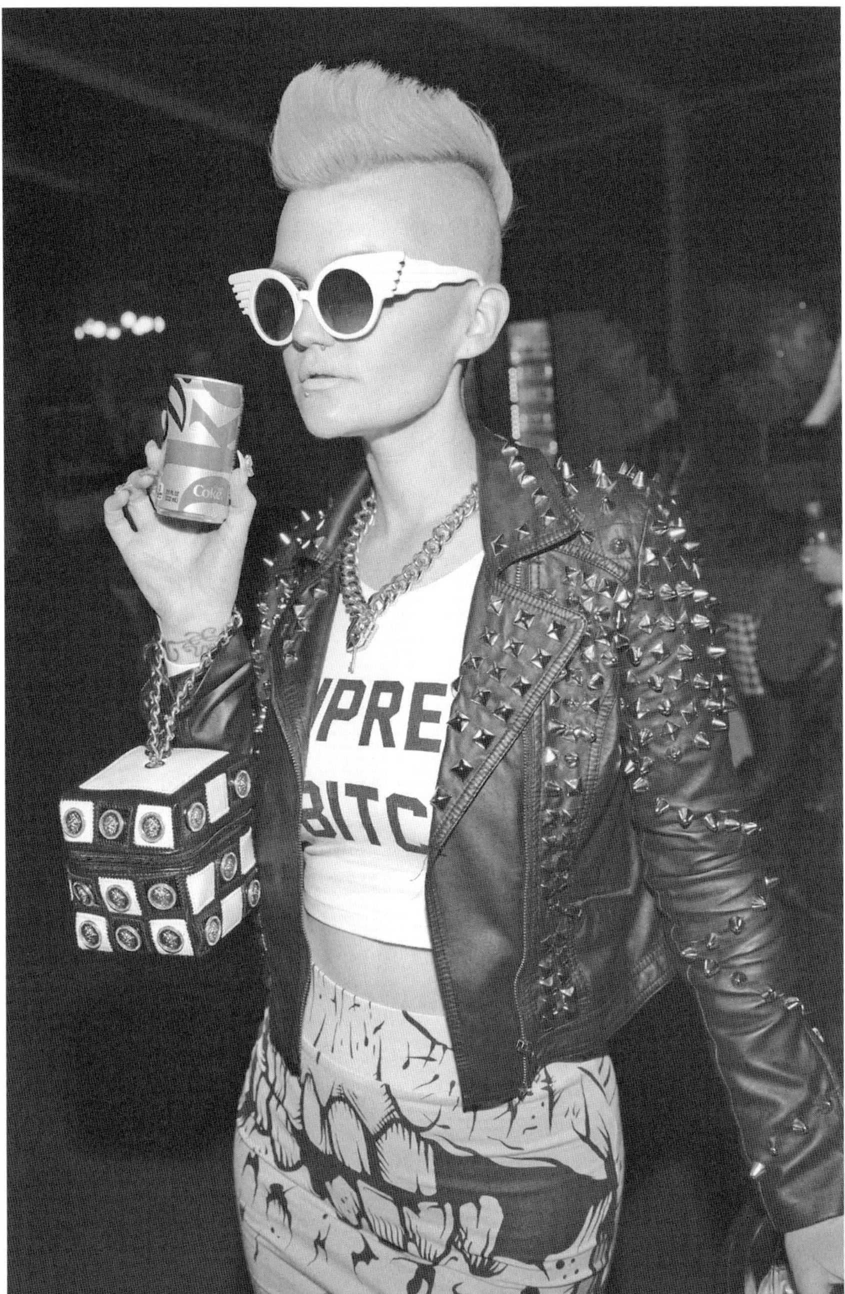

Figure 7.4 A view of *Diet Coke* during Mercedes-Benz Fashion Week Fall 2014 at Lincoln Centre on 7 February 2014, in New York City. (Photo by Mike Pont/Getty Images for Diet Coke.)

artificial. In her study of Barbie dolls, Kim Tofaletti argues that Barbie (although initially designed for adults),

> is said to teach girls codes of femininity through standards of dress, bodily ideas and modes of behaviour. She is rigid and slender, always smiling and immaculately groomed and attired . . . by playing with Barbie dolls girls learn that in order to be successful and popular women, just like Barbie, they must look good.[50]

In other words, Barbie encourages girls to be consumers in the same way that the Diet Coke marionettes encourage young women to not only to consume Diet Coke, but products from fashion magazines, to clothes and make-up. In the United Kingdom the collaboration with cosmetic brand Benefit included a 5 pound voucher code on the can which was redeemable for purchases over 20 pounds. The Facebook app, called 'Get Glam' brings together fashion, glamour, beauty, style, friends, boys and parties. Users can discover whether they are romantic, a rock chick or a fashionista and learn to apply make-up and dress in the latest fashionable styles. In his examination of fashion dolls, Adam Geczy notes that records date back to as far back as the end of the fourteenth century, where dolls were used as supports for prototypes or copies of clothing so that these could be communicated to other courts for guidance as to what was desirable to wear. In French the term *mannequin* is still used for 'model', indicating its roots in the doll and the dummy (it literally means 'little man' in Dutch).[51] So the model's body was always linked to something uniform and mechanized like the marionette. It was also something that emphasized manoeuvrability and movement. In the early decades of the twentieth century, just as generic dummies, uniformity, and regularity was encouraged, irregularity discouraged.

The three fully articulated marionettes had expressive eyes and mouths and were used along with several supporting characters for a number of Diet Coke campaigns, including television, print media and digital platforms. The first commercial in the series was called 'There's One Left' and featured Eleanor, Bernadette and Irene fighting amongst each other for the last can of Diet Coke remaining in the fridge. 'Fashion, femininity and fun is at the centre of our brand,'[52] comments Cathryn Sleight, marketing director for Coca-Cola. The campaign focused on the light-hearted attitude of young women aged between seventeen and twenty-nine, Coca-Cola's core target consumer. In keeping with their likes of fashion and music, Coca-Cola contracted the digital resource hub FullSix to develop a series of webisodes that were also housed on YouTube. Each short film featured the 1980s anthem 'Maniac' (Michael Sembello, 1983) from the cult dance film *Flashdance* (1983, Adrian Lynn). Young women were able to interact directly with the feisty fashion marionettes by leaving messages, sharing with friends on Twitter via a social media sharing tool bar and download the soundtrack via a link to iTunes. Additional rewards such as wallpaper, ringtones and competitions appeared via a link to *Coke Zone, Coca-Cola*'s loyalty site and a link to the online portal *Netvibes* delivered music, fashion tips and relationship advice.

The 'Love it Light' campaign firmly entrenches fashion in the domain of the feminine as frivolous and fun rather than a serious preoccupation and maintains stereotypes of gender and sexuality. The advertisement, webinars and associated digital media platforms target heterosexual girls rather than lesbians, homosexual boys or even a gender non-defining audience. Sarah Gilligan writes that 'costume, fashion and merchandising enables the formation of tactile transmediality for the spectator by bridging the gap between virtual 'worlds' on-screen and the lived material body.'[53] While Gilligan's comment and analysis of tactile transmediality is geared towards the immersive nature of contemporary gaming, the same evaluation can be applied to *Diet Coke*'s social media platforms. It is through the haptic pleasures of adornment, that the spectator gains access to the fashionably popular 'girl gang' culture by sharing fashion advice, make-up tips, music and so on.

Two years later in 2013, *Diet Coke* appointed Jean Paul Gaultier as its first creative director. 'The brand asked me to explore it's fun personality and to style the bottle.'[54] Gaultier said, 'I want to show people the codes and signatures I love. The bottles have the shape of a woman's body, so it was great fun to "dress" them.'[55] The design of the bottles were based on the Gaultier's signature perfume bottles, Le Male for men and Classique for women (Figure 7.5). A year earlier, Gaultier appeared in a new instalment of the 'Love it Light' campaign starring himself as the 'Serial Designer', or 'puppet whisperer', a character that comes to rescue Bernadette from her fashion crisis. In the opening scene Bernadette is lying on a couch drinking a can of Diet Coke, whilst talking to her psychiatrist (also played by Gaultier wearing a messy white wig resembling a mad scientist) about her dream. Bernadette wakes up from her dream nursing an alcoholic hangover and starts to panic when she realizes that she is late for a job interview just as Gaultier appears as a ghostly apparition. Opening a can of Diet Coke and smacking his lips from its cool refreshing taste (a popular hangover cure) Gaultier dresses Bernadette into his signature blue and white *marinière* dress with matching hand bag. ' Do you think this will do for a job interview?' asks Bernadette, 'Of course,' replies Gaultier, 'it is light, it is right.'

The cult of slenderness is an ideology that places the shape of a slender body at a premium in ideal body images of men and women. These definitions of desirability are constructed by interest groups (fashion labels, modelling agencies and so forth) in the fashion industry that maintain a vested interest. This highlights one of the grimmer paradoxes in the fashion industry, especially in the way that the language of luxury and plenty is told (and read) on the body, or in spite of it.

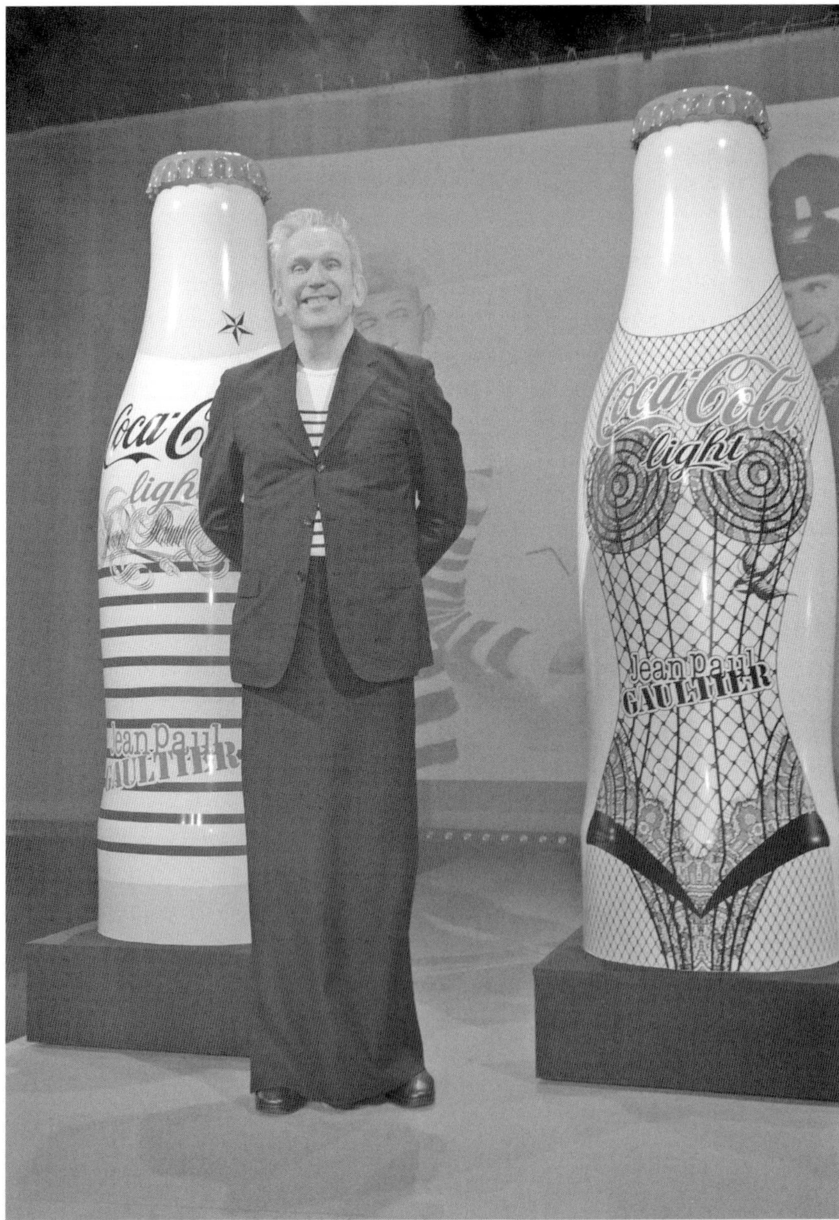

Figure 7.5 *Coca-Cola light*, *Diet Coke* and Jean Paul Gaultier host the launch party for their limited edition bottle collection at Le Trianon in Paris. (Photo by PA Images via Getty Images.)

8
FASHION, FOOD AND ART

Food in art and fashion can be said to begin with the work of Giuseppe Arcimboldo, that most eccentric of painters, who is now best known for his amusing and intricate compositions of foods, flora and other natural paraphernalia formed into faces and anthropomorphic shapes (he also used other objects as well, very little was sacred). Largely forgotten after his lifetime, Arcimboldo was very much a man of his age, active throughout the sixteenth century which not only witnessed the flourishing of the courtly masque and feast, but also the amassing of curiosities in what were the first museums, the *Wunderkammern* and *Kunstkabinette*, otherwise known as the 'Cabinets of Curiosities'. His patron, Rudolph II of Prague, was one of the first great keepers of such collections, which had themselves become important symbols of courtly prowess beyond military might in amassing intellectual capital. In 1590 Arcimboldo painted Rudolf II as a composite of fruits and vegetables with a pumpkin for a forehead, a turnip in place of his Adam's apple, peapods for eye lids and an ear of corn for his ears. (Figure 8.1). He looked more like a fruit platter than a distinguished royal, but there was a reason behind Arcimboldo's capriciousness and wit. Although the paintings were meant to amuse, they also symbolized the great power that the emperor wielded over everything – even nature and hence food and, by default, clothing.

In Arcimboldo's painting the body is adorned with fruit that takes the place of clothes. On a symbolic level, the 'fruit' garments communicate the identity of the wearer as sovereign. Like the English libertine Restoration poet John Wilmont, Earl of Rochester, who used words and wit as a form of political satire to comment on King Charles II, his enemies and his vast kingdom,[1] Arcimboldo's role as a court artist was to organize pageants and tournaments which were a form of political propaganda and served to display the authority of the ruling merchant class. So popular were Arcimboldo's paintings that the emperor commissioned him to design ceremonial costumes based on the painting's imagery for the royal pageants – which were a kind of dramatic performance[2] that reflected peoples rank and role according to the order in which they appeared in the procession. Arcimboldo's costume designs were whimsical illustrations penned in brown and blue wash of garments, masks and shoes that displayed exotic flora and fauna that are now stored in the Galleria degli Uffizi in Florence.

Figure 8.1 Vertumnus. A portrait depicting Rudolf II, Holy Roman Emperor as Vertumnus the Roman god of the seasons, *c.* 1590–91. Skooloster Castle, Sweden. (Wikipedia Commons, Public Domain.)

After centuries of neglect, the artist's name resurfaced in a monograph from 1885, but only became something of a household name in artistic circles with the Surrealists from the 1920s onwards. In a major exhibition of the Surrealists in New York in 1937, Arcimboldo's work was included as among the significant precursors to the movement. Directly or not, Arcimboldo is the historical touchstone of the convergence of art, food and fashion, since he painted what stood for clothing as well. He is also a precursor to less fortunate off-shoots, such as 'food art', but also the far more structured performances of contemporary haute couture. He may also have been on the minds of artists such as Salvador Dalí when he collaborated with Elsa Schiaparelli to make the *Lobster Dress*. Like his fellow Dadaists and Surrealists, Dalí was always open to the possibility of shattering the purportedly restrictive, and tired old conventions of art, embracing the ephemeral in addition to the permanent. As guided by the laws of transience, fashion and food were welcome bedfellows. Since the end of the twentieth century, to varying degrees, food, fashion and art have enlisted one another as vehicles for reflecting on the evanescence of life as well as life's pleasures and bounties.

The lobster and the dress

Salvador Dalí and Elsa Schiaparelli made several items together, including the *Desk Suit* (1936), *Tear Dress* and the *Skeleton Dress*, which were part of her 1938 'Circus Collection'. But none is better remembered than the *Lobster Dress* (Figure 8.2). Since serially copied, troped and riffed on in dress designs to the present day, it was originally, in the words of Schiaparelli's biographer, Meryle Secrest,

> A sleeveless evening gown in white organza with a gently flaring skirt on which a gigantic lobster had been screen printed with sprigs of parsley strewn about here and there. The idea that someone would want to waltz away the evening in a dress whose main emblem was something to eat seemed preposterous.[3]

The meticulous print had been administered by Sache, among the leading silk designers of the day and made its debut as part of Schiaparelli Summer–Fall 1937 collection. Lobsters had a special place within Dalí's iconography. Like asparagus, oysters (which Casanova called 'a spur to the spirit of love') caviar, honey and truffles (favoured by the Marquis de Sade, Casanova and Madame de Pompadour) lobsters are considered to contain aphrodisiac qualities.[4] Given that it was well known in popular mythology as a love potion, Dalí used the lobster as a symbol of sexual desire. It crops up in various places in his *œuvre*, most memorably as the handle of a telephone. Dalí's explanation for his love of crustations is offered in his biography,

> I do not understand why, when I asked for a grilled lobster in a restaurant, I am never served a cooked telephone. I do not understand why champagne is always chilled and why on the other hand telephones, which are frightfully warm and disagreeable sticky to the touch, are not also put in silver buckets with crushed ice around them.[5]

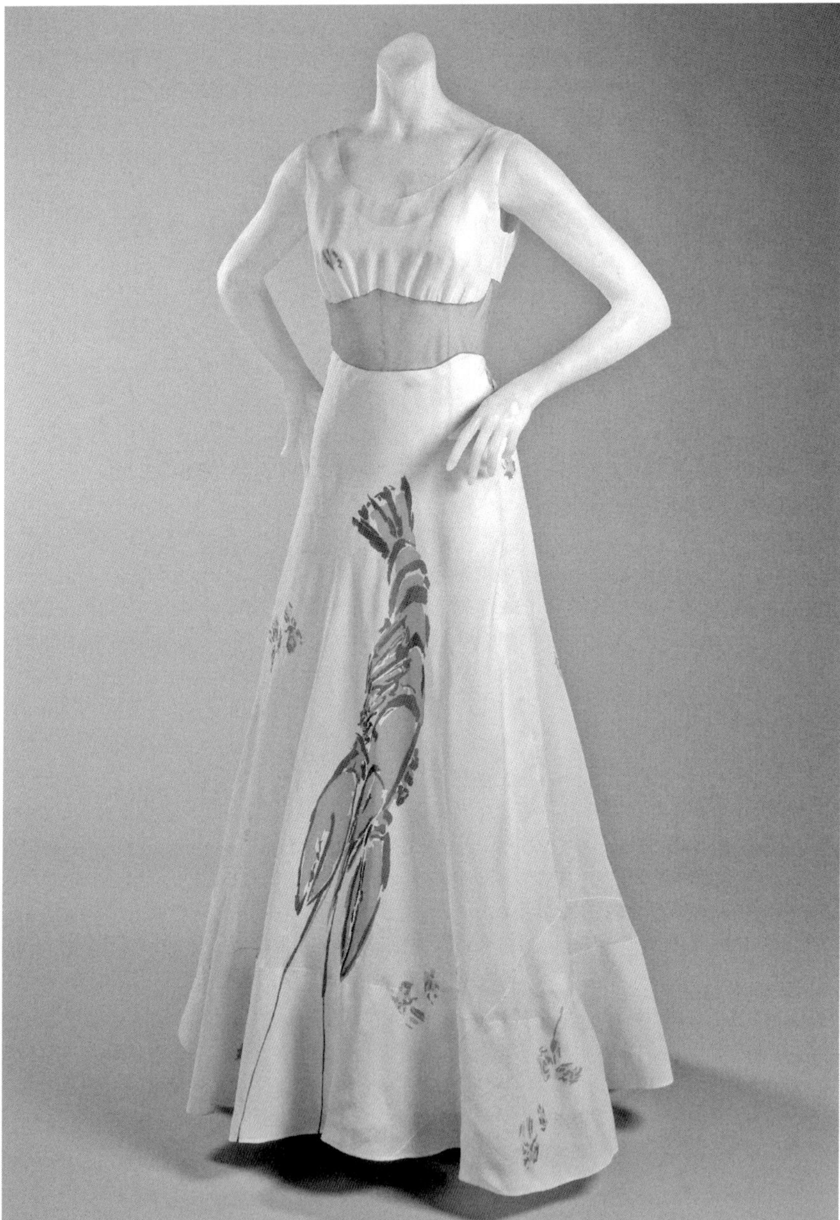

Figure 8.2 Women's Dinner Dress designed by Elsa Schiaparelli, February 1937. Printed silk on organza, synthetic horsehair. Gift of Mme Elsa Schiaparelli, 1969. Made in Paris, France. (Philadelphia Museum of Art.)

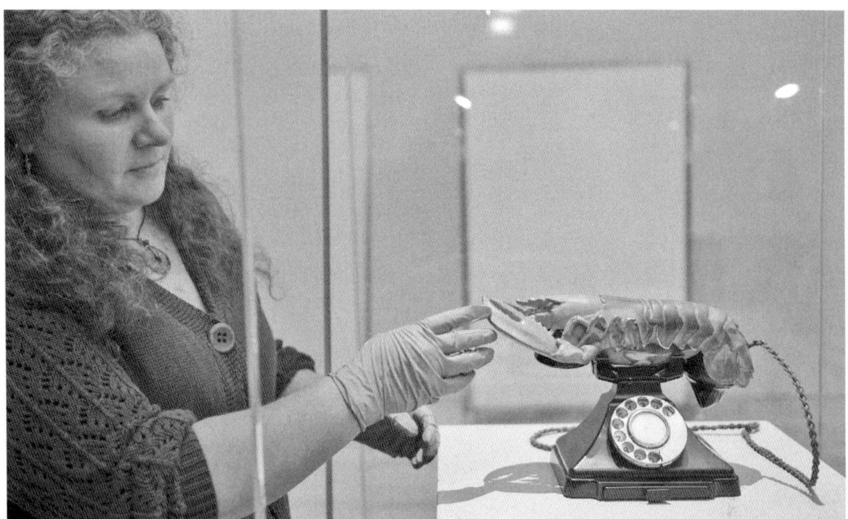

Figure 8.3 Conservator Micheline Forde unpacks Salvador Dalí's *Lobster Telephone* in preparation for the exhibition 'Salvador Dali: Liquid Desire', at the National Gallery of Victoria, in Melbourne on 3 June 2009. One of the most famous artistic creations of the twentieth century, this sculpture is one of only ten Lobster telephones that Dalí created during the 1930s, all of which were fully functioning telephones. (WILLIAM WEST/AFP via Getty Images.)

When the *Lobster Telephone* (Figure 8.3) was first exhibited in 1936 the work was called *Aphrodisiac Telephone*, which associated the telephone as a love object used by lovers to share erotic conversations. Many other iterations of the lobster followed, including a graphite and ink drawing of comedian Harpo Marx sitting at his harp with a lobster on his head, balancing an apple on its tail. This retelling of the story of William Tell who shot an apple off his son's head casts the lobster with its serrated claws as a metonym for castration and fear of emasculation. Eventually, as Nancy Frazier notes, Dalí's anxiety 'sent the lobster on a new mission – to express his fear of female cannibalism.'[6] So how did a lobster find its way onto a dress and how did that dress find its way into the wardrobe of an American socialite who would change the course of British history?

During the interwar years fashion and art came mutually together in the Surrealist movement to amuse, shock and to question art itself and the contradictory nature of fashion. Schiaparelli was born into a wealthy and distinguished Roman family and so her entry into artistic and intellectual circles was relatively easy. She was introduced to Marcel Duchamp and the Dadaists in New York in the 1920s and upon her return to Paris in 1922 met Man Ray who first escorted Schiaparelli to the famed Parisian cabaret bar, *Le Boeuf sur le Toit*

(The Ox on the Roof). Le Boeuf, as it was affectionally called by its patrons, was a gathering place for intellectuals, jazz musicians and the avant-garde art scene (including Schiaparelli's rival Chanel). It was at Le Boeuf that Schiaparelli met Picasso (who affectionately called her 'Sciap'), Jean Cocteau and Georges Braque. It was only a matter of time before she would meet Dalí, and together they would create garments with outlandish motifs and designs.[7] Her salon on the Rue Vendôme 'overflowed with the wild, the whimsical and even the ridiculous.' [8] By the 1930s, affirms Valerie Steele, Schiaparelli 'had become the most talked about fashion designers in Paris.'[9]

The audacity of the *Lobster Dress* soon found itself reaching the approval of Wallis Simpson, the American socialite for whom Edward VIII of England would abdicate his thrown. Ironically enough, Wallis had never been a stranger to men, and was known for her healthy sexual appetite, but that was hardly grounds for her choice. Concerned over her own rather uneven public image, she believed that recent pictures of her in the press made her look too plain and dowdy, causing her to choose an avant-garde option to augment her image. In 1936 Cecil Beaton conducted a rigorous eight-page photo-shoot of Wallis in the dress for *Vogue* magazine, taking over one hundred photographs at Château de Candé in the Loire valley. The château would later become the site of Wallis and Edward's wedding and Beaton would take their wedding photos as well. The Dalí–Schiaparelli creation instantly become a couture classic and found its way into Wallis Simpson's wedding trousseau as part of her Spring wardrobe (as well as seventeen other garments from Schiaparelli's collection). The eccentric and scandalous dress had found its appropriate match capturing the elements of Simpson's fame at the time – scandal, fashion, sex and power.[10] The dress had become the uncanny embodiment of the 'Dalinian *vagina dentata* of the castrating and predatory *femme fatale*.'[11]

The *Lobster Dress* would garner yet more fame when it was worn by a number of society dames and socialites, including Elizabeth Winifred 'Jane' Clark, wife of the celebrated art historian and director of the National Gallery in London, Sir Kenneth Clark, in effect conferring the dress 'art' status if a de facto way. (Reprising the theme of lobsters and lust, Jane did have her share of extramarital affairs, but not to the extent to those of her husband.) In 2012 Anna Wintour, Chief Editor of *Vogue* served as the chairperson for the *Schiaparelli/Prada: Impossible Conversations* (10 May–19 August) exhibition at the Costume Institute, Metropolitan Museum of Art in New York. The exhibition, which celebrated Miuccia Prada and Schiaparelli's work, their similarities, and their affinities, was curated by Andrew Bolton and Harold Coda. In a tribute to Schiaparelli, Wintour asked Miuccia Prada to recreate a version of the *Lobster Dress* to wear to the Met Gala ball for the exhibitions opening (Figure 8.4). In Prada's rendering of the dress, the lobster was embroidered with silver stones and was completely transformed from its predatory embodiment to a tame

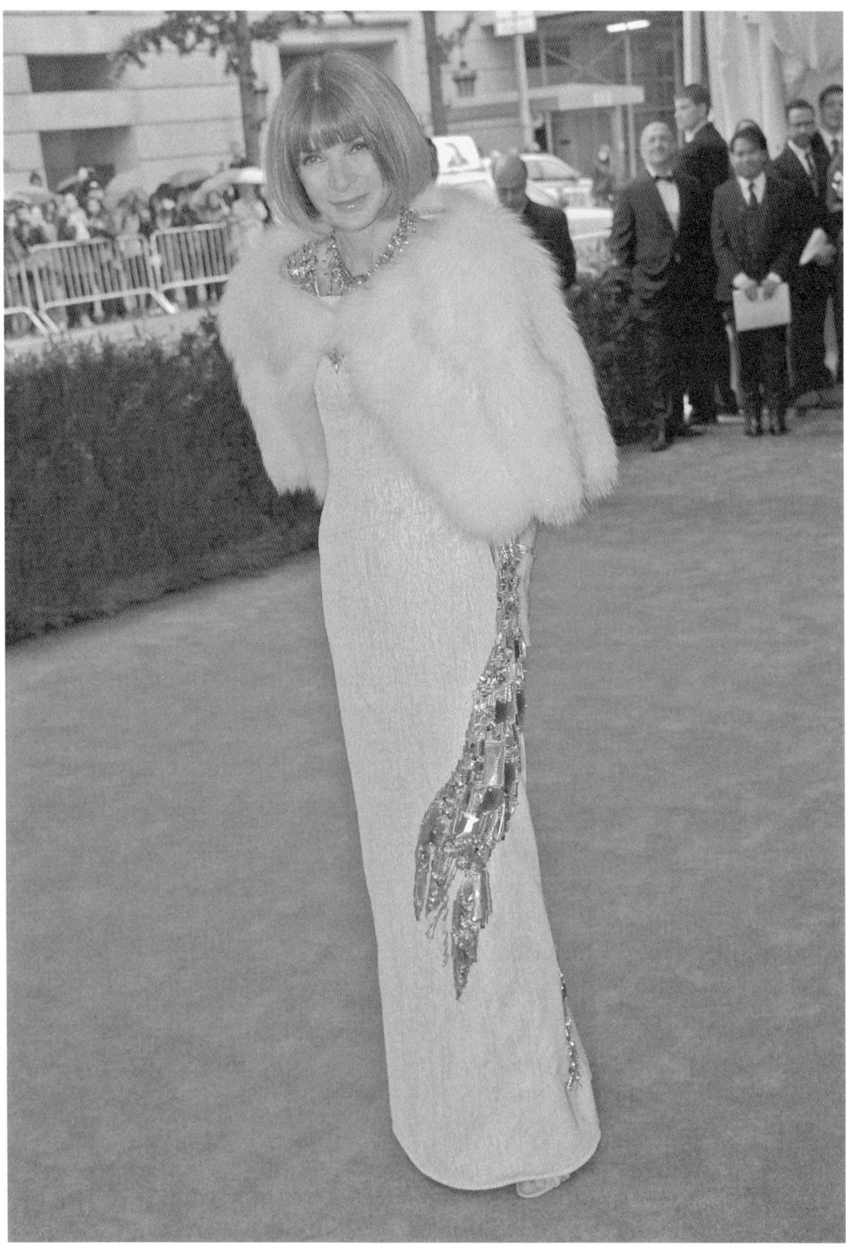

Figure 8.4 American *Vogue* editor-in-chief Anna Wintour attends the 'Schiaparelli and Prada: Impossible Conversations' Costume Institute Gala at the Metropolitan Museum of Art on 7 May 2012, in New York City. (Photo by Larry Busacca/Getty Images.)

evening dress. Writing on the event, journalist Mona Molasky remarked that for the Gala,

> Miuccia Prada re-imagined Schiaparelli's red lobster as a glittering, golden creature that swirled down Anna Wintour's long white gown. Tipped with sparkling jewellery and an elegant white jacket, the predator was as denatured as a crustacean can get. Lobster? What lobster? All is safe at *Vogue* and the House of Prada.'[12]

This was not however the end of the *Lobster Dress*, presenting his Schiaparelli Spring–Summer 2017 haute couture collection at its Place Vêndome salon, creative director Bertrand Guyon included what Mark Holgate called 'a time-honoured Elsa-ism'[13] a pink chiffon adaptation of the *Lobster Dress*, except that it was a 'featherweight version'.[14] Literally. The dress was made of two layers of silk tulle and the lobster appliqué was hand sewn onto the bias-cut skirt.

Let them eat bread

Salvador Dalí's fascination with food did not begin nor did it end with the lobster, as a Catalonian and an artist he was drawn to the creative potential that food offered. Food was at the top of his agenda, for right from the very beginning of the movement, the Surrealists (and Schiaparelli) were attracted to the object and the ideas of displacement operative in Sigmund Freud's dreamwork. Dalí's aim was to rescue objects and by extension language from their mundane meaning and function in daily life. A telephone mouthpiece becomes a lobster, eggs appear on a *Plate without a Plate* (1932) and in the *Persistence of Memory* (1931) a watch takes the form of melted cheese that once appeared in a dream. Food was the leitmotif in Dalí's paintings. The centrality of food for Dalí was evident when he wrote at the very start of his autobiography, 'when I was six, I wanted to be a cook, at seven, I wanted to be Napoleon . . . and my ambition has been steadily growing ever since.'[15]

In 1973 Dalí, together with his great love and muse Gala (Elena Inanovna Diakonova), wrote a cookbook that was republished by Taschen in 2016. The cookbook contained recipes from the opulent dinner parties that they hosted which were legendary for the strange food that they served. Recipes included Conger of the Rising Sun that instructed to remove the skin and the backbone of the conger eel, wrap in strips of bacon, and cook on a skillet with a tablespoon of butter for 40 minutes. There was the Peruvian crayfish prepared in a fish broth with white wine, tequila, carrots and onions with a dash of cayenne pepper. As well as mulligan of oxtail, eel pâté and grilled lamb's head. A whole chapter is devoted to frog and snail dishes and the cookbook contains such strange recipes as minced almonds and tequila perched on top of rye bread and bacon-wrapped eel stuffed inside a fish.[16] Dalí and Gala would host lavish dinner parties and invite celebrity guests who were required to wear elaborate costumes and bring along exotic pets. They hired the best chefs from fashionable Michelin-starred Parisian restaurants – Maxim's, Lasserre, Tour d'Argent and Le Train Bleu (originally known as Buffet de la Gare de Lyon). Even Babou, Dalí's pet ocelot, roamed freely amongst the food on the table. In 1941 Dalí and Gala hosted a themed dinner party, 'Night in a Surrealist Forest', in the ball room at the Hotel Del Monte in Monterey California to raise funds for artists displaced by the war. Dalí wore huge ear flaps representing anatomy and Gala was dressed as a unicorn. She spent the entire evening reclined on a bed bottle feeding a lion cub while monkeys scurried around the room. Guests were served dishes of fish that were plated on satin slippers and live frogs were served as the main course.[17]

Among Dalí's favourite culinary staple was bread – even before he became a Surrealist, he painted *The Basket of Bread* (1926) depicting four slices of bread (one is bitten) spread with butter in a basket. He later painted another version of *The Basket of Bread* (1945) or *Basket of Bread–Rather Death then Shame*, but instead of slices of bread, it depicts a half a bread loaf in a basket placed near the edge of a table. Dalí wrote that 'bread has always been one of the oldest subjects of fetishism and obsession in my work, the first one to which I have remained faithful.'[18] Julia Pine even goes so far as to call bread Dalí's 'personal device or trademark . . . the Dalí Brand.'[19] Dalí first arrived in New York in 1934 abroad the steamship *Champlain* to attend his exhibition at the Julien Levy Gallery on Madison Avenue. As he walked down the plank of the ship, he enthusiastically waved an oversized baguette as a performative gesture to New York bystanders who lapped up his European eccentricity. The biannual magazine published by the St Regis Hotel where Dalí and Gala wintered in a private suite ever year for forty years wrote that Dalí

> would happily swish around in his golden cape of dead bee's or 'accidently' let loose a large box of flies. With arms stretched wide, cane held high, moustache pointing to the heavens, nobody knew better how to make the grandest entrance. Soon not just fans but also tourists would congregate around the hotel hoping for a sighting of him on the steps of East 55th Street, growling his war cry, each loud sung syllable: 'Da-lí . . . is . . . he-re!'[20]

Before travelling to New York, Dalí had just completed *Retrospective Bust of a Woman* (1931) a sculpture made from a painted porcelain bust. An inkwell on top of a baguette crowns her head, cobs of corn dangle like earrings or a necklace around her neck and ants swarm along her forehead gathering breadcrumbs. Death, decay and consumption are themes that prevail in this work. In 1958 Dalí himself was photographed wearing a loaf of bread on his head as a surrogate hat

(Figure 8.5), another display of eccentricity that would appear many times throughout the course of his life.

But Dalí was not alone, nor was he the first to work with bread, in 1905 Pablo Picasso painted *The Bread Carrier* (1905) a portrait of a woman wearing a headscarf balancing two loaves of bread on her head. Years later when Picasso

Figure 8.5 Spanish surrealist artist Salvador Dalí (1904–1989) wears a hat shaped like a loaf of bread on his head, 5 November 1958. (Photo by Keystone/Hulton Archive/Getty Images.)

had become a world-renowned artist, Robert Doisneau photographed him in at his kitchen table with two loaves of *Mains de Nice* (Hands of Nice) positioned at the edge, so that it looked like the bread loaves were Picasso's hands (Figure 8.6). Picasso wears a Breton shirt characteristically worn by seamen in the French navy. The garment would become a staple of French fashion and a favourite item of Jean Paul Gaultier who would adopt the *marinière as* part of his signature look along with a Scottish kilt, or leather pants and military leather boots.

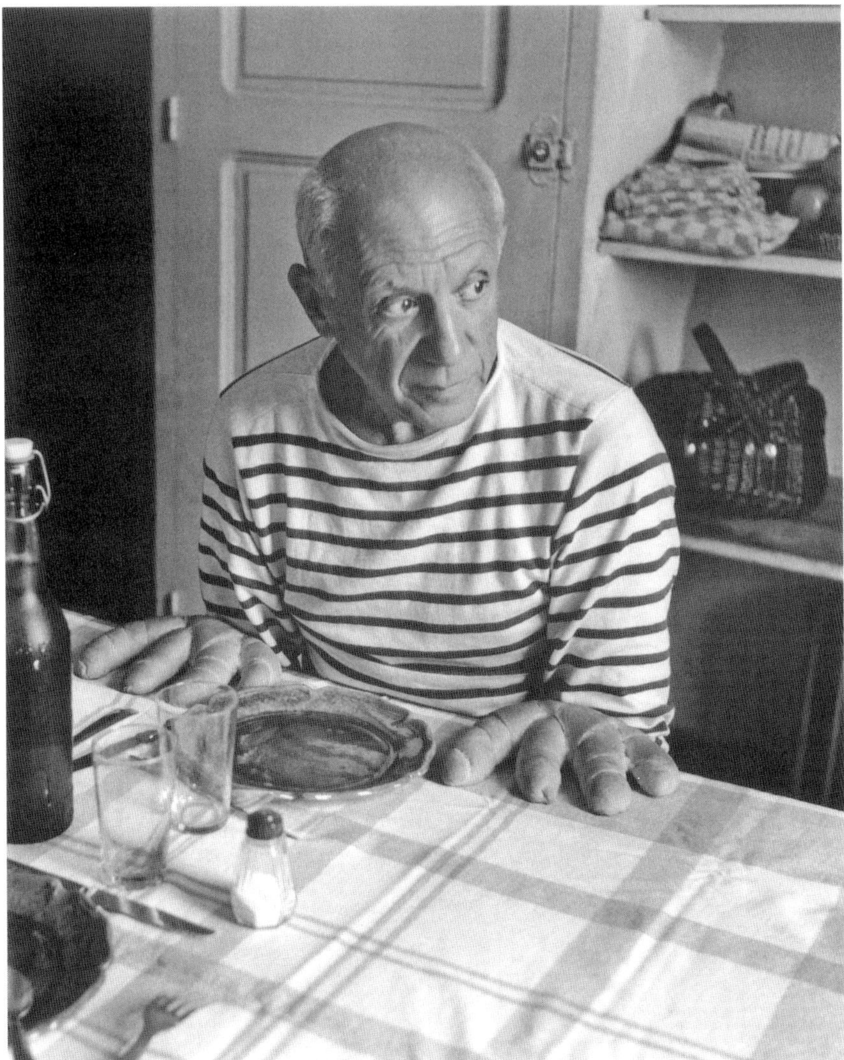

Figure 8.6 Picasso, France *c.* 1952. (Photo by Robert DOISNEAU/Gamma-Rapho/Getty Images.)

In the summer of 2004 Jean Paul Gaultier collaborated with the French Bakers Guild (known as *Temeliers*, or flour sifters when they first formed in the Middle Ages and were considered important citizens) to create a collection of his iconic designs made from bread. *Pain Couture* (High Fashion Bread) was exhibited at the *Fondation Cartier pour l'art contemporain*, in Paris and whilst the public roamed amongst the quirky life-size garments the scent of warm baking bread lingered in the air. Wicker baskets contained several baguettes that formed the garments shape, like that of a whale-boned petticoat (Figure 8.7) and Madonna's

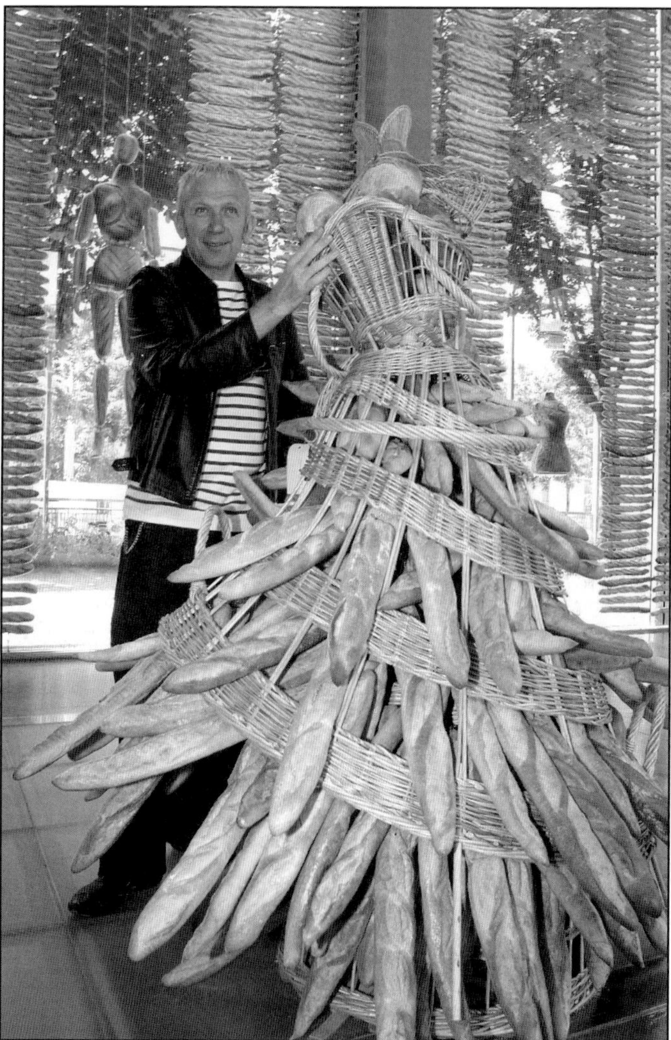

Figure 8.7 Jean Paul Gaultier mixes fashion and bread with his exhibit 'Pain Couture' at the Cartier Foundation in Paris, France on 6 July 2004 (Photo by Frederic SOULOY/Gamma-Rapho via Getty Images.)

conned bustier bra featured brioche cups. Models were dressed in traditional aprons and bakers wore uniforms designed by Gaultier. The concept behind the installation was simple, the creative process of artisan bread-making and garment design and construction were similar. Fashion, like bread eventually becomes stale and crumbles.

In early 2021, Estonian conceptual artist (and rapper) Tommy Cash (Thomas Tammemets) collaborated with Maison Margiela on a capsule collection that included a pair of bread loaves as slippers as well as a co-branded oversized sweater and black T-shirt. The trompe l'oeil 'home loafers' were co-branded and packaged in a clear plastic bag like the kind of bag that bread is packaged in supermarkets. The release of the capsule collection was accompanied by a song track titled 'Mute'. The single was billed 'a real pandemic banger' and contained three-and-a-half minutes of silence rather than music. Instead of being bombarded by sounds of everyday consumption in 'an endless flood of escapist fare',[21] the daily sounds of streets, nature and home are replaced by the silence of the pandemic lockdown.[22] No shopping, no spending, no consumption as bread is intended as a metaphor for money. Baking bread, in particular sourdough, became a trend during the pandemic as supermarket shelves emptied of yeast and flour during the coronavirus panic buying. According to its home baking report, Packaged Facts noted an increase of 24 per cent of bake-related products to $26.5 bn in the US in 2020 during quarantine compared to pre-Covid 2019.[23] The scent of baking bread and its association with warmth, nourishment and wellbeing provided a sense of security during a time of anxiety and uncertainty.

For the cover of the single, Cash parodied a group photograph taken by Herb Ritz during the 1990s of supermodels Cindy Crawford, Naomi Campbell, Stephanie Seymour and Tatjana Patitz. But instead of using naked supermodels, Cash, with his skinny body, pencil thin moustache and blunt cut bob is cuddled up with a group of young Estonian boys who are wearing white underwear like those designed by Calvin Klein. The underwear acts as an intertextual device that links the image of Tommy Cash to Calvin Klein's unisex underwear campaigns of the 1990s. The super sexy advertisements featured supermodels Jenny Shimuzu and Kate Moss whose glamourized skeletal bodies and stringy unwashed hair started the 'heroin chic' trend. The look of disillusionment captured the mood of retaliation against the mass consumption and excess of the 1980s. Included in the capsule's theme of food was also a collectable packet of vacuum-packed ramen noodles that was not intended for consumption. The fine print on the plastic packet warns the consumer to 'eat at your own risk'.[24] Cash said that the noodles were 'every student's food . . . everyone eats it when you're in a broke spot.'[25]

Bread is a metaphor for money or in the case of sliced white bread, a metaphor for modernity and industrialization. As an idiomatic expression, white bread is used in American popular culture to describe a certain class of Caucasian people. The statement implies bigotry and is synonymous with 'white trash' a derogatory racial slur against poor white working-class people with limited access to education and resources. 'White bread' has also come to symbolize fast food culture whose high level of carbohydrates quickly break down into sugar resulting in weight gain and high cholesterol. The 1960s counterculture made white bread a symbol of everything that was wrong with middle-America. It was 'bland, homogeneous, and suburban [as well as] plastic and corporate'[26] prompting the columnist and then *Vogue* editor Diana Vreeland to proclaim that 'people who eat white bread have no dreams.'[27]

When Anna Wintour took over the helm of American *Vogue* magazine in 1988, she hired the Harvard-educated, food-obsessed lawyer Jeffrey Steingarten and gave him a food column which he still avidly writes today. In the July 1988 issue, Steingarten wrote an article on 'Breaking Bread' in which he noted that the 'true' French baguette began to disappear in the economic pressures of the 1960s. The soft and creamy French flours used in artisan bakeries were replaced by high-gluten American and Canadian flours that were needed to run the automated high-speed mixers in factories. 'The traditional bread began to disappear,'[28] writes Steingarten and in its place 'was a tasteless, fluffy, pale and bleached imposter.' Bread had lost its nutritional reputation and became a fattening, high carbohydrate substitute with a bad name.

In 2008 New York-based photographer Ted Sabarese started thinking about people and their relationship to food which led him to develop the Hunger *Pain* Series, referencing the French word for bread as well as the physical experience of having hunger pains from lack of food. 'The idea behind "Hunger Pains",' Sabarese said, 'was to visually suggest an actual meal the model was craving by having them wear it.'[29] The concept behind the series was how the thin-obsessed fashion industry whose culture of ideal body image deprives models of food and creates eating disorders. More of which we discuss at length in Chapter 7 of this book. Working in collaboration with SOTU Productions, a costume designer brand for film, fashion and television, Sabarese asked the models what food they would like to eat at that very moment, then he took the food they described and working with a team of fashion designers turned the food into garments. In one particular image a model wears a skirt made from sliced baguettes and a top made from croissants with brioche shoulder pads. She is holding a matching clutch bag and wears accessories made from bread, including a baguette hat.

Protest fashion: That meat dress

So, when Lady Gaga decided to wear a dress constructed entirely from fresh flank steak, designed by Franc Fernandez, and styled by Nicola Formichetti, including matching platform shoes, clutch purse and hat to the 2010 MTV Music Video Awards, it wasn't anything new (Figure 8.8.1). If anything, it was scandalous and attention-grabbing which was exactly what Gaga intended. Instead of being escorted to the awards by black-suited bodyguards, she arrived with an entourage of ex-military personal that had recently been discharged under the discriminatory policy. The crowd was uncomfortable, the media went wild. Five days before the music awards, Gaga appeared naked on the cover of *Vogue Hommes* Japan wearing nothing but pieces of raw meat held together with string, what looked like a meat bikini. The controversial cover did not raise an eyebrow, 'Oh, Lady Gaga's job is to do outlandish things,'[30] said PETA's[31] President Ingrid Newkirk, and this certainly qualifies as outlandish.'[32] This was Lady Gaga and it was expected, unlike PETA's response to episode 4 of the television series *America's Next Top Model* (2008), which had models wrapped in raw meat and posing in an abattoir for a photo shoot in New York's meat-packing district. 'Meat represents bloody violence and suffering, so if that's the look they were going for—they achieved it.' [33] Returning to the MTV Music Video Awards, Gaga's meat dress was worn in protest against the Don't Ask, Don't Tell (DADT, 1993–2012) policy that prohibited Gays, bisexuals, transexuals and lesbians from serving in the United States armed military forces.

Eight days later, on 20 September, Gaga attended a rally along with 2,000 protesters at Deering Oaks Park, Portland ahead of a key Senate vote to urge two US senators to appeal the discriminatory policy. Standing at a lectern in front of the American flag, she gave a speech dressed in a blue suit, blue and white star-spangled tie and large black-rimmed glasses (Figure 8.8.2). 'Equality is the prime rib of America,' she shouted, 'Shouldn't everyone deserve the right to wear the same meat dress that I do? Repeal "Don't Ask, Don't Tell" or go home.'[34] Keeping the meat metaphor in place, she likened the American constitution to a buffet, asking if military personal should be allowed to choose which parts of the Constitution to defend. 'Are you listening?'[35] she exclaimed, before finishing her speech and giving the audience a peace sign. U2's single, 'Beautiful Day', considered a protest anthem played in the background. When U2 recorded 'Beautiful Day', there were storm clouds over Dublin . . . things were not as they might have been. 'But the song is not a description of where we were at,' said Bono, 'It was a prayer for where we could go.'[36]

This scenario could have been a scene taken from the film *Good Morning, Vietnam* (1987, Barry Levinson), where Robin Williams played the role of a radio DJ, or it could have been the scene from *Gump* (1994, Robert Zemeckis) where Tom Hanks dressed in a military uniform gives a speech at an anti-Vietnam protest rally. So strong were the intertextual references to both movies. Except, in this case Gaga was wearing a suit and tie performing being man, whilst performing being a discharged US military officer. Taking on his voice and subject position, Gaga gesticulated, raised her finger and shouted for homophobes to

Figure 8.8.1 Lady Gaga poses in the press room at the 2010 MTV Video Music Awards held at Nokia Theatre L.A. Live on 12 September 2010 in Los Angeles, California. (Photo by Steve Granitz/WireImage.)

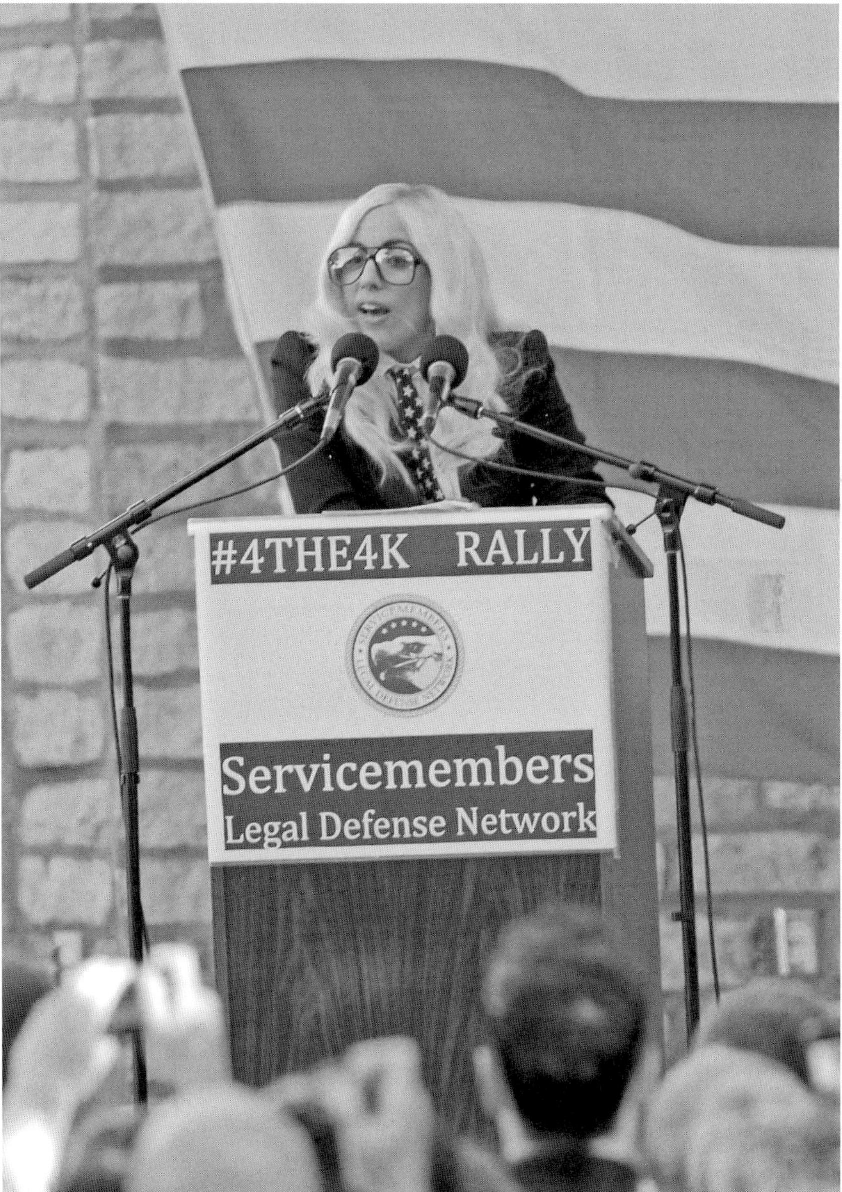

Figure 8.8.2 Lady Gaga speaks during the Servicemembers Legal Defence Network Grassroots Rally in support of repealing 'Don't Ask, Don't Tell' at Deering Oaks Park near the University of Southern Maine campus on 20 September 2010 in Portland, Maine. (Photo by Cliff Kucine/Getty Images.)

leave the military and go home. In her 'Prime Rib' speech and in attending the MTV Video Awards, Gaga was using dress (and the analogy food), as a vehicle to address a political issue and call for social change. As Quentin Bell wrote in his article published in 1951, just before the political and social movements of the 1960s and the explosion of popular culture and subcultural style, 'The history of dress is, to a very large extent, the history of protests.'[37] In a recent article published in the special issue of *Fashion Theory* on 'Fashion as Politics, Dressing Dissent', Monica Titton writes that there has been a unprecedented explosion of 'political fashion' since 2017. LGBTQI* rights, anti-racism and environmental issues have been high on the fashion agenda as symbols of protest that have been appropriated into dress as messages of dissent. 'Fashion,' she writes 'has always been part of the dictionary of political protest.'[38]

Returning to 2010, Gaga's meat dress and meat bikini evoke various analogies, acting as a trope for the ways in which the gendered body operates in culture. One is the way that the meat dress renders the commodification and consumption of the female body as an object of the male gaze visible and active. In *The Sexual Politics of Meat* (1990) Carol Adams argues that in Western hegemony women are reduced to the status of animals and presented by popular media as entities to be consumed. Adams applies the term 'absent referent' to describe the way that women and animals are rendered invisible in the violent act of consumption, or flesh eating, which separates the object from the individual. In this instance, one might think of Gaga's meat dress as a form of power whose meaning circulates within a network of discourses, institutions, practices and technologies producing positions of dominance and subordination. Gaga's meat garments bear an uncanny resemblance to Jana Sterbak's *Vanitas: Flesh for an Albino Anorectic* (1987) whether intentional or not (Figure 8.9).

Sterbak's work consisted of slices of flank steak sewn together to construct a dress which was then displayed on a tailors mannequin. Nearby, there was a photograph of a model wearing the dress in a pose characteristic of a fashion magazine editorial. As time passed the dress began to decay and desiccate taking on the form of a dressmakers dummy. The artwork evokes the field of fashion as a disciplinary force that constructs discourses of age, beauty and slimness which establishes the body as a site of propensity and domination. Although Sterbak's and Gaga's dress reduce the body to its basic metaphysical state of fleshiness, the dress operates in opposition acting as a signifier of self, or subjectivity. As Marni Jackson writes of *Vanitas*: 'It's a way of filleting the self into spirit and flesh for a moment, so the "I" can feel the sensation of this ungainly and perishable body. Flesh Dress undresses us down to the spirit.'[39] At the same time, the meat garments conjure the binary concepts of nature and culture. In its most fundamental natural state the naked body is raw flesh, culture then inscribes the body with meanings and leaves its mark.

Figure 8.9 A picture taken on 11 February 2011 shows 'Vanitas: Flesh Dress for Anorexic Albinos' of Jana Sterbak, exposed at the Maison Rouge gallery during the Cannibalism exhibition on 11 February 2011 in Paris. (JACQUES DEMARTHON/AFP via Getty Images.)

It might also be argued that *Vanitas* flounders under its own specificity overshadowing anything else that Sterbak subsequently did in her career. What distinguishes Sterbak's work from Gaga's intervention was that Sterbak poses in a vacuum, effectively turning the work into an artefact and skirting a hegemonizing discourse, a discourse that she seeks to critique. On the other hand, Gaga's take on the dress is vampish and coquettish and is lived, its existence conferred through so-called real life. That is, her dress is used as a multivalent device in her activity as a rock star, 'cyborg' (as she once said she wanted to be known) and activist. In so doing, the component of transience in the use of meat as clothing, is provocatively preserved. The lived aspect jars with the deadness and perishability of the meat, with all the abject associations of its decay, and, for all of that, the imminent decay of our own flesh. In any case, Gaga's reappropriation glaringly begs the question: 'Which one is better?' In this regard, her activity – version/intervention/recreation – calls to mind Yves St Laurent's redeployment of Piet Mondrian, bringing an artistic style meant to be a sublation of life into real life and in so doing turning the artist from someone revered by a specialist few into a household name.

In *The Raw and the Cooked, Introduction to a Science of Mythology: 1* (1964) structural anthropologist Claude Levi-Strauss notes that the 'empirical categories the raw and the cooked, the fresh and the decayed, the moistened and the burned, etc. . . . can be used as a conceptual tool with which to elaborate abstract ideas and combine them in the form of propositions.'[40] He categorizes the raw into two basic levels; *cooked food* which is the cultural transformation of the raw and *rotten food* which is the natural conversion of the raw. Various intermediary states emerge; cooking in air such as roasting and smoking and cooking in water, such as boiling. Each category is derived from culture, except that roasting which is cooked in the open air and remains relatively raw is considered closer to nature. Whereas boiled errs on the side of culture because it undergoes a complete process of cooking submerged in water (i.e. pot as a designed implement). Each category is then assigned different levels of prestige, some food is exclusive to men, others to women or children, some foods can only be eaten at particular times and others are forbidden to children or religious orders. Boiled is associated with endo-cuisine with the private sphere of the family and the feminine (such as casseroles or stews). On the other hand, the roasted is associated with exo-culture, the exterior public space of the outdoors which is associated with masculinity. Cooked food becomes the cultural transformation of the raw, the less the food is cooked the higher its social status. Food that requires little or no human intervention, such as caviar or oysters, maintains the highest prestige Forest. In other words food, whether raw or cooked is classed and gendered.

Gaga's fleshy wardrobe draws attention to the military body as a site of hegemonic power that serves to protect the nation state. In her 'Prime Rib or America' speech, she aligns the consumption of meat with the constitutional rights of freedom and equality. Meat is 'the prime rib of America', and the standing rib roast is the most superior (and expensive) cut of beef available to consumers. Why eat offal if you can afford to eat steak? Gaga uses the metaphor of the beef rib, which is located on the back of a cow, as a metaphor for the pillars of the American nation, the 'back bone of America'. 'I thought this was a prime rib buffet,'[41] Gaga cried out in during her speech, 'I thought that equality meant everyone, but apparently for certain value meals, for certain civil rights, I have to pay extra because I am gay.'[42] Applying Levi-Strauss' culinary triangle, meat is assigned a high level of prestige, afforded only to the dominant privileged. Approximately two months after the MTV Music Video Awards, President Barak Obama signed a bill that set in motion the repeal of DADT which was formally disbanded in September 2011. Military personal that were previously discharged because of their LGBTQI* status were reinstated. Although Gaga's meat dress was heavily criticized by the food and fashion industry as being wasteful in the face of worldwide poverty (which was the same criticism Sterbak received for *Vanitas*) and an affront to animal rights. Gaga's meat dress became a visible example how food-as-fashion is used as a communication tool to illicit political discourse for the purpose of instrumenting social change.

The intersection of food, art and fashion very much brings the role of perishability to the fore. This also means the many perishable aspects of the human character and condition: the perishability of our loves and desires, ourselves as agents in the inexorable passage of time. In many ways, the nexus of food, art and fashion is one that is a campaign against the relic: these works require action, noise, movement and the general messiness of circumstance. Their display is in time, just as the thought of a great meal exists almost as beautifully as a lingering memory.

9
DESIGNER COOKBOOKS AND CELEBRITY CHEFS

Toward the beginning of this book, we established that celebrity chefs grew out of the rise in restaurant culture and the increasing ability for cooks to move from place to place, patron to patron. The first celebrity chef, Carême, was a child of the old regime, who took full advantage of the Revolution to become a taste-maker in his own right, and to be treated as a trophy by those for whom he cooked. His career is mirrored by those of artists, composers and musicians such as Beethoven and Paganini, whose livelihoods were shaped according to commissions and ticket-sales, and thus their ability to attract audiences. In the new age of the virtuoso, Carême's sumptuous architectonics were on par with the bravura performances of contemporaries in other fields and disciplines, whose livelihoods depended on the level of attention they could command. As with the fashion industry, this inevitably meant that such people had to deal in variety and novelty to keep audiences interested. Cookbooks raised chef's reputations to star status and with television, the status of chefs took a new turn, as the emphasis was increasingly that of personality and performance over that of producing something that is physically consumed. The innocuous and generic 'cook' disappears as the servile and workaday associations of professional cooking is dispelled. Since the early 1990s, when Marco Pierre White, Jamie Oliver and Nigella Lawson tickled television viewers palette with aspirations, sex appeal and a cornucopia of culinary styles the celebrity chef has become much of the same breed as the designer and the stylist. Using lifestyle and social aspiration as a formula of success, by fetishizing taste and romanticizing ingredients celebrity chefs are linked to brands and commerce which drives sales and consumption.

Curated food: guidebooks, magazines and designer cookbooks

As we have seen already, one of the de rigueur platforms for celebrity status had long been the cookbook, which in Lévi-Straussian terms can be viewed as the 'transition between food and culture.'[1] Much like etiquette books (beginning in the Middle Ages) that served as a guide to appropriate manners and deportment in public spaces, the cookbook allowed the chef to circulate outside the boundaries of their kitchen, it acted as a kind of sacred text, that could exist for posterity as a culinary testament. In other words, etiquette books and cookbooks act as guides for an aspirational lifestyle or to gender and social class expectations and status. The etiquette book, written from the point view of the upper class to maintain control by structuring class behaviour, instructed one how to dress on different occasions, whether at parties, balls or dinner, how to write letters or compliment cards and gave directives on correct conversation and manners. In *The Civilizing Process* (1939), Norbert Elias locates manners as having arisen as an aspect of group living and were a way of maintaining social order that were fundamentally bound to a person's social status.[2] The cookbook is a guide to sourcing seasonal produce, how to prepare a meal, preserve ingredients, whilst some cookbooks offer advice on setting a table or planning a meal. Stephen Mennell extends Elias's work to the field of culinary arts arguing that this 'civilising appetite' involves changes in social and economic power as well as changing perspectives on meals and eating.[3]

From the eighteenth century onward, it was the cookbook that allowed women visibility as offering a serious contribution to gastronomy. These began as guides to domestic life, the most popular at the time was Eliza Smith's *The Complete Housewife, or Accomplished Gentlewoman's Companion* (1727) which also included 'recipes' for 'Medicines, Salves and Ointments'.[4] It was also the first cookbook to be printed in America (1742). Subsequent successful titles by women included *The Art of Cookery, Made Plain and Easy* (1747), by Hannah Glasse, *The Experienced English Housekeeper* (1769) by Elizabeth Raffald, and *American Cookery* (1796) by Amelia Simmons. In the nineteenth century, popular cookbooks in America such as *The Ladies Receipt Book* by Miss Leslie (1847), Mary Randolf's *The Virginia Housewife* (1838) and Mary Henderson's *Practical Cooking and Dinner Giving* (1876) began to identify ladies tastes with a preference for light lunches and creamy deserts while men were expected to partake of game and wine.[5] Women's culinary efforts were not directed at pleasing her husband exclusively but was expected to cook what she thought were appropriate meals for herself and her family. It was not until the twentieth century beginning in the 1920s and especially in the following two decades that cookbooks began to be addressed to men and designed to tell women what men liked.[6] The influence that such books, which were in ample circulation exerted on tastes and methods, is hard to gauge, but twentieth-century examples provide a good indication.

In any case, the etiquette book and the cookbook are comparable with each other and align with women's magazines (and later men's magazines) forming a triangle in a Lévi-Straussian sense. Beginning in the eighteenth century, magazines guided middle-class women on good housekeeping, sewing tips, embroidery notes, recipes and the latest fashions. Magazines (like etiquette and cookbooks) appealed (and instructed) women on how to be socially and morally correct and to create an idealized vision of themselves and their home. Conducting a comparative interpretive analysis of photographs of food in two competing women's magazines, French *Elle* and *L'Express*, for his essay 'Ornamental Cookery' (1972 [1952]), Barthes argues that one of the major developments of genteel cooking is 'ornamentation', a process where 'natural food' turns into 'prepared food'[7] in the process of representation, what Barthes calls 'rococo cooking'. Surfaces are glazed, rounded off and buried under sauces and jellies, whose consumption is accomplished by simply looking. 'Golden partridges [are] studded with cherries, a faintly pink chaud-froid, a mould of crayfish surrounded by their red shells, a frothy charlotte prettified with glacé fruit designs, multicoloured trifle, etc.'[8] Ornamentation occurs in two dialectically opposed ways that are contradictorily reconciled, 'fleeing from nature' and the process of artifice in which food turns into petit -bourgeois art, an elaborate form of trinketry, in the same way that dress becomes fashion through artifice. Taste in food, has become like fashion, a signifier of style trickling down or bubbling up.

When Taylor Antrim was finishing the last touches to her edited book, *Food in Vogue* (2017) she asked *Vogue* Editor in Chief Anna Wintour why *Vogue* covers food. Wintour replied, 'It's part of our world, it's part of our lives. It never occurred to me not to include it.'[9] Wintour's predecessor, Diana Vreeland, who edited American *Vogue* in the 1960s and was known to enjoy a peanut butter and marmalade sandwich with a glass of Scotch whisky, covered the latest diets and recipes amongst its fashion pages, but it was not until 1988 under Wintour's stewardship that *Vogue* became preoccupied with food featuring images from photographers Irving Penn, Bruce Weber, Helmut Newton and Annie Leibovitz amongst others. Like 'the openly dream-like cookery'[10] described by Barthes in French *Elle* magazine 'which never show the dishes except from a high angle, as objects once near and accessible,'[11] the photographs in *Vogue* were like modernist still lifes of food. It was Barthes 'rococo cooking' at its finest – a razor slicing a steak, a chicken in high heels, a giant turkey neck, a rabbit squeezing into a small casserole dish, 'brown banana slices – even an apple – look[ed] like art.'[12]

The creative process behind cooking and designing clothes are similar, each involves inspiration, a willingness to experiment, the selection of ingredients or fabrics and endless test kitchen revisions, or toiles. Christian Dior's good friend Raymond Thuilier remembers that Dior often compared cooking with couture, 'The ingredients we use when cooking are just as noble as the materials used in couture,'[13] Dior would regularly quip. Christian Dior's love of food was so great and so well known that once when he was in New York he consumed five hotdogs after finishing a five course meal.[14] Dior liked to eat. His favourite dish combined oysters and foie gras, or eel and trout cooked with *Dom Pérignon* champagne. He also liked to cook. At one point, Dior even considered taking up a culinary career. 'I know lots of recipes, and, who knows, one day I might need something to fall back on,'[15] he told his managing director, Jacques Rouët. 'We could do a Dior ham, or a Dior roast, perhaps?[16] Fifteen years after Dior's death of a heart attack in 1957 (his third and final) the House of Dior released a cookbook, *La Cuisine Cousu-Main* (1972) (*Tailor-Made Cuisine*) crammed with all Dior's favourite recipes from soups, salad, game, sauces and soufflés.

It comes as no surprise then, that fashion designers have been preoccupied with eating as much as dressing. In the May 2020 issue of *Vogue* magazine fashion designers shared their favourite lockdown recipes during the coronavirus pandemic. Laura Kim, creative director of Oscar de la Renta (with Fernando Garcia) shared her recipe for the French stuffed cabbage dish, *Chou Farçi* and Carolina Herrera her grandmother's recipe for oatmeal cookies that has been passed down from generation to generation in her family. Thai-born American designer Phillip Lim offered his mother's recipe for Salt and Pepper Shrimp, a dish that she would often cook for him and appears in his cookbook *More Than Our Bellies*, published in 2019. Two years earlier, Zac Posen released a cookbook *Cooking with Zac. Recipes from Rustic to Refined. A Cookbook* (2017) that was organized by fashion seasons, Spring and Summer, Resort, Fall, Winter and holiday. Like Dior, Posen believes that fashion and food share an expressive synergy, their 'creative process takes research, takes preparation, takes trial and error, practice, [and] technique.[17]

Food has been used to tell the story of the Missoni brand with advertising campaigns photographed by Juergen Teller and Steven Meisel that focus on intimate feasts with the Missoni clan. So, when Francesco Maccapani Missoni, the heir of the Italian fashion dynasty published *The Missoni Family Cookbook* (2018), the concept of food and fashion had already been explored by the brand. Creative director Angela Missoni says that 'Cooking is our way of enjoying our time together. Even on a normal night at dinner can quickly grow from six to eight to twelve people. It's very much about taking care of yourself and those around you.' Missoni have also expanded into homewares with cushions, throws and bath towels and a limited edition melamine dinner and a serve ware collection for Target.

Celebrity chefs and television

The first celebrity chef, in the modern sense, was Xavier Marcel Boulestin, a French Anglophile who ran the celebrated Restaurant Boulestin in London and appeared on two cinema documentary shorts, *A Scratch Meal with Marcel Boulestin* and *Party Dish by Marcel Boulestin* in 1936. Directed by Arthur Elton, the shorts were commissioned by the British Gas Association and the Gas Light and Coke Company to promote gas cooking.[18] Dressed in a grey tweed suit, white shirt with matching tie and brilliantined hair, Boulestin would *flambé*, *sauté* and *julien*. Utensils and ingredients were always close at hand in Boulestin's kitchen, spices were easy to reach, and ingredients were cut and portioned in advance, as Boulestin, with a smooth, unassuming voice instructed his viewers on the techniques and preparation of French cuisine. The same friendly tone that he used for all his cookbooks, beginning in 1923 with *Simple French Cooking for English Homes*. Boulestin dabbled in several occupations before arriving in London from Paris in 1906, including securing employment as an art dealer, interior decorator and a music critic. At one point he worked as a ghost writer and secretary to the libertine rake Henry Gauthier-Villars whose nom de plume was Willy and was married to the novelist Colette.[19] The three became close friends moving together in fashionable and artistic circles. Boulestin even appears as a clever dandy with an exaggerated demeanour in Colette's novel *Minne* (1905) and Willy's *Une Plage d'amour*, published in 1906.

The same year, with a small inheritance from his doting grandmother, Boulestin immigrated to London where he met Lord Alfred Douglas (Oscar Wilde had died in Paris in 1900) and became intertwined with the clandestine gay scene. He established an interior decorating shop *Décoration Moderne* in 1911 at the fashionably wealthy suburb of Belgravia which soon went bust, but in the process of liquidating his business he met Theodore Bayard, publishing director for Heinemann books and pitched the idea of a cookbook. By this stage, Boulestin had been writing a cooking column for British *Vogue* magazine (1923–1929) and was very familiar with the food scene in London and abroad.[20] The rest, as they say, is history: *Simple French Cooking for English Homes* (1923) and its successor *A Second Helping, or More Dishes for English Homes* followed in 1925. The same year Boulestin opened a catering company with his boyfriend Henry Adair and catered an exclusive luncheon party for Virginia Woolf and British *Vogue* editor Dorothy Todd and her girlfriend Madge Garland at their exclusive Chelsea home where they held notoriously good parties. Todd, who was the second editor of British *Vogue* had a vision of the magazine as an intelligent and thoroughly modern publication that included literature, art and cooking. Todd persuaded Woolf, Vita Sackville-West and the flamboyant Nöel Coward to write articles and essays for the magazine. Gertrude Stein contributed poetry, Cecil Beaton photography, Vanessa Bell art criticism and Boulestin food writing. The *Vogue* circle was a queer clique and Boulestin was very much a part of it.

So successful was his catering business that Boulestin opened Restaurant Français in May 1925 supplanted by the aptly named Restaurant Boulestin in Wolseley near Convent Gardens. Edward Larocque Tinker, the food editor for *The New York Times* wrote on 27 March 1938, that 'Marcel Boulestin, whose small restaurant near Convent Gardens . . . decorated with Marie Laurencin murals . . . [where one can get] the most perfect recherché dinner to be found in all London.'[21] The restaurant, with its circus-themed Laurencin murals and Roaul Dufy yellow silk brocade curtains attracted high society clientele with its eclectic menu and gained a reputation for being the most expensive eating establishment in the city.[22] Boulestin's reputation as a chef had spread far and wide, but it also helped that he mixed in rarefied circles. When not cooking at his restaurant or writing for *Vogue* magazine, Boulestin was conducting cooking classes at the London grocery shop, Fortnum and Mason, where he was approached by director Arthur Elton.

Elizabeth David, whose *A Book of Mediterranean Food*, published in 1950, all but single-handedly introduced such food to the then drab British table. David held Boulestin in great regard, adopting many of his dictums and praising him in her numerous cookbooks. Although still suffering from food shortages in the aftermath of the war, David's book spoke of eggplants, garlic and olive oil, which were then deemed exotic and foreign. As scarcity eased, she proved to have a sizeable effect on British cookery, taste and cultural awareness. The books that followed, *French country cooking* (1951) and *French Country Cooking* (1960) had an undeniable hold on British cookery, making it highly fashionable to turn to the continental for what was culinarily desirable and *Spices, Salts and Aromatics in the English Kitchen* (1970) was, 'the most sophisticated compendium of all that is good in British cooking.'[23]

David was what one would describe as beautiful if not striking which goes a long way for popularity votes especially for a public figure. She had an aquiline nose, high cheek bones, pencil thin eyebrows and wore her hair styled in a perm which was the height of fashion in the 1950s and early 1960s (Figure 9.1). She

Figure 9.1 Elizabeth David *c.* 1960. Unknown Photographer. (Wikipedia Commons, Public Domain.)

dressed in open collar white shirts with sleeves rolled up (which became her trademark style), pencil skirts and kitten heel pumps. David was very fashionable; this was in part that she landed a job as a food correspondent for *Harper's Bazaar* magazine in 1949 on her return to England after having spent the early years of the Second World War in Greece and Egypt. David had a privileged upbringing, was rebellious and self-possessed. At sixteen she was sent to Paris where she studied art and was exposed to good food and designer fashion. She worked briefly as a sales assistant for the House of Worth which was still operating under Worth's descendants. She returned to England, joined a theatre troupe, only to elope soon after on a yacht with a married actor. The affair soon came to an end and a string of tumultuous relationships followed before a series of marriages that soon too fell apart.

David was instrumental in a new generation of those who did not just eat, but prepared the food, discussed its preparation and ingredients with others, and began to look to the spaces and implements of preparation.[24] A century earlier, such discussion would have been disparaged as beneath any middle or upper-class woman. Now cookery had become its own industry that could wager its own stakes in the social landscape of taste. Making Southern European food fashionable was moreover a far cry from the inclinations of eighteenth-century England which reviled garlic and olive oil as repellently pungent and unpleasantly greasy. For centuries, the English, except for the élite, had prided themselves on the plainness and simplicity of their food.[25] Nutritional science would shortly have a role to play in popularity in several decades to come.

David was also decisive in bringing a literary flair and sophistication to cookbook writing, elevating it to an independent literary genre. In *Italian Food* (1954) David's prose is elegant as she describes the food markets near the Rialto in Venice.[26]

> The light of a Venetian dawn in early Summer – you must be about at four o'clock in the morning to see the market coming to life – is so limpid and so still that it makes every separate vegetable and fruit and fish luminous with a life of its own, with unnaturally heightened colours and clear stencilled outlines. Here the cabbages are cobalt blue, the lettuces clear pure green, sharp as glass.

(In a slightly different vein, tilted more toward literature than table, was *The Alice B. Toklas Cookbook* [1954] by the eponymous companion of Gertrude Stein. Mixing recipes with reminiscences, it is now best remembered for a recipe for chocolate brownies laced with marijuana.) Abigail Dennis asserts that most of the ingredients being out of reach at the time of publication may have added to the book's appeal, as David offered description and pictures of comfort and plenty against sparkling, bounteous backdrops, into which the reader could freely insert themselves and escape from the gloom that was post-war England.

As Melissa Pasanen observes, David 'went beyond recipes, her descriptions made people want to cook the food'[27] that marked the beginning of the lifestyle cookery book. The text and its illustrations sell themselves not as an instructional guide for recipes to be made – clearly, many readers were simply unable to realize the dishes the book described – but as an escape from the drabness of post-war British food and lifestyle.[28] In this David's book anticipated the lavish and 'ostentatious display books that were to become popular in the 1980s.'[29] The lifestyle magazines that grew out of these would be serious competition with fashion and style magazines, to the extent that, by the 1980s, boundaries were blurred: home magazines had sections on fashion, while fashion magazines featured recipes and nutritional guides.

David became a celebrity in her own right, transforming food writing into a respectable and intellectual pursuit. She was elected a Fellow of the Royal Society of Literature, was named a Commander of the Order of the British Empire for her contribution to the gastronomic arts and France honoured her with a *Chevalier du Mérite Agricole* (Order of Agricultural Merit). Years later after her death in 1992, James Kent directed the British television film *Elizabeth David: A Life in Recipes* (2006) starring Catherine McCormack as David. She did, however, not have the power of television, (which had now become affordable to the masses) to take that celebrity and influence on a level that felt like it was universal. Born around the same time as David, Julia Child is perhaps the first television celebrity chef in the modern mould (Figure 9.2). Like David, her early studies were in art (David art, Child, art history), but her real influence was to demystify classic French cuisine to American audiences. *Mastering the Art of French Cooking* (1961), which she wrote together with Simone Beck and Louisette Bertholle, was an instant success, and frequently referred to as one of the most influential books of gastronomy ever written. The book appeared just as America was in the flush of its post-war economic boom, and the dramatic changes that technological appliances introduced into the household. The ease of access within the kitchen, the increased efficiency of stoves and refrigerators had the natural effect of cultivating interest in home cookery.

In retrospect, it is not hard to see how the first cooking shows fell into place. For women, with more time on their hands, and with television as the centrepiece of the middle-class living room, to be taken step-by-step, free of charge, in their own home, through the newly touted cuisine was an attractive prospect. For French cuisine in the early 1960s was still considered a specialized affair, only available in restaurants, led by men trained in France. As Amy Trubeck explains, Child's success was not limited to an approachable personality, but also her intuitive understanding that 'television, especially cooking on television, integrated professional and culinary worlds. She used television to teach home cooks to cook artful food and understand French cuisine as an art form.'[30] Moreover, while as we have seen there have been cookbooks since the early age of the printing

Figure 9.2 Julia Child in her kitchen as photographed by Lynn Gilbert, Cambridge Massachusetts. 1978. (Wikipedia Commons, Public Domain.)

press, by and large, the transmission of culinary knowledge has long been practical and verbal. Her televisual formalization allowed for a convenient blending of such communication between mother and daughter, chef and apprentice. Child was effectively a bridge between the feminized domestic world of cookery and the masculine professional world of gastronomy. Such material conditions help to explain why the first cookery shows were from women, since men were disinclined to be associated with the domestic space, and the daytime audience, at a time when femininity and domesticity was encouraged and promoted. So, a year later in 1962, because of her co-authored book, Child was asked to do a fill-in segment after a cancellation of a different show. Her cooking demonstration was so well received, after a few pilots, she was invited to host her own television show, *The French Chef*, first aired in 1963, one of several successful shows, that aired in ten seasons until 1973. Thus, the origin of the first television cooking show owes itself to sheer happenstance. When director and screenwriter Nora Ephron moved to Manhattan in 1962 as a young reporter for *Newsweek*, 'two historic events had occurred: the birth-control pill was invented, and the first Julia

Child cookbook was published. As a result, everyone was having sex, and when the sex was over you cooked something.'[31] With Child's book, coupled with the keeping-up-with-the-Joneses in domestic products, made specialized home cookery desirable and with television, highly fashionable. Ephron remembers that owning Child's cookbook was 'an emblem of adulthood, a way of being smart and chic and college-educated where food was concerned.'[32] Years later, when Ephron's obsession with food and cooking did not wane, she wrote and directed *Julie & Julia* (2009) starring Merryl Streep as Julia Child. The film tells the parallel story of call centre operator Julie Powell who blogs about cooking the 524 recipes that make up *Mastering the Art of French Cooking* and Julia Child. Like David, Child didn't consider herself a chef, but more of a cook and like David, Child was born into money, serious money. Born in Pasedena in 1912, Child's father was a wealthy Californian landowner and her mother an heir to the New England Weston Paper fortune that cushioned Child's life. Unlike David who was poised and elegant, Child described herself as 'a rather loud and unformed social butterfly.'[33] Less of a clothes horse and more of a battering ram. Child wore colourful buttoned-up shirts, simple knee-length skirts or pants and flat sensible shoes, a style which remained the same throughout her years on television.

It is significant that the rise of the modern celebrity chef is coterminous with television. Television shows are serialized where audiences can relate to the presenter, and such shows are built on expectation that this will happen, in seeing him or her in different contexts, facing different challenges. On a small number of occasions, Child's outcomes were not as expected, which had the salutary effect of humanizing her to the audience. Child's appeal, as we can only expect, were manifold, as it was based on culinary authority *and* warm domesticity. Her demonstrations could also be read as offerings, which is essentially the case with television food shows which subsequently would involve another chef (if the ego of either could stand it), or a less knowledgeable counterpart, who would be the proxy for the viewer. Their transaction would double as a form of sharing, to compensate for the ultimate lack of real food for the viewer at the end, but a consolation made in a promise. The domesticity of cooking shows is doubled by the domesticity of the viewing setting, and, as David Marshall relates there is a different kind of intimacy that contrasts with the film star:

> The aura of the television celebrity is reduced therefore because of three factors: the domestic nature of television viewing, the close affinity of the celebrity with the organization and the perpetuation of consumer capitalism, and the shattering of continuity and integrity of character that takes place through the interspersal of commercials in any program.[34]

Although he does not mention cooking shows, we can see how they would become important within the television repertoire, and active symbiosis. Cooking shows are all about ingredients and guidance, making them ripe for all kinds of product placement and straight-out endorsement. It is now part of everyday shopping life in the developed world to have product lines endorsed by celebrity cooks or other celebrities, a venerable example is now 'Newman's Own', line of salad dressings, that has a longevity well after the actor, Paul Newman's death.

While Child was the epitome of the adept housewife-cum-chef, as befitting her time, she fitted smoothly into the mould of carer and teacher, the bearer of knowledge and bounty, a new kind of presentational model would emerge that would bring the age-old association of food and sex to the fore that would culminate in the term 'gastroporn'. If there is some parallel to point to, as David's books became popular in the early 1950s, *Playboy* magazine was founded in Chicago in 1953, Child's *Mastering the Art of French Cooking* in 1961, *Penthouse* in 1963 and *Hustler* in 1974. In the meantime, Mrs Beeton brought out her revised *All About Cookery* in 1961 and *Time-Life* published *The Picture Cookbook* in 1968, both of which displayed, according to Dennis, a notable 'shift from the instructional to the temptational.'[35] Representing food had now taken its cue from the fashion shoot. For in the early days of the model, the purpose was a kind of objective demonstration of the garment on the body. But this soon gave way – the first fashion shoot is attributed to Steichen of garments by Poiret in 1911 – to a much more complex interplay between garment, props and narrative. Similarly, by the 1960s, representations of food were no longer the result of the cooking process, but a world unto themselves, complete with props (fetishes) and against salubrious surroundings or come-hither landscapes, the food being only an anchor for a much more semantically saturated message of success, money, happiness and hedonism. Colours were high-key, and textures, including gleams and glints, were writ large. 'Such illustrations,' Dennis contends,

> represent the beginnings of food photography both as art and what has come to be called "food pornography" or "gastroporn." The vicarious sensual thrill of the visual stimulation of food photography, often accompanied by evocative and descriptive text, and its high-class equivalent, the cookbook as *objet d'art*, are paralleled with the physical and mental gratification of sexual pornography.[36]

This tended to expand the connotative potential of food in representation. Andrew Chan observes that even the way objects are arranged in cookery shows have formal affinities to pornography: 'The idealization of cooking is subtly evident in the surreally coloured foods, anatomically perfect chickens, and super-sized "vertical" displays of cooking shows, comparable to the cosmetically-altered, human sex-toy actors in porno films.'[37] Further still, pornography is filled with extreme bodies, but without any trace of the rigours needed to acquire them (exercise, surgery), while slim cooks use ingredients and make foods that defy their own physical shape. (Chubby celebrity cooks exist but they are never in fullest favour.)

Just as the representation of fashion is of world free of myriad impediments and logistics such as cleaning the garment or of fluctuations of temperature, let alone all the messy impediments of life, the food shoot and the cookery show is an idealized world in which all the appliances work and are state-of-the-art (more product placement), where all ingredients are on hand, where the implements sparkle, where all surfaces are free of mildew or unwanted residue. As Chan continues: 'In the TV program's fantasy kitchen there is copious space and ventilation; there are no dishes to wash, no mounds of trash to throw out.' We need not wait for things to cook as we have editing for that: 'Everything has also been meticulously edited and orchestrated, often to the strains of classical music, so that the master chef and his happy minions can sauté and garnish to the melodies of Vivaldi or Mozart.'[38] Such shows are of a piece with lifestyle commercials – clothes cars, travel, real estate – except packaged as wholesomely educational.

Gastrofashion and gastroporn: Jamie and Nigella

The celebrity chef who combatted the pristine world of stylized cookery (or ostensibly so), while making gastroporn a mainstream family affair is Jamie Oliver. Facing gastroporn head-on in the title of his first and most famous television show series, *The Naked Chef* (BBC), which offered a 'wraparound culture of youth, food, cool music, clothes, scooters and friends.'[39] Oliver approached food production with an affable, no-nonsense approach that was pitched at 'everyone'. In his broad British Essex accent and his cheeky grin, he was Mr Everyman bringing food to the people. As Gilly Smith writes in her study of lifestyle cooking programs, Jamie portrayed a world of old British values and rustic Italian fare. But behind the scenes,

> Jamie Oliver's world was quickly branded by the tabloids as stylish, youthful, and healthy and everything within his reach; while his old school mates featured in his on-screen barbecues, off-screen he was Brad Pitt's new best friend.

Words that have been used for both Oliver's style are 'approachable', 'pared-down', and 'unpretentious'. First aired on the BBC in 1999, he and his show arrived at a time when the public was casting out for economic alternatives to restaurant-going, and the rival of DIY culture. The show was grunge for epicureans, with many components adding to the garage-band feeling of it all. Oliver would jump around unaffectedly and chat casually with the camera as if in a concert. As opposed to Child, who was the paragon of poise and refinement,

Oliver would never let his enthusiasm be curbed, cooing and sighing over ingredients, talking about them with a winning boyishness reminiscent of the excitement over a new toy. Whereas Child transacted the universal truths of French cuisine, Oliver approached food as a novelty and a new discovery. Oliver would pride himself on approaches that to refined cookery would be considered unnecessarily audacious or downright crude. A favourite gesture was to tear off the head of a bunch of parsley rather than go through the rigmarole of removing the individual leaves before chopping them. Oliver ritualizes the no-fussiness, the 'naked' version of the stylized and monitored professional kitchen.

It is in the title itself that we can observe the positive symbiosis of food and fashion. The way 'naked' is deployed by Oliver makes use of its various semantic possibilities that are also mythic. That is, Oliver purported to offering a no-nonsense, unalloyed and therefore honest experience, appealing to the modern popular subconscious rooted back to the Enlightenment philosopher Jean-Jacques Rousseau. 'Nakedness' ramified in many directions, such as to grass-roots activists, cult of the organic, and, by extension the ecology movement, which was gaining significant momentum at the time of the show's airing into the early 2000s. Nicola Perullo writes about 'naked' and 'dressed' gustation in a manner that is considerably in thrall of a Rousseauian paradigm which, from the mythologies that *The Naked Chef* rides on, is nonetheless instructive: 'Naked gustatory pleasure can be valuable, free, primitive, and a regenerating endowment. If properly understood, it can be a powerful tool of resistance against dominant and hegemonic discourses on taste, made by the dominant class.'[40] When food is clothed, it is given rules, protocols and its own language-games, as already noted. Again, the paradigmatic terminology of which Perullo avails herself proves useful in deciphering the assumption that Oliver's show explored: 'The infant becomes an adult. Nude pleasure gets dressed, imbuing itself with new layers of meaning and with sharing and negotiating . . . [the] fluid, dynamic difference between two levels of taste experience – naked pleasure and dressed taste – marks the thin line between the first and second access to eating.'[41] Folding the 'naked' with the 'dressed' is precisely what Oliver performs: offering insight and knowledge but from a vantage point that this is grass-roots, unalloyed, unpretentious and accessible, and therefore all you need to know.

Oliver's raw actions and direct talking is all about not having airs and graces: while they could be read as vaunting the vernacular of cooking, the easy and understandable action as opposed to the finesse of the professional trainee, could also be grasped in a sexual way. Chan astutely observes that starting '[w]ith the title as teaser and come-on, our imaginations run amok. Sexual scenarios become manifest with every gesture, as when Oliver pokes at meat he is preparing, verbalizes his desires and preferences for certain combinations of ingredients.'[42] Chan contends that the unsteady movements add to a fetishized spectacle, as if 'observing Oliver's moves as a sexual predator might.' It is also evident that Oliver is addressing someone off-camera. Hence '[t]he idea of nakedness is further reinforced in the sense that the chef is perceptibly vulnerable and does not know we are there.'[43]

Not overly tall, with a boy-next-door friendliness ('approachable' again), and therefore not dominant or prepossessing, Oliver became the optimal culinary exemplar of the mediated 'New Lad' which emerged in the late 1990s as a backlash against the emotionally skilled and narcissistic 'New Man'. Unlike the New Man, who was body, health and fashion conscious – fit, muscular and well-groomed – the New Lad was loutish and drank too much, preferred the company of his mates, watched copious amounts of football, and didn't really think much of women except as sexual partners – but he liked stylish clothes (Figure 9.3). So, Oliver showed, or better *demonstrated*, that the New Lad could cook without foregoing any of his manly brashness or obtuseness. His message was simple 'cook well, impress your friends and you too can have it all.'[44] The bachelor apartment; a Vespa scooter, a VW Combi Van, good mates, a social life and even a down-to-earth, girl-next-door girlfriend like Jools, whom he later marries and has five children that all appear in his later television programmes. The New Lad turned dad.

Jamie's dress is consonant with his demeanour: informal in the extreme with T-shirts with logos, jeans and sneakers – just an everyday guy or 'bloke'. 'The

Figure 9.3 Chef Jamie Oliver visits BuzzFeed's 'AM To DM' to discuss his new book *Ultimate Veg: Easy & Delicious Meals for Everyone* on 9 January 2020, in New York City. (Photo by Slaven Vlasic/Getty Images.)

New Lad is echoed in Oliver's figure,' explains Jonatan Leer, 'not only by his "Oasis" look and his informal "street" diction, but also his lack of seriousness. Life and food "gotta be a laugh"!'[45] Leer notices how Oliver does alter roles on different occasions. 'The show suggests that this kind of balancing act is expected of a man in the post-traditional era, where identity and gender roles are fluid' and are measured against different social encounters.[46]

Another clever aspect of each show was that it was oriented around a particular theme drawn from Oliver's own life, such as babysitting, which gave a sense of reason to the proceedings, a narrative that viewers could relate to, as well as providing a tacit 'how-to' as to the culinary dimension of such occasions. Oliver played a large part in grafting food and cooking as an activity onto any domestic occasion. It was thanks to Oliver that more men were comfortable to enter homeware stores, buy specialty foods, cook, and buy cookbooks. Oliver's first book became a No. 1 bestseller in Britain. Oliver would subsequently become the champion of various causes, which included teaching underprivileged mothers how to cook nutritious meals for their children and giving young unemployed youth the opportunity to retrain as chefs, as well as establishing a programme that encouraged schoolchildren to be more conscious of the foods they ate.

Oliver's career progressed by maintaining an emphasis on workability and practicality (to go with 'approachability'). Following *The Naked Chef* shows were simply named *Jamie's Dinners* (2004) and *Jamie's School Dinners* (2005), banking on the confidence that his celebrity need now only carry his first name. The latter show, pitched at what he saw as the poor standard of food served in large public schools (in the show's case in Greenwich, London), had an obvious altruistic edge, but gave the value-added perception that Oliver's unalloyed approach was always motivated toward the larger public good. On this basis, Oliver has built an empire with restaurants, signature brands and specialty foods sold in supermarkets ready for home-preparation. His smiling face on labels and leaflets is the benign assurance that the everyday person can accomplish, with his intervention, what they had not thought possible. Trubeck comments that Oliver in example and influence is a salient sign that 'the borders between public and private cooking have become completely porous.'[47] He has taken Child's homely personability to vernacular extreme, his continuing popularity owing to 'his commitment to democratizing cooking.' His ability to penetrate into the lives of so many people – such as to be a household world in the anglophone sphere – has in turn transformed 'aspirations and expectations . . . [which have shaped] the form and content of cooking categories.'[48] Certainly, Oliver has demystified cooking, while at the same time causing other chefs to avail themselves of technical feats which are unfathomable to the home cook – Heston Blumenthal comes to mind.

The television celebrity to have monopolized on gastroporn 'to the point of parody' as Dennis suggests, is Nigella Lawson, whose show aired no longer during a day-slot but in the evening. Lawson, who was married to journalist John

Diamond (then advertising magnate and art collector Charles Saatchi) would sway her buxom hips and just out her bosom during presentations. Tasting food would commonly be in close-up, with Lawson pursing and smacking her lips, raising eyebrows, and rolling her eyes back in faux-orgasmic delight. Beginning in 1999, the title of the show, *Nigella Bites* did not help matters (the cover of the 2002 book based on the show has her putting a morsel of food into her open mouth). It is, according to Chan, 'the natural successor to *The Naked Chef*.' But where Oliver did retain elements of professionalism in the deftness with the way that he handled his implements and his ease around the kitchen space, Nigella draws attention to her many mild ineptitudes, thus ingratiating herself with television audiences. Chan continues: 'She assures the viewer that it's perfectly natural and not shameful to cook like she does, or at least to watch her cook – and like spectators at a nudist camp, we buy into her libertine ways.'[49]

Nigella stands out from her contemporaries because she carefully curates her image through the television series produced by her own company, Pabulum Productions. She is Oxford University educated, financially intelligent and was born into publishing aristocracy. Her father, Nigel Lawson, Lord Lawson of Blaby was a journalist and Margret Thatcher's chancellor, and her brother is the influential journalist, Dominic Lawson. Her introduction to food and cooking came very early by way of her mother whose family owned J. Lyons and Co. the food and catering company. It was partly her pedigree and partly her food column for British *Vogue* magazine that Nigella was primed to succeed. The author of numerous books, while some have had more suitably decorous titles in later years, the early ones took the liberties that make liberal use of semantic overlap between 'sensuous' and 'sensual'. Her first book in 1998 is titled *How to Eat*, which vaguely gestures to *The Joy of Sex* (1972). Her subsequent book in 2000 made no ambiguity about its references to tantric delights: *How to Be a Domestic Goddess*. Understandably, Lawson was welcomed by many women who wanted to uphold feminist values but also wanted to reclaim femininity and domesticity. Lawson's triumph, writes Gilly Smith, 'was in the mainstreaming of popular feminism through the re-imagining of domestic life . . . Nigella became the pin-up girl for post-feminism.'[50] Lawson performs at being a 'goddess' reclaiming the nurturing power of women 'by feeding her friends and family, revelling in her curves, and reclaiming the right to feast. Her recipes are handed down from her grandmother and mother and are full of the legacy and lifestyle of the women in her life.'[51] In a 2019 interview with Smith celebrating the vintage edition of *How to Eat*, Nigella said that 'the enchantment of cooking lies in its ordinariness, it's a bit like a spell: you are making a potion.'[52] Lawson's comment reinforces her image as a seductress.

In the photograph below (Figure 9.4) Nigella is sitting in front of a bowl of cherries holding two between her forefinger and thumb that are poised just above her cleavage. The viewers gaze is directed towards the cherries, then

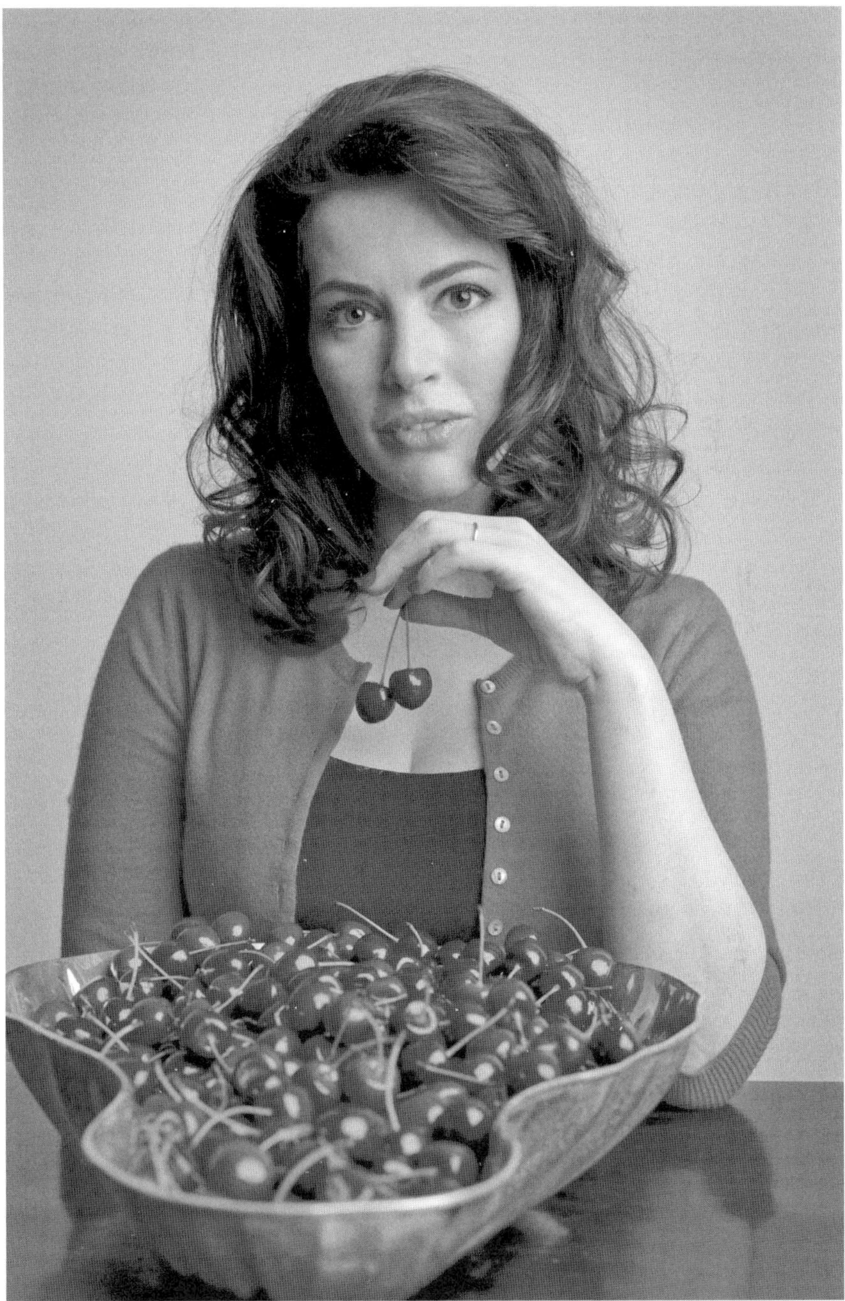

Figure 9.4 Food writer and broadcaster Nigella Lawson is photographed for *The Observer* on 15 November 2005, in London, England. (Photo by Harry Borden/Contour by Getty Images.)

onto her breasts. Her tussled hair suggests that she is has either woken up from an erotic slumber, or that she may be sexual aroused. Either or, the cherry (and its ripeness) has been associated with sex in Europe since the sixteenth century when it was used as a motif to describe the 'sins of the flesh' and later as a cultural reference to young virgins. The fruit has become a popular pattern in contemporary clothing and lingerie for adolescent girls suggesting purity (and its eventual loss). In this case, the meaning in the photograph is quite explicit, Nigella is inviting the audience to 'pop her cherry'. Her style, persona and other markers of feminine masquerade are deployed in the virtuoso skill that she manoeuvres between alternate visions of herself as a domestic goddess, a seductress and a diva. She embodies a glamorous retro-Italian style, performing a 1950s femininity that is steeped in the power of Italian women as mothers, wives and voluptuous sirens that men fear and yet are attracted to. Nigella modelled her image on Italian film stars such as Gina Lollobrigida and Sophia Loren, wearing cardigan and blouse twin sets to enhance her breasts and belts to narrow her waist and extend her hips much like the silhouette captured by Christian Dior in his 'New Look' first introduced in 1947. As Stephen Gundle writes in his history of glamour, 'glamorous people belonged to the world of representation, where playacting and fakery were commonplace.'[53]

In addition to discrete limited episode series (such as *Simply Nigella* in 2015 or *Nigella: At My Table* in 2019), Nigella is a frequent guest chef for competitive cooking programmes such as *Taste* in the United Kingdom and *MasterChef* in Australia and the United States. Having an appeal to both men and women: for men she is the domesticated vixen who is sexually available but still bound to the home, for women she is the saucy girlfriend with all the answers. She is also a model for women, since she is not shy about eating which means you do not have to forego food to be attractive. She presides over a full larder, and a well-stocked fridge, cooking fabulous food while also taking care of her children, and by tacit implication, her man. *Naked Chef* and *Nigella Bites*, revelled in the final unveiling, the climax of the show in the literal and the sexual sense, what in pornography is known as the 'money shot'.

Culinary bad boy Marco Pierre White

As we have seen already, cooks became chefs when they had their own autonomy, and when they had ownership or custodianship over a restaurant. This meant that the cook had more than skills, he had a proprietorial interest, and therefore authority. This was something of which Paul Bocuse, arguably the most famous chef of the post-war period, was duly conscious. In the tradition of celebrity chefs and self-promotion, Bocuse had an innate flair not only for cooking and innovation but for marketing. His brand extended well beyond himself and his cookery to brands. This he took from his contemporary Pierre Cardin, who already in the 1960s had developed a licence system that allowed different companies to manufacture a wide range of products that carried his name as the logo. Just as Cardin's name became affixed to anything from handkerchiefs and pens, so Bocuse put his name onto pepper mills and wine coolers. In addition to amassing a small empire, Bocuse was able to advocate for his profession, and to inaugurate yet another claim to nouvelle cuisine. His own version invited parody, as it consisted of small portions, and was associated with the health and food culture that burgeoned from the 1980s onward. Bocuse and his contemporaries were distinctive for their application of scientific knowledge to food that refers to what the biologist Édouard de Pomaine in the 1930s called 'gastrotechnology'. This gained momentum in 1984 with Harold McGee's *On Food and Cooking* which put into laymen's terms the chemical processes involved in cooking.

During the period in the 1990s when celebrity cooks were working at downplaying their technical and trained prowess as 'chefs' per se, there were as many attempts to elevate chefs to a pedestal, albeit in a theatricalized kitchen-set, or as someone imbued with star quality. Marco Pierre White first appeared in 1990 on the cover of his cookbook *White Heat* dressed as a rock star, with long unruly dark hair, penetrating eyes, and a smouldering cigarette dangling from his lips. Photographed by Bob Carlos Clark in White's kitchen at Harveys, the image captured White's 'fiery, gastro-punk energy'[54] and the chaos of running a restaurant. 'In the culinary world White [was] the equivalent of Kurt Cobain,'[55] the *enfant terrible* of the British restaurant scene. At thirty-two he was the youngest chef to be awarded three Michelin stars at thirty-eight he was burnt out from hard work, then he did the unthinkable, he gave back his three Michelin stars and quit cooking. 'I'd realised my dream. I'd spent 21 years of my life trying to do so,' said White, 'and the truth is when you get there it's really boring. Winning three stars is the most exciting journey of any chef's life. Retaining them is boring.'[56] The title of his autobiography, *White Slave. The Godfather of Modern Cooking* (2006), released in America under the title *The Devil in the Kitchen, Sex, Pain, Madness and the Making of a Great Chef*, (2008) with Clark's iconic photograph on the cover, details the long hours and hard labour entailed in becoming a chef. Suffice to say, the titles of the books say it all. The image below (Figure 9.5) taken by photographer John Stoddart sums it all up, White standing in front of an oil painting at his restaurant Harveys, arms outstretched, knees drawn together, a crucified Christ.

White Heat was a game changer, it created an image of a chef as a sexy beast, (albeit if it was stylized) rather than plump and jolly, or matronly like Julia Child. White looked like an artist with a fiery temper or a wild woodsman brandishing a meat cleaver. The British press lapped up the whole story, including photographing him feeding supermodels ortolans; suddenly every aspiring

Figure 9.5 British chef Marco Pierre White, photographed at his restaurant on 7 December 1988. (Photo by John Stoddart/Popperfoto via Getty Images.)

young male chef wanted to be like him. 'It was an image which would launch a new generation of chefs,'[57] including Jamie Oliver and White's protégé Gordon Ramsay, a former footballer, who was brash and prone to verbal abrasiveness like White.

Style became the single most important quality, next to personality and talent that would create the celebrity chef. This was distinct from the kind of bourgeois refinement and respectability that Escoffier and the best of his generation wanted to assert. 'In this tendency,' comments Jonathan Leer, 'which I call "re-chefisation," signs of professionalism and references to the iconography of the great past masters of the restaurant tradition are blended with more individualized expressions.'[58] The blending is key, since the celebrity chef is supposed to offer truths about cooking, things that are workable and consumable, delivered by an individual voice, as if only he or she could bring this to you.

Marco Pierre White was one of the most successful publicity campaigns in food history with exceptions such as Oliver and Nigella and were part of the Cool Britannia campaign launched in 1996 that rebranded British culture considered stuffy and conservative to one that was young, cosmopolitan and cool, especially in art, fashion, music and food. British fashion came back in vogue under Vivienne Westwood, Alexander McQueen and John Galliano, while British cooking with its perceived bland palette, became sexy and stylish under White, Oliver and Nigella turning cooking into a lifestyle brand that expanded cooking beyond the *bon vivants*.

Virtual cooking and culinary mastery

The celebrity chef of the new millennium had become comfortably absorbed into a media system that had become wide-eyed with the audience numbers and the profits generated from the gastronomy industry – well beyond restaurants themselves. Gwen Hyman comments on American fame culture and its effect on food celebrities: 'Our celebrity chefs are strange animals: manual labourers in Gucci shoes; Page Six denizens who wear uniforms.'[59] They are now a normal and expected component of television and streaming services:

> they are TV stars, scene-makers, gossip-page regulars with glamourous lives, famous home kitchens, and famous girlfriends. Chefs appear naked but for a blender on advertisements; on TV, they straddle motorcycles and savour fine Burgundies and taste fried-insect delicacies in remote corners of the world. The stratospheric incomes of the rich and famous chefs are published in the *Wall Street Journal;* their apartments are profiled in the *New York Times*, they hawk cookbooks, pots, dishes, and knives, represent charities, and draw crowds and groupies. This ain't your grandma's Galloping Gourmet. The restaurant world is the most exciting theatre around, these days, and chefs are the coolest.[60]

Most recently, Massimo Bottura of the three-Michelin star restaurant Osteria Francescana in Modena, Italy was part of the Gucci and *GQ* magazine *Performers Campaign* (2021), a five-part film series and advertising campaign that celebrates the achievement of five creative and influential men. Each film documents the inspiration that shaped each man's vision of their craft. Dressed in Gucci, Bottura travels by bicycle to Tetro Lirico where jazz musician Thelonious Monk played in concert in 1961, recounting how the pianist has influenced his cooking. Even naming a dish after the great impresario – seared cod with burnt herbs and dehydrated sea urchin served on a bed of green onion, celery and daikon noodles in a squid ink broth. The black-and-white plate mimics the keyboard of a piano. Japanese casualwear label Uniqlo featured an advertisement campaign with Momofuku's David Chang who believes that 'looking at a pair of Uniqlo jeans is like looking at a Momofuko menu' where a hoodie and a bowel of ramen noodles intersect.[61] Known for his wacky menu (kung pao pastrami) and idiosyncratic fashion styling, David Bowie of the Sichuan-fusion restaurant Mission Chinese Food in Manhattan and San Francisco was photographed by *GQ* magazine with bright green dyed hair wearing a pair of Vetements patchwork cropped jeans and a baggy red T-shirt. The internet has fused restaurants with fashion labels creating chefs as unlikely style icons as restaurants are using fashion to connect people with food vis-à-vis. Virtual cooking has exploded into the mainstream: blogging and YouTube have not only made cooking more domestic but has also provided mainstream celebrity chefs with new channels by which to assert their presence.

Despite fandom, the celebrity chef is still rooted in work, but there is every attempt made to separate the activities of cooking from its roots in servility. When it comes to upper-end restaurants, exclusive fare and fine wines, we are brought home to the extent to which the spectacle of food as is presented to us, and which most of us are unable to experience for ourselves, is one of class-production. This is one way the chef oversteps all the residual connotations of labour and class. The other is their capacity for alteration, and transformation. Hyman adds: 'Chefs are alchemists who transform the everyday act of eating into something greater, more transcendent, at once imbued with and productive of taste and class.' Knowing the historical class roots of cookery, the celebrity chef battles with hiding, displacing and transcending it in ways that the fashion designer need not. For although the couturier has become an haute couturier, the designer can be seen to design, to have ideas, and to relegate the base labour to others. Yet if the chef cannot demonstrate his or her skills then he or she is nothing but a dilettante, a gourmand, an observer, an interloper no better than a travel-writer or critic – so the social semantics go, at least.

So far, we have seen the way in which culinary celebrity has coincided with media culture, specifically television (now streaming and YouTube), and that it struggled between maintaining the prestige of the specialized space of the professional kitchen and that of the everyday kitchen, keeping prestige while maintaining accessibility. Through mass media, the celebrity chef evolved decisively from that of star of the élite, in the tradition of Carême and Escoffier, to an item in anyone's living room and kitchen, and thus an object of public consumption. In the assertion of this newly-formed and carefully curated persona, the celebrity chef found him or herself contending with the servile origins of the trade. As Marco Pierre White would repeatedly say in talks and interviews, 'service is service', echoing his earliest days of gruelling apprenticeship in the late 1970s and early 1980s. Despite the many efforts to slough off the connotations of servility, and thus of class, these met with only mixed success. For in the traditional cooking show, that is, based in the semi-didactic step-by-step, there is always the sense, no matter how remote, that the chef is performing a service for us, for it is we who have the free choice to tune in or not. The master–slave dialectic is very much in play, where the viewer is both master and slave, and the chef slave and master, depending on the vantage point.

The media space has now caused the number of people offering guides and tips on cookery to proliferate, as with guides and tips on almost everything. This, and the need to contend with the age-old association of cookery and service, has been addressed through the powerful assertion of expertise and authority, implying a level of mastery that is well beyond the bounds of service, and well outside the hands of hobbyists and enthusiastic YouTubers. In reference to this phenomenon, Trubek adds: 'There is acting with authority, there is being understood as an authority, and there is defining your culinary identity with authority.'[62] The trick is that the pre-eminent celebrity captures and commands all three. It is an authority that also embraces a traditional manliness, the exceptions only serving to reinforce the rule.

CONCLUSION

Most likely anyone visiting the Louvre in Paris for the first time will make it their first mission to see Leonardo da Vinci's *Mona Lisa*. There are even prompting arrows around the museum to direct prospective viewers in the right direction. The experience of the painting is usually a mixture of awe and disappointment, not only for its relatively small size but because it is so heavily obscured behind protective bullet-proof glass. You join the sizeable huddle of visitors most of whom raise their smartphones and partake in looking at themselves looking. In this blindness of spectacle, the casual visitors enact another blindness. For most have their backs to a painting which, for many different reasons, is a painting easily as great. That is Paulo Veronese's *Wedding Feast of Cana* (1563) (Figure 10.1) that relates the Biblical episode of the eponymous event where Jesus turns water into

Figure 10.1 Paolo Veronese (1528–1588), *Wedding Feast at Cana* (*Nozze di Canna*), oil painting, Dimensions: Height: 660 cm (21.6 ft); Width: 990 cm (32.5 ft). (Wikipedia Commons, Public Domain.)

wine. Originally hung in the San Giorgio Monastery situated on the island off the city of Venice, it was plundered in the French Revolutionary wars and in 1797 it was brought to the Louvre where at 660 cm x 990 cm (21.6 ft x 32.5 ft) is stands as the most expansive in the entire museum.

To say that the oil painting relates the Biblical story obscures the fact that the story is but an excuse for a visual panoply of feasting and fashion of untold proportions. It is a signal example of the primacy of Venetian painters to colour: the guests are lavishly dressed in brocaded silks and flowing satins, in the richest of hues. The bodies do not so much sit as intertwine and weave around the table. Any austerity that the original Biblical tale may have suggested is dispelled in an instant, while the figure of Jesus is eclipsed by his glamorous company, which include cameos by Emperor Charles V, Sokollu Mehmet Pasa (an Ottoman statesman), and Vittoria Colonna (a poetess). In the foreground are portraits of his contemporaries, Jacopo Bassano and Titian playing musical instruments for the company as they relish their meals. The colours and textures are such that they too incite appetite, desire. In short, the sacred apparatus is simply a support for a secular display of ornate and sumptuous clothing as they share bread and wine together. The relationship of enjoying appearances together while relishing food in ceremony and celebration, or just for the sake of doing so, is as old as civilization and sociability itself.

It would be difficult to imagine any reader of this book who has not dressed up for dinner, who has not, indeed, gone to dinner just for the sake of going out and dressing up. In the formal occasions, that are invariably public and co-substantial, it is hard to see which component comes first, the dressing up, the fashion, or the food. And then there is the comingling of the two in fashionable foods, fashionable restaurants, fashionable décor and so on.

Where this convergence is most visible and dynamic is with the rise of consumerism together with the individual, all the concomitant factors of modernism and modernization that necessitate a language and syntax of consumption, hence the fashion system as it emerged in the eighteenth century. It is an all too obvious fact that is sometimes hiding in plain sight that fashion's development from this time on occurs together – not quite in strict parallel but in distinct similarity – with the broadening of gastronomy, restaurants, travel, which in turn created a language of food that went beyond the local, the exceptional or the anecdotal. Food was given names of celebrities or of the chefs themselves who had become celebrities due to the intricate and yet immeasurable merging of taste and appearance, where taste was both physical and metaphysical. Cooks and dressmakers became chefs and haute couturiers.

Taste, such an important innate concept of the elite in the seventeenth and eighteenth century became increasingly marketable, transactable and manipulable. These chefs and haute couturiers vied with artists and among themselves for their creations to be on par with fine art, while the places where their creations appeared became something similar to temples, to whose importance was measured not just according to popularity and critical acclaim but also to the celebrities and people of note who patronized them.

Food and fashion, fashion and food are both an archaic and a very modern marriage. While contemporary debates and commentaries rage over sustainability, the relationship has special resonance. Sustainable fashion is a notion that, again, runs in (almost) lockstep with sustainable food. The current demands on the environment, be they in the scale of production and the devastating effects of intensive farming, are calling for a reorientation of skills, processes and outlooks. We can only look positively forward that this mounting conscience will be the new fashion in fashion and food. For albeit in different ways, clothing and food are key in bringing people together.

NOTES

Introduction

1 Joanne Finkelstein, *Dining Out*. A Sociology of Modern Manners, New York: New York University Press, 1989, 17.

2 Geczy and Karaminas, *Fashion Installation: Body, Space and Performance*, London and New York: Bloomsbury, 2019.

3 Roland, Barthes, 'Towards a Psychosociology of Contemporary Food Consumption', *Food and Culture*. A Reader, third edition, edited by Carole Counihan and Penny Van Esterik, New York and London: Routledge, 2013, 23–30.

4 Baldessare Castiglione, *The Courtier*, trans. Thomas Hobby, London, 1588, 10; https://www.bl.uk/collection-items/the-book-of-the-courtier-1588

5 See Geczy, *The Artificial Body in Fashion and Art: Marionettes, Models, and Mannequins*, London and New York: Bloomsbury, 2017, 91.

6 Valerie Taylor, 'Banquet plate and Renaissance culture: a day in the life', *Renaissance Studies*, Vol. 19, No. 5, November 205, 622.

7 Ibid., 622–623.

8 Ibid., 623.

9 Cit. Paul Metzner, *Crescendo of the Virtuoso: Spectacle, Skill, and Self-Promotion in the Age of Revolution*, Berkeley and London: University of California Press, 1998, 64.

10 Priscilla Parkhurst Ferguson, 'Writing of the Kitchen: Carême and the Invention of French Cuisine', *Gastronomica*, Vol. 3, No. 3, Summer 2003, 40.

11 Beatrice Fink, 'Enlightened Eating in Non-Fictional Context and the First Stirrings of Ecriture Gourmand', *Dalhousie French Studies*, Vol. 11, Fall/Winter, 1986, 9.

12 Metzner, *Crescendo of the Virtuoso*, 80.

13 Henry Notaker, *A History of Cookbooks: From Kitchen to Page over Seven Centuries*, Los Angeles: California University Press, 2017, 283.

Chapter 1

1 See Geczy, *Fashion and Orientalism: Dress, Textiles and Culture from the 17th to the 21st Century,* London and New York: Bloomsbury, 2013, 50–51.

2 Mergim Ozdamar, 'United Coffeedom: The History of London's Coffee Houses', *Londonr*, 14 February 2019, https://londnr.com/united-coffeedom-the-history-of-londons-coffee-houses/ (accessed 11 August 2019).

3 Brian Cowan, *The Social Life of Coffee: The Emergence of the British Coffeehouse*, New Haven and London: Yale University Press, 2005, 18.

4 Pierre Andrieu, *Fine Bouche. A History of the Restaurant in France*, trans. Arthur Hayward, London: Cassell and Co., 1956, 56.

5 Cit. Cowan, *The Social Life of Coffee,* 132.

6 Ibid.

7 Troy Bickham, 'Eating the Empire: Intersections of Food, Cookery and Imperialism in Eighteenth-Century Britain,' *Past and Present,* No. 198, February 2008, 74.

8 Ibid., 80.

9 Cowan, *The Social Life of Coffee*, 180.

10 Eugène Briffault in J. Weintraub, 'The Restaurants of Paris: A Translation from *Paris à table*,' *Gastranomica*, Vol. 14, No. 1, Spring 2014, 34.

11 , Jean Anthelme Brillat-Savarin, *Phyiologie du goût, øu meditations de gastronomie transcendante* (1825), Paris: Éditions Lagaran, 2015 (2 vols.), II: 165. See also Rebecca Spang, *The Invention of the Restaurant: Paris and Modern Gastronomic Culture*, Cambridge MA: Harvard University Press, 2000, 140.

12 Andrieu, *Fine Bouche*, 27.

13 Ibid., 43.

14 Cit. Rebecca Spang, 'L'Individu au menu: l'invention du restaurant à Paris au XVIIIe siècle', *Ethnologie française*, Vol. 44, No. 1, January 2014, 13.

15 Ibid., 14.

16 Metzner, *Crescendo of the Virtuoso,* 64.

17 Louis-Sébastien Mercier, *Le nouveau Paris*, Paris 1795, v. 4, 167–169.

18 Ibid., 169.

19 Mercier, *Le nouveau Paris*, v. 3, 25–26.

20 Ibid., 26–27.

21 Andrieu, *Fine Bouche*, 56.

22 Esther Aresty, *The Delectable Past: The Joys of Table, From Rome to the Renaissance, From Queen Elizabeth I to Mrs. Beeton*, London: Allen & Unwin, 1965, 27.

23 Abigail Dennis, 'From Apicius to Gastroporn: Form, Function, and Ideology in the History of Cookery Books', *Studies in Popular Culture*, Vol. 31, No. 1, Fall 2008, 3.

24 Ibid.

25 Metzner, *Crescendo of the Virtuoso,* 60.

26 Marie de Rabutin-Chantal, marquise de Sévigné, *Receuil des lettres de Madame de Sévigné*, 9 vols., Paris: Libraires Associés, 1806, Vol. 1, 159–160.

27 Metzner, *Crescendo of the Virtuoso,* 60.

28 Fink, 'Enlightened Eating', 12.

29 Menon aka François Marin, *Les Dons des Comus, ou l'art de la cuisine, réduit en pratique*, Paris: Chex la Veuve Pissot, revised edition, 1750, iii.

30 Menon aka François Marin, *Les Dons des Comus*, xix-xx. See also Metzner, *Crescendo of the Virtuoso,* 59.

31 Arnold Hauser, *The Social History of* Art, 4 vols., London and New York: Routledge (1962) 1999, vol. 3, 149.

32 S. K. Wertz, 'Taste and Food in Rousseau's *Julie, or the New Héloïse*', *The Journal of Aesthetic Education*, Vol. 47, No. 3, 2013, 25.

33 Ibid.

34 Ibid., 29.

35 Fink, 'Enlightened Eating', 15.

36 Wertz, 'Taste and Food in Rousseau's *Julie*, 30.

37 Ibid., 33.

38 'Les mets de la cuisine française portent au contraire les noms les plus illustres de la noblesse de France: à la Reine, à la Dauphine, à la Royale, à la d'Artois, à la Xavier, à la Condé, à la d'Orleans, à la Chartres, à la Penthièvre, à la Soubise, à la Conti, à la Montomorency, à la Villeroi, à la Pompadour, à la Mirepoix, à la Matignan, à la Montgolfier, à la Mazarine, à la Richelieu, à la Colbert. Je puis encoure ajouter a ces noms illustres et très français: à la Parisienne, à la Française, à la Lyonnaise, à la Bordelaise, à la Provençale, à la Périgord, à la Périgueux, à la Montpellier, à la Normande, à la Bretonne, à la Bourguignotte, à la Magnoinnaise, à la Saint-Denis, à la Saint-Cloud, à la Compiègne, et tant d'autres semblables qui échappent à mon mémoire.' Marc-Antoine Carême, *The Cuisiner parisienne: ou l'art de la cuisine française au dix-neuvième siècle* (1828), Paris: Ligaran, 2015, 13.

39 Priscilla Parkhurst Ferguson, 'A Cultural Field in the Making: Gastronomy in 19th-Century France,' *American Journal of Sociology*, Vol. 104, No. 3, November 1998, 612.

40 Ibid., 611.

41 Fink, 'Enlightened Eating', 17.

Chapter 2

1 Joseph Berchoux, *La gastronomie*, Paris: Giguet et Michaud, fourth edition, 1805, 7–8.

2 Ibid., 62.

3 Jane Levi, 'Charles Fourier Versus the Gastronomes: The Contested Ground of Early Nineteenth-Century Consumption and Taste', *Utopian Studies*, Vol. 26, No. 1, 2015, 43.

4 Parkhurst Ferguson, 'A Cultural Field in the Making', 627.

5 Levi, 'Charles Fourier', 46.

6 Octavio Paz, 'Eroticism and gastrosophy', trans. Sara Klaren, *Daedalus,* Vol. 117, No. 3, 1988, 235.

7 Levi, 'Charles Fourier', 49.

8 Fabrice Teulon, 'Le Voluptueux at le gourmand: économie de la jouissance chez la Mettrie et Brillat-Savarin', *A Quarterly Journal in Modern Literatures*, Vol. 52, No. 3, 178.

9 Ibid., 188–189.

10 Brillat-Savarin, *Phyiologie du goût,* I: 8.

11 Ibid., 9.

12 Judith Pike, 'Brillat-Savarin's Occidentalizing of the Orientalist Origins of French Cuisine', *The French Review*, Vol. 84, No. 5, April, 2011, 937.

13 Ibid., 10.

14 Luke Bouvier, 'A Taste for Words: Gastronomy and the Writing of Loss in Brillat-Savarin's "Physiologie du gout"', *Mosaic: An Interdisciplinary Critical Journal*, Vol. 38, No. 3, September 2005, 99.

15 Brillat-Savarin, *Phyiologie du goût*, 218.

16 Ibid., II: 186.

17 Ibid., 190.

18 Ibid., 191.

19 Ibid., 193.

20 Geczy and Karaminas, *Fashion Installation: Body, Space and Performance*, London and New York: Bloomsbury, 2019, 105.

21 Cit., Andrieu, *Fine Bouche,* 71.

22 Roland Barthes, *The Rustle of Language*, trans. Richard Howard, Berkeley and Los Angeles: University of California Press, 1989, 251.

23 Ibid.

24 Ibid., 251–252.

25 Philippe Dubois, 'Savarin/BalZac: Du gout des excitants sur l'écriture modern', *Nineteenth-Century* Studies, Vol. 33, No. 1/2, Fall–Winter 2004–2005, 77

26 Ibid., 87.

27 Honoré de Balzac, *Physiologie du marriage, ou meditations de philosophie éclectique*, Paris: Charpentier, 1840, 35.

28 Ibid., 47.

29 Ibid., 123.

30 Charles Baudelaire, 'le Peintre de la vie modern', in *Œuvres completes*, Paris: Gallimard Pléiade, 1954, 910.

31 Ibid., 911.

32 Hiroshi Matsumara, 'La physiologie, la table et la modernité: de Brillat-Savarin au *Père Goriot*', *L'Année balzacienne*, No. 19, 2018, 94.

33 Cit. ibid., 95.

34 Cit. ibid., 96.

35 Ibid., 99–100.

36 Parkhurst Ferguson, 'A Cultural Field in the Making', 628.

37 Barthes, *The Rustle of Language*, 261.

38 Bouvier, 'A Taste for Words', 110.

39 Roland Barthes, *The Fashion System* (1967), trans. Matthew Ward and Richard Howard, Berkeley and Los Angeles: University of California Press, (1983) 1990, 235.

40 Ibid., 235–236.

41 Ibid., 237.

42 Ibid., 238.

43 Ibid., 239.

44 Ibid., 240. See also Geczy, 'Modernity' in Geczy and Karaminas, *Fashion and Art*, Oxford and New York: Berg, 2012, 55–56.

45 Jean-Robert Pitte, *French Gastronomy: A History and Geography of a Passion* (1991), trans. Jody Gladding, New York: Columbia University Press, 2002, 28.

46 Mars, *A History of the French in London: Liberty, Equality,* Opportunity, London: University of London, 2013, 234.

47 Ibid.

48 Laurence Senelick, 'Consuming Passions: Eating and the Stage at the Fin de Siècle', *Gastronomica,* Vol. 5, No. 2, Spring 2005, 45.

49 Pierre Andrieu, *Fine Bouche. A History of the Restaurant in France*, trans. Arthur Hayward, London: Cassell and Co., 1956.

50 Ibid., 65.

51 Ibid.

52 Ibid., 123–124.

53 Kenneth James, *Escoffier: The King of Chefs*, London and New York: Bloomsbury, 2012, 149.

54 Luke Barr, *Ritz and Escoffier: the Hotelier, the Chef, and the Rise of the Leisure Class*, New York: Clarkson Potter, 2018, 79–81.

55 Senelick, 'Consuming Passions', 46

56 Ibid., 109.

57 Ibid., 109–110.

Chapter 3

1 Spang, *The Invention of the Restaurant*, 236.

2 John Merriman, 'Dynamite Club: The Anarchists,' https://www.youtube.com/watch?v=vVGsoiE3zQQ (accessed 16 April 2020).

3 John Merriman, *Ballad of the Anarchist Bandits: The Crime Spree that Gripped Belle Époque Paris*, New York: Nation Books, 2017, 34–46.

4 Ibid., 242.

5 Philippa Lewis, 'Stomaching the Salon: The Sense of Taste in *Le Tintamarre*'s "Boulangerie du Louvre" and Baudelaire's *Salon de 1846*', *Nineteenth-Century French Studies*, Vol. 42, No. 1/2, Fall/Winter 2013–2014, 36–37.

6 Ibid., 39.

7 Ibid., 47.

8 Margaret Visser, *The Rituals of Dinner: The Origins, Evolution, and Meaning of Table Manners*, Harmondsworth: Penguin, 1992, 202.

9 Parkhurst Ferguson, 'A Cultural Field in the Making', 606.

10 Annie Gray, '"Perfection and Economy": Continuity and Change in Élite Dining Practices, c. 1780–1880', in Alasdair Brooks ed., *The Importance of British Material Culture to Historical Archaeologies of the Nineteenth Century*, Lincoln: University of Nebraska Press, 2015, 228.

11 Ibid., 231.

12 Senelick, 'Consuming Passions', 44.

13 Visser, *The Rituals of Dinner*, 203.

14 Gray, in Alasdair Brooks ed., *The Importance of British Material Culture*, 229.

15 Bertram Gordon, *Second World War France from Defeat and Occupation to the Creation of Heritage*, Ithaca: Cornell University Press, 2018, 22.

16 Ibid., 25.

17 Cit. ibid., 26.

18 Marcel Proust, *Remembrance of Things Past*, trans. C. K. Scott Moncrieff and Terence Kilmartin, Harmondsworth: Penguin, (1983) 1987, II: 887.

19 Ibid., I: 717.

20 Spang, *The Invention of the Restaurant*, 222.

21 Merriman, *Ballad of the Anarchist Bandits,* 175.

22 This subheading takes from the unattributed title for Ritz that he was the 'king of hoteliers and the hotelier of kings', while Escoffier earned the same title except he was the 'king of chefs and the chef of kings'.

23 Barr, *Ritz and Escoffier*, 55.

24 James, *Escoffier*, 90.

25 Cit. ibid., 109.

26 Ibid., 111.

27 Culinary Institute of America, 'The Chef's Uniform', *Gastronomica*, Vol. 1, No. 1, Winter 2001, 90.

28 Ibid., 90–91.

29 Ibid., 89.

30 James, *Escoffier*, 113.

31 Ibid., 115.

32 Ibid., 119.

33 George Painter, *Marcel Proust* (1959), Harmondsworth: Penguin, 1990, 2 vols, II: 255.

34 Ibid., 284.

35 Proust, *Remembrance of Things Past*, II: 855.

36 Ibid., 855–856.

37 Ibid., 856.

38 Barr, *Ritz and Escoffier*, 103.

39 Proust, *Remembrance of Things Past*, I: 712–713.

40 Ibid., 713.

41 Ibid.

42 Ibid., 742.

43 Ibid., 743.

44 Ibid., 743.

45 Jean-Yves Tadié, *Proust*, Paris: Gallimard, 1996, 765.

46 Philippe Michel-Thiriet, *The Book of Proust,* trans. Jan Dalley, London: Chatto and Windus, 1989, 172.

47 Proust, *Remembrance of Things Past*, I: 867–868.

48 Ibid., 868.

49 Barr, *Ritz and Escoffier*, 61.

50 James, *Escoffier*, 129.

51 Cit. Alison Gernsheim, *Victorian and Edwardian Fashion: A Photographic* Survey, New York: Dover, 1963, 78.

52 Barr, *Ritz and Escoffier*, 106.

53 Ibid., 121.

54 Ibid., 33.

55 Ibid., 62.

56 Gabriela Cruz, *Grand Illusion: Phantasmagoria in Nineteenth-Century Paris,* Oxford and New York: Oxford University Press, 2020.

Chapter 4

1 Rachel Mathews, 'Contemporary Fashion Tastemakers: Starting Conversations that Matter', *Catwalk the Journal of Beauty and Style*, vol. 4, no.1, 2015, 52.

2 John Dewey, *Art as Experience*, New York: Perigreen, [1934] 1980, 36.

3 Ibid, 49.

4 Ibid.

5 See Pierre Bourdieu, *Distinction. A Social Critique on the Judgement of Taste*, translated by Richard Nice, London: Routledge, [1979], 2002.

6 Mary Douglas, 'Deciphering a Meal,' Daedalus, 1'01 (1), 1972, 62.

7 See Chapter 7 of this book for a comprehensive understanding of the Michelin star and the *Gault et Millau hat* as a restaurant quality rating system.

8 Wesley Monroe Shrum, *Fringe and Fortune. The Role of Critics in High and Popular Art*, Princeton, New Jersey: Princeton University Press, 1996, 41.

9 Stephen Mennell, *All Manners of Food: Eating and Taste in England and France from the Middle Ages to the Present*, Oxford: Basil Blackwell, 1985, 185, 267.

10 See also Metzner, *Crescendo of the Virtuoso,* 63.

11 Ibid., 67.

12 Carême, *The Cuisiner parisienne*, 16–17.

13 Parkhurst Ferguson, 'Writing of the Kitchen,' 43.

14 Darra Goldstein, 'Russia, Carême, and the Culinary Arts,' *The Slavonic and East European* Review, Vol. 73, No. 4, October 1995, 693–694.

15 Carême, *The Cuisiner parisienne*, 9.

16 Ibid., 14.

17 Parkhurst Ferguson, 'Writing of the Kitchen,' 46.

18 Metzner, *Crescendo of the Virtuoso*, 72.

19 Parkhurst Ferguson, 'Writing of the Kitchen,' 47.

20 Ibid., 50.

21 Metzner, *Crescendo of the Virtuoso*, 76–77.

22 Valerie Mars, *A History of the French in London: Liberty, Equality,* Opportunity, London: University of London, 2013, 225.

23 Diana de Marley, 'Worth. Father of Haute Couture', *The History of Haute Couture, 1850–1950,* New York: Holmes, 1980, xiii.

24 Chantal Trubert-Tollu, Françoise Tétart-Vittu, Jean-Marie Martin-Hattemberg and Fabrice Olivieri, *The House of Worth 1858–1954. The Birth of Couture*, London: Thames and Hudson, 2018, 34.

25 Aileen Robeiro, 'Painting: Refashioning Art – Some Visual Approaches to the Study of the History of Dress', Geczy, in Adam Geczy and Vicki Karaminas (eds) *Fashion and Art*, London: Bloomsbury, 2012, 175.

26 Therese Dolan, 'The Empress's' New Clothes. Fashion and Politics in Second Empire France', *Women's Art Journal,* Spring–Summer, 1994, Vol. 15, No. 1, 26.

27 Ibid.

28 Ibid, 156

29 M. Griffiths, 'Paris Dressmakers', *Strand Magazine* 48, vol, VIII, July to December 1894. http://www.avictorian.com/fashion_paris_dressmakers.html (accessed 4 January 2022).

30 Ibid

31 Ibid.

32 Ibid.

33 Ibid.

34 Amy de la Haye and Valerie Mendes, *The House of Worth: Portrait of an Archive*, London: V&A Publishing, 2014, 14.

35 Hippolyte Taine, *Notes on Paris*, translated by John Austin Stevens, New York: Henry Holt, 1875, 150

36 Ibid, 151.

37 Abigail Joseph, 'A Wizard of Silks and Tulle: Charles Worth and the Queer Origins of Couture', *Victorian Studies*, Volume 56, no. 2, 268.

38 Ibid.

39 Ibid.

40 Ibid.

41 Ibid.

42 Ibid, 269

43 Jess Berry, *House of Fashion. Haute Couture and the Modern Interior*, London and New York: Bloomsbury, 2018, 31.

44 Èmile Zola, *The Kill*, translated by with an introduction and notes by Brian Nelson, Oxford: Oxford University Press, 2004, 90.

45 Ibid.

46 Griffiths, 'Paris Dressmakers'.

47 Berry, *House of Fashion*, 30.

Chapter 5

1 Finkelstein, *Dining Out*, 26.

2 https://www.opentable.com.au/the-polo-bar

3 In 1890 Harry Gordon Selfridge the manager of Marshal Fields department store in Chicago opened the first tearoom in America. In 1908 he left his employment and migrated to England where he opened Selfridges department store.

4 Paul Freedman, 'Women and Restaurants in the Nineteenth-Century United States', *Journal of Social History*, vol. 48, no. 1, (2014), 1.

5 Ibid.

6 William R. Leach, 'Transformations in a Culture of Consumption: Women and Department Stores, 1890–1925', *The Journal of American History*, Sept.1984, Vol. 71, No.2, 327.

7 Ibid.

8 Ibid.

9 Mary Firestone, *Dayton's Department Store*, Arcadia: Chicago, 2007, 6

10 Viviene Stewart, 'The Way they Were: A Sydney Department Store in the 1920s', *Heritage Australia,* vol. 9, no. 4, Summer 1990, 23.

11 Ibid.,

12 Freedman, *Women and Restaurants*, 11.

13 Jan Whitaker, *The Department Store, History, Design, Display,* London: Thames and Hudson, 2011, 235.

14 Rosalind. H. Williams, *Dream-Worlds: Mass Consumption in Late Nineteenth Century France*, Berkley: University of California Press, 1982, 67.

15 Leach, Women and Department Stores, 327.

16 Susan Porter Benson, *Counter Culture: Saleswomen, Managers, and Customers in American Department Stores, 1890–1940*, Champaign: University of Illinois Press, 1987, 115.

17 Leach, 1984, 328.

18 Ibid.,

19 Whitaker, 235.

20 Natalie Smith, ‘Food and Fashion: Establishing a Critical Distance from the . . . Mess,’ in *Art and Food*, ed. Peter Stupples, Cambridge: Cambridge Scholars Press, 2014, 134.

21 Finkelstein, *Dining Out*, 150.

22 Ibid., 145.

23 Smith, Food and Fashion, 134.

24 Jan Whitaker, *Service and Style. How the American Department Store Fashioned the Middle Class,* New York: St Martins Press, 2006, 270.

25 Whitaker, *The Department Store,* 236.

26 Palmer Lunn Architects, *Kensington Roof Garden Pavilion Internal Strip Out Works, Design and Access Statement, Vol. 1*, June 2020, 7, https://www.rbkc.gov.uk/idoxWAM/doc/Other-2398023.pdf?extension=.pdf&id=2398023&location=Volume2&contentType=application/pdf&pageCount=1 (accessed 13 September 2021).

27 Whitaker, *The Department Store*, 230.

28 Rob Baker, ‘Mini Skirts, Soviet Spies and the Chelsea Palace – The Fascinating History of the Kings Road,’ The Telegraph, 16 April 2016, https://www.telegraph.co.uk/travel/destinations/europe/united-kingdom/england/london/articles/kings-road-london-history/ (accessed 28 September 2021).

29 Mary Quant, *My Autobiography*, London: Header and Hodder, 2012, 134.

30 Jess Berry, *House of Fashion. Haute Couture and the Modern Interior*, London: Bloomsbury, 2018, 154.

31 Lauren Sams, ‘Mary Quant. The Great Liberator’, *Financial Review*, 12 March 2021, https://www.afr.com/life-and-luxury/fashion-and-style/mary-quant-the-great-liberator-20210215-p572mm (accessed 24 September 2021).

32 Quant, *My Autobiography*, 123.

33 Barbara Hulanicki, *From A to Biba*, *The Autobiography of Barbara Hulanicki*, London: Hutchinson, 1983, 144.

34 Ibid. 137.

35 Ibid., 78.

36 Alwyn W. Turner, *The Biba Experience*, (London: Antique Collectors Club, 2007), 6.

37 http://www.bbc.co.uk/britishstylegenius/content/21800.shtml (accessed 4 September 2021).

38 Turner, *Biba Experience*,78.

39 https://kasiacharko.wordpress.com/2013/08/03/the-rainbow-room-big-biba/ (accessed 4 September 2021).

40 https://jannaludlow.co.uk/Biba/DT_Rainbow_Room_Roof_Gardens.html (accessed 4 September 2021).

41 Hulanicki, *From A to Biba*, 136.

42 Ibid., 137.

43 Ibid.,137.

44 Ibid.,137.

45 Barbara Hulanicki, in Turner, *Biba Experience*, 95.

46 Lauren Cochrane, 'Paris' Colette, the "Trendiest Store in the World" – Set to Close,' *The Guardian*, https://www.theguardian.com/fashion/2017/jul/12/pariss-colette-the-trendiest-store-in-the-world-set-to-close (accessed 1 October 2021).

47 'Kate Moss Regrets Nothing Tastes as Good as Skinny Feels,' *BBC News*, 14 September 2018, https://www.bbc.com/news/newsbeat-45522714 (accessed 1 October 2021).

48 https://london.doverstreetmarket.com/rose-bakery (accessed October 1 2021).

Chapter 6

1 Kate Fletcher, 'Slow Fashion' *Ecologist*, https://theecologist.org/2007/jun/01/slow-fashion (accessed 19 October 2021).

2 Ibid.

3 Anna Bates, 'Li Edelcoort', *ICON*, icon 064, October 2008, https://www.iconeye.com/icon-064-october-2008/li-edelkoort (accessed 18 October 2021).

4 Li Edelcoort, 'On Why doing Less is More,' Time Sensitive, Episode 29, https://timesensitive.fm/episode/trend-forecaster-li-edelkoort-doing-less-is-more/ (accessed 19 October 2021).

5 See William McDonough and Michael Braungart, *Cradle to Cradle: Remaking the Way We Make Things*, New York: North Point Press, 2002.

6 Anne Teresia Wanders, *Slow Fashion*, Niggli: Berlin, 2009, 101.

7 Max Berlinger, 'How Erewhon Became L.A's Hottest Hangout', *The New York Times*, 17 February 2021, https://www.nytimes.com/2021/02/17/style/erewhon-los-angeles-health-food.html (accessed 10 December 2021).

8 Ibid.

9 William Shurtleff and Akiko Aoyagi, *History of Erwhon-Natural Foods Pioneer in the United States (1966–2011), An Annotated Bibliography and Sourcebook*, California: Soyinfo Centre, 2011, 25.

10 Warren J. Balasco. *Appetite for Change. How the Counterculture Took on the Food Industry*, Ithaca: Cornel Uni. Press, 2007 [1989, 1993], x.

11 Jonathan Kauffman, *Hippie Food. How the Back-to-Landers, Longhairs and Revolutionaries changed the way we Eat*, New York: William Morrow, 2018.

12 David Bell and Gill Valentine, *Consuming Geographies. We are Where We Eat*, London: Routledge, 1997, 3.

13 Dylan Clark, 'The Raw and the Rotten: Punk Cuisine', in *Food and Culture. A Reader*, Third Edition, edited by, Carole Counihan and Penny Van Esterik, London and New York: Routledge, 2013, 232.

14 Ibid.

15 Clarkson Potter, 'Chef Alice Waters Memoir Tells Tales of Her Youth and Loves,' *The Salt Lake Tribune*, 9 September 2017, https://www.sltrib.com/artsliving/2017/09/08/chef-alice-waters-memoir-tells-tales-of-her-youth-and-loves/ (accessed 10 December 2021).

16 Vanessa Friedman, 'Let them Wear Cake,' *The New York Times*, 21 February 2020, https://www.nytimes.com/2020/02/21/style/milan-fashion-week-prada-moschino.html (accessed 10 December 2021).

17 Patrizia Calefato, *Fashion as Cultural Translation. Signs, Images, Narratives*, London: Anthem Press, 2021, 77.

18 Ibid.

19 Pierre Bourdieu, 'Distinction: A Social Critique of the Judgement of Taste', 31–39.

20 Hannah Marriott, 'Fast Food Fashion: Moschino Accused of "Glorifying" McDonalds Logo', *The Guardian*, https://www.theguardian.com/fashion/2014/jul/13/moschino-glorifying-mcdonalds-logo-fashion, 13 July 2014 (accessed 26 December 2021).

21 Lizzie Widdicombe, 'Barbie Boy. How Jeremy Scott Remade Moschino for the Instagram Era', *The New Yorker*, 14 March 2016, https://www.newyorker.com/magazine/2016/03/21/jeremy-scotts-new-moschino (accessed 20 December 2021.

22 https://fashion.mam-e.it/moschino/ (accessed 15 December 2021.

23 Sarah Tinoco, 'Jeremy Scott the Peoples Designer, Vlad Yudin (2015)', Review, *Critical Studies in Men's Fashion*, Vol. 3, Number 1, 2016, 51-54.

24 Holly Brubach, 'Franco Moschino. Talk of the Town', *The New Yorker*, 9 January 1989, https://www.newyorker.com/magazine/1989/01/09/franco-moschino (accessed 15 December 2021.

25 Justine Picardie, *Coco Chanel: The Legend and the Life*, London: Harper Collins, 2010, 307.

26 Tierney McAfee and Liz McNeil, 'How Jackie Kennedy Invented Camelot Just One Week after JFK's Assassination', *People*, 22 November 2017, https://people.com/politics/jackie-kennedy-invented-camelot-jfk-assassination/ (accessed 10 July 2020).

27 Xan Brooks, 'Jackie: Behind the Creation of JFK, America's Once and Future King', *The Guardian*, 7 January 2017, https://www.theguardian.com/film/2017/jan/07/jackie-natalie-portman-behind-the-creation-of-jfk-camelot-movies (accessed 10 July 2020).

28 Roland Barthes, 'The Face of Garbo,' *Mythologies*, trans. Richard Howard, London: Paladin, 1979, 56.

29 Ibid.

30 Noah Raymon, 'How a McDonalds Restaurant Spawned the Slow Food Movement', *Time*, 10 December 2014, https://time.com/3626290/mcdonalds-slow-food/ (accessed 21 December 2021).

31 Mary Davis Suro, 'Romans Protest McDonalds', *The New York Times*, 5 May 1986, https://www.nytimes.com/1986/05/05/style/romans-protest-mcdonald-s.html (accessed 15 December 2021).

32 Roland Barthes, 'Steak and Chips,' *Mythologies*, London: Penguin, 1973, 70.

33 Arie Sover and Orna Ben-Meir, 'Humour Food and Fashion: The Use of Humour and Food in Fashion Shows', *European Journal of Humor Research*, 5, (1), 81.

34 Ibid.

35 Ibid.

36 John F. Mariani, *How Italian Food Conquered the World*, New York: Palgrave McMillan, 2011.

37 Jack Goody, 'Industrial Food: Towards the Development of a World Cuisine', edited by Carole Counihan and Penny Van Esterik, *Food and Culture. A Reader*, Third Edition, New York and London: Routledge, 2013, 72.

38 Ibid, 6.

39 Alberto Capati and Massimo Montanari, *Italian Cuisine. A Cultural History*, translated by Aine O'Healy, New York: Columbia University Press, 2003, 278.

40 Masimo Montanari, *Italian Identity on the Kitchen, or Food and the Nation*, translated by Beth Archer Brombert, New York: Columbia University Press, 2013, 43.

41 Sneja Gunew, *Framing Marginality Multicultural Literary Studies*, Melbourne: Melbourne University Press, 1994, 234.

42 Simona Segre Reinach, 'The Meaning of Made in Italy in Fashion', *Craft + Design Enquiry*, edited by Kay Lawrence, Canberra: ANU Press, 2015, 137.

43 Ibid, 144.

44 Ibid, 136.

45 Arie Sover and Orna Ben-Meir, 'Humour Food and Fashion', 82.

46 https://www.cameramoda.it/en/associazione/news/920/ (accessed 25 December 2021).

47 Erin Schwartz, 'Everything you see Moschino Owes to Spaghetti,' https://www.ssense.com/en-us/editorial/fashion/everything-you-see-moschino-owes-to-spaghetti (accessed 25 December 2021.

48 Laird Borrelli-Persson, Moschino, Spring 1994 Ready-to-Wear, Vogue Runway, 3 May 2019, https://www.vogue.com/fashion-shows/spring-1994-ready-to-wear/moschino (accessed 26 December 2021.

Chapter 7

1 Kristen Andersen, 'How I would Fix Fashion. 5 Industry Insiders tell us', Vogue Runway, September 2016, https://www.vogue.com/article/fashion-calendar-problems-spring-2017-shows (accessed 7 June 2021).

2 Ibid.

3 Toby Slade and M. Angela Jensen, 'Letter from the Editors', *Fashion Theory the Journal of Dress, Body and Culture*, Special issue on Decoloniality and Fashion, Volume 24, Issue 6, 2020, 810.

4 Paolo Velonté, 'The Thin Ideal and the Practice of Fashion', *Journal of Consumer Culture*, 2019, Vol. 19 (2), 252.

5 Ibid.

6 Ibid.

7 Suzanne Daly and Ross G. Forman 'Cooking Culture: Situating Food and Drink in the Nineteenth Century', *Victorian Literature and Culture*, 2008, vol. 36, no.2, 365.

8 Laura Frazer, 'The Inner Corset. A Brief History of Fat', *The Fat Studies Reader*, Esther D. Rothblum and Sondra Solovay, eds., New York: New York University Press, 2009, 12

9 Ibid, 13.

10 Emma Griffin, 'Diet, Hunger and Living Standards During the British Industrial Revolution, *Past and Present*, 2028, Volume 239, issue 1, 71–111.

11 Ibid.

12 Paul Clayton and Judith Rowbotham, 'How the Mid Victorians worked Ate and Died', *International Journal of Environmental Research and Public Health*, 2009, issue 6, 1235–1254.

13 Thorstein Veblen, *The Theory of the Leisure Class*, trans. Robert Hullot-Kentor, New York: Random House, 2001,127.

14 Pricilla Pankhurst Ferguson, *Accounting for Taste. The Triumph of French Cuisine*', Chicago and London, The University of Chicago Press, 2006, 153.

15 Pierre Bourdieu, *Distinction: A Social Critique of the Judgement of Taste*, London: Routledge and Kegan Paul, 1986.

16 Suzanne Daly and Ross G. Forman, 'Cooking Culture: Situating Food and Drink in the Nineteenth Century', *Victorian Literature and Culture*,2008, vol. 36, no.2, 367.

17 Marianne Thesander, *The Feminine Ideal*, London: Reaction, 1997, 85.

18 Ibid.

19 Ibid., 179.

20 Jennifer Harris, Sarah Hyde and Greg Smith, *1966 and All That. Design and the Consumer in Britain 1960–1969*, London: Trefoil Publications, 1986, 130.

21 Barbara Hulanicki, *From A to Biba, The Autobiography of Barbara Hulanicki*, London: Hutchinson, 1983, 98.

22 Pamela Church Gibson, 'The Deification of the Dolly Bird: Selling Swinging London, Fuelling Feminism', *Journal for the Study of British Cultures*, Special Issue, Fashioning Society, volume 14, no. 2, 2007, 100.

23 Elizabeth Wilson, *Adorned in Dreams. Fashion and Modernity*, London: I.B Tauris, 1985, 148.

24 Visser, *The Rituals of Dinner*, 204.

25 Wendell Steavensen, 'The Rise and Fall of French Cuisine', *The Guardian*, 16 July 2019, https://www.theguardian.com/food/2019/jul/16/the-rise-and-fall-of-french-cuisine (accessed June 2021).

26 Ibid.

27 Roland Barthes, 'Towards a Psychosociology of Contemporary Food Consumption', *Food and Culture*. A Reader, third edition, edited by Carole Counihan and Penny Van Esterik, New York and London: Routledge, 2013, 24.

28 Ibid.

29 Rachel McCormack, 'Caviar, Explained: Where to Source the Very Best and How to Serve it', *Robb Report*, 16 December 2019, https://robbreport.com/food-drink/dining/what-is-caviar-where-to-source-the-very-best-and-how-to-serve-it-2884402/ (accessed 17 June 2021).

30 Mary Rizzo, 'Embodying Withdrawal. Abjection and the Popularity of Heroin Chic', *Michigan Feminist Studies*, Special issue, Desire, Vol. 15, 2001, https://quod.lib.umich.edu/cgi/t/text/text-idx?cc=mfsfront;c=mfs;c=mfsfront;idno=ark5583.0015.004;g=mfsg;rgn=main;view=text;xc=1 (accessed 16 June 2020).

31 Rebecca Arnold, 'Heroin Chic', *Fashion Theory*, Volume 3, issue 3, 1999, 280.

32 Susan Bordo, 'Not Just "a White Girl's Thing": The Changing Face of Food and Body Image Problems', in *Food and Culture, A Reader*, edited by Carole Counihan and Penny Van Esterik, third edition, New York and London: Routledge, 2013, 267.

33 Joanne Entwistle and Elizabeth Wissinger, *Fashioning Models: Image, Text and Industry*, London and New York: Berg, 2012, 1.

34 Kirstie Clements, 'The Truth about Size Zero', *The Guardian*, 5 July 2013, 5, https://www.theguardian.com/fashion/2013/jul/05/vogue-truth-size-zero-kirstie-clements (accessed 20 June 2020).

35 Lizzie Deardan, 'France Bans Unhealthy thin Models with Law Requiring Doctor's Certificate', *Independent*, 6 May 2017, https://www.independent.co.uk/news/world/europe/france-bans-unhealthily-thin-model-bmi-doctors-certificate-photoshopped-images-a7721211.html (accessed 20 June 2020).

36 'Skinny Model Furor: Not All Fashion's Fault, Say Designers, Editors', *Women's Wear Daily*, Vol. 193, Issue 21, 30 January, 2007, http://web.a.ebscohost.com.ezproxy1.library.usyd.edu.au/bsi/detail/detail?vid=0&sid=743b296d-e3dd-4361-b3af-01592c40fd12%40sdc-v-sessmgr01&bdata=JnNpdGU9YnNpLWxpdmU%3d#AN=23978126&db=bsu (accessed 25 March 2020).

37 Ibid.

38 Ibid.

39 Joanne Entwistle and Don Slater, 'Models as Brands: Critical Thinking of Bodies and Images', *Fashioning Models: Image, Text and Industry*, edited by Joanne Entwistle and Elizabeth Wissinger, London and New York: Berg, 2012, 15–33.

40 Karl Largerfeld, https://getrawenergy.co/karl-lagerfeld-eats/#.YLpMCV6xUl4 (accessed 3 June 2021).

41 Kiki Meola, 'Diet Secrets: Beyonce Reveals the Super strict Diet she Started at 218 Pounds Post Twins: I'm Hungry', *US Weekly*, 17 April 2019, https://www.usmagazine.com/celebrity-body/news/beyonces-coachella-diet-after-twins-no-sugar-carbs-dairy-meat/ (accessed 18 June 2020).

42 Christine Muhlke, 'Paris is Losing it,' *The New York Times Magazine*, 1 May 2005, https://www.nytimes.com/2005/05/01/magazine/paris-is-losing-it.html (accessed 1 June 2021).

43 Ibid.

44 Ta-Nahisi Coats, 'The Largerfeld Diet', *The Atlantic*, 7 March 2012, https://www.theatlantic.com/health/archive/2012/03/the-lagerfeld-diet/254018/ (accessed 4 June 2021).

45 Jessica Booth, 'Karl Largerfeld used to Drink 10 Diet Cokes a Day and Called Toast a Luxury', *Insider*, 20 February 2019, https://www.insider.com/karl-lagerfeld-food-nutrition-diet-coke-2019–2 (accessed 4 June 2021).

46 Christa de Souza, 'How Diet Coke became Fashions Favourite Fizz', *The Guardian*, June 2013, https://www.theguardian.com/fashion/2013/jan/12/diet-coke-fashion-favourite-fizz (accessed 5 June 2021).

47 Ibid.

48 Ibid.

49 Mark Sweney, 'Diet Coke Swaps Duffy for Puppets', *The Guardian*, 11 March 2010, https://www.theguardian.com/media/2010/mar/11/diet-coke-duffy-puppets (accessed 4 June 2021).

50 Kim Toffoletti, *Cyborgs, Feminism, Popular Culture and Barbie the Posthuman Dolls*, London: I.B Tauris, 2007, 60.

51 See Adam Geczy, *The Artificial Body in Fashion and Art:* 91ff., and Caroline Evans, 'The Ontology of the Fashion Model', *AA Files*, Vol. 63, 2011, 56–69; Entwistle and Wissinger, *Fashioning Models*, 3–4.

52 Ibid.

53 Sarah Gilligan, 'Heaving Cleavages and Fantastic Frock Coats: Gender Fluidity, Celebrity and Tactile Transmediality in Contemporary Costume Cinema', *Film, Fashion and Consumption*, volume 1, number 1, 2012, 25.

54 Josie All Chin, 'Case Study: Diet Coke and its Creative Designers', *Marketing Week*, 6 March 2013, https://www.marketingweek.com/case-study-diet-coke-and-its-creative-designers/ (accessed 6 June 2021).

55 Ibid.

Chapter 8

1 See 'The Merry and Scandalous Court of King Charles II', in Adam Geczy and Vicki Karaminas, *Libertine Fashion: Sexual Rebellion, Freedom and Style*, London: Bloomsbury, 2020, 37–60.

2 Thomas de Costa Kauffman, *Arcimboldo: Visual Jokes, Natural History, and Still-Life Painting*, Chicago: University of Chicago Press, 2010, 341.

3 Meryle Secrest, *Elsa Schiaparelli: A Biography*, New York: Knopf, 2014, 145.

4 Nancy Frazier, 'Salvador Dali's Lobsters: Feast, Phobia and Freudian Slip,' *Gastronomica. The Journal of Food and Culture*, Vol. 9, No. 4 (Fall 2009), 16.

5 Salvador Dali, *The Secret Life of Dali*, New York: Dial Press, 1942, 271.

6 Ibid, 17.

7 See 'From Harlem to Pigale: Josephine Baker,' in Adam Geczy and Vicki Karaminas, *Libertine Fashion: Sexual Rebellion, Freedom and Style*, London: Bloomsbury, 2020, 121–148.

8 'Elsa Schiaparelli: Fashion Visionary', Legacy.com, 13 November 2013, https://www.legacy.com/news/elsa-schiaparelli-fashion-visionary/ (accessed 18 May 2020).

9 Valerie Steele, *Paris Fashion. A Cultural History*, London: Bloomsbury, [1988,1998] 2017, 220.

10 Claire Eldred, 'Encounters and Exchanges with Elsa Schiaparelli's Lobster Dress: An Object Biography', *Fashion and Contemporaneity. Realms of the Visible*, edited by Laura Petican, Boston: Brill, 2019, 81.

11 Ibid.

12 Ibid., 78

13 Mark Holgate,'Schiapparelli Spring 2017 Couture', Vogue Runway, 23 January 2017, https://www.vogue.com/fashion-shows/spring-2017-couture/schiaparelli (accessed 17 May 2021).

14 Ibid.

15 Salvador Dali, *The Secret Life of Salvador Dali*, London: Dover Fine Art, 1993, 1.

16 Salvador Dali, *Les Dîners de Gala*, New York: Taschen, 2016.

17 '*Dizzy Dali Dinner*', 1941 News reel. YouTube, 14 September 2006, https://www.youtube.com/watch?v=vg6i4E0Woak (accessed 20 May 2021).

18 Salvador Dali, *Dalí*, New York: Bignou Gallery, 1945, *n,p.*

19 Julia Pine, 'Breaking Dalinian Bread: On Consuming the Anthropomorphic, Performative, Ferocious, and Eucaristic Loaves of Salvador Dali,' *Invisible Culture: An Electronic Journal for Visual Culture*, Issue 14: Aesthetics and Eaters – Food and the Arts, Winter, 2000, www.rochester.edu/in_visible_culture/Issue_14/pdf/jpine.pdf (accessed 20 May 2021).

20 St Regis Magazine, in Dalí in New York, *Dalí Universe*, 20 November 2017 https://www.thedaliuniverse.com/en/news-dali-new-york (accessed 19 May 2021).

21 Rachel Fried, 'Tommy Cash and Maison Margiela drop Haute Couture Carbs', *CR Fashion Book*, 21 March 2021, https://www.crfashionbook.com/fashion/a35903084/tommy-cash-maison-margiela-haute-couture-carbs/ (accessed 30 May 2021).

22 Ibid.

23 Mary Ellen Shoup, 'Homebaking Continues in 2021 Giving rise to Comfort and Wellness Trends,' *Food Navigator-usa.com*, 22 March 2021, https://www.foodnavigator-usa.com/Article/2021/03/22/Home-baking-continues-in-2021-giving-rise-to-comfort-and-wellness-trends (accessed 30 May 2021).

24 Thom Wait, 'Tommy Cash Drop Maison Margiela Noodles and More Bizzare Merch', *Dazed* magazine, 18 March 2021, https://www.dazeddigital.com/fashion/article/52253/1/tommy-cash-drops-maison-margiela-noodles-bread-slippers-more-bizarre-merch (accessed 21 May 2021).

25 Liana Statetsen, 'Tommy Cash and Maison Magiela Collaborate on the Weirdest Merch Yet,' *Vogue*, 18 March 2021, https://www.vogue.com/article/tommy-cash-maison-margiela-bread-slippers-collaboration (accessed 30 May 2021).

26 Arron Bobrow-Strain, *White Bread. A Social History of the Store-Bought Loaf*, Beacon Press: Boston 2012, 165.

27 Ibid., ix.

28 Jeffrey Steingarten, 'Breading Bread', in Taylor Atrim, ed, *Food in Vogue*, New York: Abrams, 2017,188.

29 Claire O'Neil, 'Food Photo Friday: Gaga for Food Fashion,' *The Picture Show*, 3 December 2010, https://www.npr.org/sections/pictureshow/2010/12/03/131760743/fashionfood (accessed 31 May 2021).

30 Christina Everette, 'In the Flesh Lady Gaga Dons Red Meat on Cover of Hommes Japan,' *Daily News*, September 7, 2010, https://www.nydailynews.com/entertainment/gossip/flesh-lady-gaga-dons-raw-meat-cover-vogue-hommes-japan-article-1.438875 (accessed 29 May 2021).

31 PETA is an acronym for People for the Ethical Treatment of Animals, it is the largest animal rights organization in the world with more that 6.5 million members and supporters. PETA has been a vocal advocate again the use of animal products in the fashion industry.

32 Ibid.

33 Op.cit.

34 Joanne McCabe, 'Gaga Defend Homosexuals with Prime Rib Speech,' 21 September 2010, https://metro.co.uk/2010/09/21/lady-gaga-defends-american-homosexuals-with-prime-rib-speech-519254/ (accessed 29 May 2021).

35 The Meat of the Matter: A Neo-Aristotelian Analysis of Lady Gaga's 'The Prime Rib of America' Address, https://alicieinwonderland.wordpress.com/2011/09/22/the-meat-of-the-matter-a-neo-aristotelian-analysis-of-lady-gagas-the-prime-rib-of-america-address/ (accessed 29 May 2021).

36 Nick Riley, 'U2 Bono Debuts Star-Studded "Beautiful Day" Cover and Shares powerful Speech' *NME News*, 8 June 2020, https://www.nme.com/en_au/news/music/u2-bono-debuts-star-studded-beautiful-day-cover-and-shares-powerful-speech-2684185 (accessed 30 May 2021).

37 Quentin Bell, 'The Incorrigible Habit: A Study of Dress Reform in England,' *History Today*, Vol. 1, Issue 3, 1951, https://www.historytoday.com/archive/incorrigible-habit-study-dress-reform-england (accessed 29 May 2021).

38 Monica Titton, 'Afterthought. Fashion, Feminism and Radical Protest,' *Fashion Theory*, *The Journal of Dress, Body and Culture*, Special Issue on Fashion as Politics: Dressing Dissent, Volume 23, Issue 6, 2019, 752.

39 Jennifer McLerran, 'Disciplined Subjects and Docile Bodies in the work of Contemporary Artist Jana Sterbak', *Feminist Studies*, (Autumn, 1988), Vol. 24, No. 3, 539.

40 Claude Levi-Strauss, *The Raw and the Cooked*, 1.

41 Lady Gaga, *Lady Gaga's Portland Speech*, YouTube, https://www.youtube.com/watch?v=MoqOvFJ5–0c (accessed 30 May 2020).

42 Ibid.

Chapter 9

1 Claude Lévi-Strauss, *The Raw and The Cooked*, 164.

2 Norbert Elias, *The Civilizing Process*.

3 Stephen Mennell, 'On the Civilizing of Appetite', *Theory, Culture and Society*, vol. 4, no.2 (1987), 373–403.

4 E. Smith, *The Compleat Housewife, or, Accomplished Gentlewoman's Companion*, London: J. and J. Pemberton, 1739, 3.

5 Paul Freedman, 'Women and Restaurants in the Nineteenth-Century United States', *Journal of Social History*, Fall, 2014, Vol. 48, No.1, 11.

6 Ibid.

7 Roland Barthes, 'Ornamental Cookery,' *Mythologies*, London: Jonathan Cape, 1972, 85–86.

8 Ibid.

9 Taylor Antrim, *Food in Vogue*, Abrams: New York, 2017, 13.

10 Barthes, 'Ornamental Cookery', 86.

11 Ibid.

12 Ibid.

13 Shweta Ghandi, 'Christian Dior's 1972 Cookbook will Inspire your Quarantine Cooking,' 3 June 2020, https://settingmind.com/christian-dior-1972-cookbook-quarantine-cooking/, (accessed 16 October 2021).

14 Tim Blanks, 'The Last Temptation of Christian', *The New York Times Magazine*, 18 August 2002, https://www.nytimes.com/2002/08/18/magazine/the-last-temptation-of-christian.html (accessed 17 October 2021).

15 Kristin Bateman, 'Dom Pérignon and Dandelion Greens: Remembering Christian Dior's Cookbook', *Vogue*, 8 July 2017, https://www.vogue.com/article/dior-cookbook-recipes-plaza-athenee-paris (accessed 16 October 2021).

16 Ibid.

17 Hannah Walhout, 'Zac Posen on the Intersection of Food and Fashion and his new Cookbook,' *Food and Wine*, https://www.foodandwine.com/news/zac-posen-new-cookbook (accessed 15 October 2021).

18 Rachel Low, *The History of British Film 1929—1939*, vol. 5, London: Routledge, 1979, 91.

19 For a comprehensive study of Colette and libertinage and dress practices see, Geczy, Adam and Vicki Karaminas, *Libertine Fashion: Sexual Rebellion, Freedom and Style*, London: Bloomsbury, 2020.

20 Phil Lyon, *Good Food and Hard Times: Ambrose Heath's Contribution to British Food Culture in the 1930s and the War Years*, https://www.brepolsonline.net/doi/epdf/10.1484/J.FOOD.5.108964 (accessed 13 October 2013).

21 Edward Larocquetinker, 'New Editions, Fine and Otherwise, *The New York Times Book Review*, March 27 1938, https://timesmachine.nytimes.com/timesmachine/1938/03/27/99538396.html?auth=login-smartlock&pageNumber=97 (accessed 12 October 2020).

22 Lyon, *Good Food and Hard Times*.

23 Jeremy Lee, 'Elizabeth David: All that is Good in British Cookery,' *The Guardian*, 10 August 2018, https://www.theguardian.com/food/2018/aug/10/jeremy-lee-cooks-cook-elizabeth-david (accessed 8 October 2021).

24 Mars, *A History of the French in London*, 239–240.

25 David Howes and Marc Lalande, 'The History of Sensibilities: Of the Standard of Taste in Mid-Eighteenth-Century England and the Circulation of Smells in Post-Revolutionary France,' *Dialectical Anthropology*, Vol. 16, No. 2, 1991, 127.

26 Melissa Passanen, 'Enough Saffron to Cover a Sixpence. The Challenge and Pleasures of Elizabeth David,' *The Art of Eating*, no. 61, 2003, https://artofeating.com/the-pleasures-and-challenge-of-elizabeth-david/ (accessed 8 October 2021).

27 Ibid.

28 Dennis, 'From Apicius to Gastroporn,' 10.

29 Ibid.

30 Amy Trubek, *How Americans Cook Today*, Los Angeles: University of California Press, 2017, 147.

31 Nora Ephron, 'Serial Manogamy . My Cookbook Crushes,' *The New Yorker*, 5 February 2006, https://www.newyorker.com/magazine/2006/02/13/serial-monogamy?utm_source=nl&utm_brand=tny&utm_mailing=TNY_SundayArchive_090521&utm_campaign=aud-dev&utm_medium=email&bxid=5ce4489405e94e38df022314&cndid=57338746&hasha=656be797c5db6a1e93f627913eda1202&hashb=deccbcc38ede43dc0362561f1b7d58220bc6835b&hashc=67555da96b9bbf4474ed422a67c03d47bdb77e2bed30a519f3ff4c38baac94a2&esrc=Archive_NL_page&mbid=mbid%3DCRMNYR012019&utm_term=TNY_SundayArchive (accessed 5 October 2021).

32 Ibid.

33 Cynthia Zaryn, 'Portrait of a marriage Julia Child Captured in Paul Child's Shimmering Photographs,' *The New Yorker*, 2 December 2017, https://www.newyorker.com/culture/photo-booth/portrait-of-a-marriage-julia-child-captured-in-paul-childs-shimmering-photographs (accessed 6 October 2021).

34 David Marshall, *Celebrity and Power: Fame in Contemporary Culture*, Minneapolis: Minnesota University Press, 1997, 121

35 Dennis, 'From Apicius to Gastroporn,' 11.

36 Ibid.

37 Andrew Chan, '"La grand bouffe": Cooking Shows as Pornography,' in Dara Goldstein ed., *The Gastronomica Reader*, Los Angeles: California University Press, 2010, 139.

38 Ibid.

39 Gilly Smith, *Taste and the TV Chef. How Storytelling Can Save the Planet*, Bristol: Intellect, 2020, 77.

40 Nicola Perullo, *Taste as Experience: The Philosophy and Aesthetics of Food*, New York: Columbia University Press, 2016, 51.

41 Ibid., 52.

42 Chan, '"La grand bouffe",' 143.

43 Ibid.

44 Smith, Taste and the TV Chef, xv.

45 Jonathan, 'What's cooking, man? Masculinity in European cooking shows after "The Naked Chef",' *Feminist Review*, No. 114, 2016, 77.

46 Ibid.

47 Trubek, *How Americans Cook Today*, 151.

48 Ibid.

49 Chan, '"La grand bouffe",' 143.

50 Smith, *Taste and the TV Chef*, 57.

51 Ibid.

52 Ibid., 58.

53 Stephen Gundle, *Glamour. A History*, Oxford: Oxford University Press, 2008, 10.

54 Smith, *Taste and the TV Chef*, 7.

55 'The Rise of the Bad Boy Chef', *Combatant Gentlemen*, 22 November 2015, https://combatgent.com/blogs/unhemmed/bad-boy-chefs (accessed 10 October 2021).

56 Dean Carroll, 'Marco Pierre White – from "enfant terrible" to International Businessman,' *Gulf Business*, 11 June 2016, https://gulfbusiness.com/marco-pierre-white-enfant-terrible-international-businessman/ (accessed 11 October 2021).

57 Smith, *Taste and the TV Chef*, 7.

58 Leer, 'What's cooking, man?' 77.

59 Gwen Hyman, 'The Taste of Fame: Chefs, Diners, Celebrity, Class,' *Gastronomica*, Vol. 8, no. 3, Summer 2008, 43.

60 Ibid., 46.

61 Jacob Gallaghar, 'Goodbye Croc, Hello Gucci: How chefs became Style Icons,' *The Wall Street Journal*, https://www.wsj.com/articles/the-rise-of-the-sexy-chef-1525109908 (accessed 3 October 2021).

62 Trubek, *How Americans Cook Today*, 150.

BIBLIOGRAPHY

Andrieu, Pierre. *Fine Bouche. A History of the Restaurant in France*, trans. Arthur Hayward, London: Cassell and Co., 1956.

All Chin, Josie. 'Case Study: Diet Coke and its Creative Designers', *Marketing Week*, 6 March 2013, https://www.marketingweek.com/case-study-diet-coke-and-its-creative-designers/ (accessed 6 June 2021).

Andersen, Kristen. 'How I would Fix Fashion. 5 Industry Insiders tell us', Vogue Runway, September 2016, https://www.vogue.com/article/fashion-calendar-problems-spring-2017-shows (accessed 7 June 2021).

Antrim, Taylor. *Food in Vogue*, Abrams: New York, 2017.

Aresty, Esther. *The Delectable Past: The Joys of Table, From Rome to the Renaissance, From Queen Elizabeth I to Mrs. Beeton*, London: Allen & Unwin, 1965.

Arnold, Rebecca. 'Heroin Chic', *Fashion Theory*, volume 3, issue 3, 1999, 279–296.

Baker, Rob. 'Mini Skirts, Soviet Spies and the Chelsea Palace – The Fascinating History of the Kings Road', *The Telegraph*, 16 April 2016, https://www.telegraph.co.uk/travel/destinations/europe/united-kingdom/england/london/articles/kings-road-london-history/ (accessed 28 September 2021).

Balasco, Warren J. *Appetite for Change. How the Counterculture Took on the Food Industry*, Ithaca: Cornel University Press, [1989, 1993], 2007.

Balzac, Honoré de. *Physiologie du marriage, ou meditations de philosophie éclectique*, Paris: Charpentier, 1840.

Barr, Luke. *Ritz and Escoffier: the Hotelier, the Chef, and the Rise of the Leisure Class*, New York: Clarkson Potter, 2018.

Barthes, Roland. *The Rustle of Language*, trans. Richard Howard, Berkeley and Los Angeles: University of California Press, 1989.

Barthes, Roland. *The Fashion System* (1967), trans. Matthew Ward and Richard Howard, Berkeley and Los Angeles: University of California Press, (1983) 1990.

Barthes, Roland. 'Towards a Psychosociology of Contemporary Food Consumption', *Food and Culture.* A Reader, third edition, edited by Carole Counihan and Penny Van Esterik, New York and London: Routledge, 2013, 23–30.

Barthes, Roland. 'Ornamental Cookery', *Mythologies*, trans. Annette Lavers London: Jonathan Cape, 1973, 85–87.

Barthes, Roland. 'Steak and Chips', *Mythologies,* trans. Annette Lavers London: Paladin, 1973, 69–71.

Barthes, Roland 'The Face of Garbo,' *Mythologies*, trans. Annette Lavers, Paladin, 1979, 56–57.

Bateman, Kristin. 'Dom Pérignon and Dandelion Greens: Remembering Christian Dior's Cookbook', *Vogue*, 8 July 2017, https://www.vogue.com/article/dior-cookbook-recipes-plaza-athenee-paris (accessed 16 October 2021).

Bates, Anna. 'Li Edelcoort', *ICON*, icon 064, October 2008, https://www.iconeye.com/icon-064-october-2008/li-edelkoort (accessed 18 October 2021).

Baudelaire, Charles. *Œuvres complètes*, Paris: Gallimard Pléiade, 1954.

Bell, Quentin. 'The Incorrigible Habit: A Study of Dress Reform in England', *History Today*, Vol. 1, Issue 3, 1951, https://www.historytoday.com/archive/incorrigible-habit-study-dress-reform-england

Bell David and Valentine, Gill. *Consuming Geographies. We are Where We Eat*, London: Routledge, 1997.

Berchoux, Joseph. *La gastronomie*, Paris: Giguet et Michaud, fourth edition, 1805.

Berlinger, Max. 'How Erewhon Became L.A's Hottest Hangout', *The New York Times*, 17 February 2021, https://www.nytimes.com/2021/02/17/style/erewhon-los-angeles-health-food.html (accessed 10 December 2021).

Berry, Jess. *House of Fashion. Haute Couture and the Modern Interior*, London and New York: Bloomsbury, 2018.

Bickham, Troy. 'Eating the Empire: Intersections of Food, Cookery and Imperialism in Eighteenth-Century Britain', *Past and Present,* No. 198, February 2008, 71–109.

Blanks, Tim. 'The Last Temptation of Christian', *The New York Times Magazine*, 18 August, 2002, https://www.nytimes.com/2002/08/18/magazine/the-last-temptation-of-christian.html (accessed 17 October 2021).

Bobrow-Strain, Aaron. *White Bread. A Social History of the Store-Bought Loaf*, Beacon Press: Boston, 2012.

Booth, Jessica. 'Karl Largerfeld used to Drink 10 Diet Cokes a Day and Called Toast a Luxury', *Insider*, 20 February 2019, https://www.insider.com/karl-lagerfeld-food-nutrition-diet-coke-2019-2 (accessed 4 June 2021).

Borrelli-Persson, Laird. Moschino, Spring 1994 Ready-to-Wear, Vogue Runway, 3 May 2019, https://www.vogue.com/fashion-shows/spring-1994-ready-to-wear/moschino (accessed 26 December 2021).

Bordo, Susan. 'Not Just "a White Girl's Thing": The Changing Face of Food and Body Image Problems', in *Food and Culture, A Reader*, edited by Carole Counihan and Penny Van Esterik, third edition, New York and London: Routledge, 2013, 265–275.

Bourdieu, Pierre. *Distinction: A Social Critique of the Judgement of Taste*, London: Routledge and Kegan Paul, 1986.

Bourdieu, Pierre. 'Distinction: A Social Critique of the Judgement of Taste', trans. Richard Nice, edited by Carole Counihan and Penny Van Esterik, *Food and Culture. A Reader*, Third Edition, New York and London: Routledge, 2013, 31–39.

Bouvier, Luke. 'A Taste for Words: Gastronomy and the Writing of Loss in Brillat-Savarin's "Physiologie du gout"', *Mosaic: An Interdisciplinary Critical Journal*, Vol. 38, No. 3, September 2005, 95–111.

Brillat-Savarin, Jean Anthelme. *Phyiologie du goût, øu meditations de gastronomie transcendante* (1825), Paris: Éditions Lagaran, 2015, 2 vols.

Brooks, Xan. 'Jackie: Behind the Creation of JFK, America's Once and Future King', *The Guardian*, 7 January 2017, https://www.theguardian.com/film/2017/jan/07/jackie-natalie-portman-behind-the-creation-of-jfk-camelot-movies (accessed 10 July 2020).

Brooks, Alasdair ed. *The Importance of British Material Culture to Historical Archaeologies of the Nineteenth Century*, Lincoln: University of Nebraska Press, 2015.

Brubach, Holly. 'Franco Moschino. Talk of the Town', *The New Yorker*, 9 January 1989, https://www.newyorker.com/magazine/1989/01/09/franco-moschino (accessed 15 December 2021).

Calefato, Patrizia *Fashion as Cultural Translation. Signs, Images, Narratives*, London: Anthem Press, 2021.

Capati Alberto and Montanari, Massimo, *Italian Cuisine. A Cultural History*, translated by Aine O'Healy, New York: Columbia University Press, 2003.

Carême, Marc-Antoine. *The Cuisiner Parisienne: ou l'art de la cuisine française au dix-neuvième siècle* (1828), Paris: Ligaran, 2015.

Carroll, Dean. 'Marco Pierre White – from "enfant terrible" to International Businessman', *Gulf Business*, 11 June 2016, https://gulfbusiness.com/marco-pierre-white-enfant-terrible-international-businessman/ (accessed 11 October 2021).

Castiglione, Baldessare. *The Courtier*, trans. Thomas Hobby, London, 1588; https://www.bl.uk/collection-items/the-book-of-the-courtier-1588 (accessed 4 September 2019).

Chan, Andrew. '"La grand bouffe": Cooking Shows as Pornography,' in Dara Goldstein ed., *The Gastronomica Reader,* Los Angeles: California University Press, 2010, 139.

Church Gibson, Pamela. 'The Deification of the Dolly Bird: Selling Swinging London, Fuelling Feminism', *Journal for the Study of British Cultures*, Special Issue, Fashioning Society, volume 14, no. 2, 2007, 99–113.

Clements, Kirstie. 'The Truth about Size Zero', *The Guardian*, 5 July 2013, 5, https://www.theguardian.com/fashion/2013/jul/05/vogue-truth-size-zero-kirstie-clements (accessed 20 June 2020).

Cochrane, Lauren. 'Paris' Colette, the "Trendiest Store in the World" – Set to Close,' *The Guardian*, https://www.theguardian.com/fashion/2017/jul/12/pariss-colette-the-trendiest-store-in-the-world-set-to-close (accessed 1 October 2021).

Cowan, Brian. *The Social Life of Coffee: The Emergence of the British Coffeehouse*, New Haven and London: Yale University Press, 2005.

Cruz, Gabriela. *Grand Illusion: Phantasmagoria in Nineteenth-Century Paris,* Oxford and New York: Oxford University Press, 2020.

Culinary Institute of America, 'The Chef's Uniform', *Gastronomica*, Vol. 1, No. 1, Winter 2001, 88–91.

de Costa Kauffman, Thomas, *Arcimboldo: Visual Jokes, Natural History, and Still-Life Painting,* Chicago: University of Chicago Press, 2010.

Clark, Dylan. 'The Raw and the Rotten: Punk Cuisine', in *Food and Culture. A Reader*, Third Edition, edited by, Carole Counihan and Penny Van Esterik, London and New York: Routledge, 2013, 232–242.

Clayton, Paul and Rowbotham, Judith. 'How the Mid Victorians worked Ate and Died', *International Journal of Environmental Research and Public Health*, 2009, issue 6, 1235–1254.

Dali, Salvador. *The Secret Life of Dali*, New York: Dial Press, 1942

Dali, Salvador. *The Secret Life of Salvador Dali*, London: Dover Fine Art, 1993.

Dali, Salvador. *Les Dîners de Gala*, New York: Taschen, 2016.

Dali, Salvador. *Dalí*, New York: Bignou Gallery, 1945

Daly Suzanne and Forman, Ross G. 'Cooking Culture: Situating Food and Drink in the Nineteenth Century', *Victorian Literature and Culture*, 2008, vol. 36, no.2, 363–373.

Deardan, Lizzie. 'France Bans Unhealthy thin Models with Law Requiring Doctor's Certificate', *Independent*, 6 May 2017, https://www.independent.co.uk/news/world/europe/france-bans-unhealthily-thin-model-bmi-doctors-certificate-photoshopped-images-a7721211.html (accessed 20 June 2020).

Dennis, Abigail. 'From Apicius to Gastroporn: Form, Function, and Ideology in the History of Cookery Books', *Studies in Popular Culture*, Vol. 31, No. 1, Fall 2008.

de la Haye, Amy and Valerie Mendes. *The House of Worth: Portrait of an Archive*. London: V&A Publishing, 2014.

De Jean, Joan *The Essence of Style. How the French invented High Fashion, Fine food, Chic Cafes, Style, Sophistication and Glamour,* New York: Free Press, 2005.

de Marley, Diana. *The History of Haute Couture, 1850–1950,* New York: Holmes, 1980.

de Souza, Christa. 'How Diet Coke became Fashions Favourite Fizz', *The Guardian,* June 2013, https://www.theguardian.com/fashion/2013/jan/12/diet-coke-fashion-favourite-fizz (accessed 5 June 2021).

Dewey, John. *Art as Experience*, New York: Perigreen, [1934],1980.

Douglas, Mary. *Food in the Social Order*, London and New York: Routledge, 1984.

Douglas, Mary. 'Deciphering a Meal', *Daedalus*, 101, (1), 1972, 61–81.

Therese Dolan, 'The Empress's' New Clothes. Fashion and Politics in Second Empire France', *Women's Art Journal,* (Spring–Summer, 1994), Vol. 15, No. 1, 22–28.

Dubois, Philippe. 'Savarin/BalZac: Du gout des excitants sur l'écriture modern,' *Nineteent-Century* Studies, Vol. 33, No. 1/2, Fall–Winter 2004–2005, 75–88.

Edelcoort, Li. 'On Why doing Less is More', Time Sensitive, Episode 29, https://timesensitive.fm/episode/trend-forecaster-li-edelkoort-doing-less-is-more/ (accessed 19 October 2021).

Eldred, Claire. 'Encounters and Exchanges with Elsa Schiaparelli's Lobster Dress: An Object Biography', *Fashion and Contemporaneity. Realms of the Visible*, edited by Laura Petican, Boston: Brill, 2019, 69–87.

Elias, Norbert. *The Civilizing Process, Vol.1: The History of Manners*, Edmund Jephcott, trans. New York: Pantheon Books, 1982.

Entwistle, Joanne and Elizabeth Wissinger. *Fashioning Models: Image, Text and Industry*, London and New York: Berg, 2012.

Entwistle Joanne and Slater, Don 'Models as Brands: Critical Thinking of Bodies and Images', *Fashioning Models: Image, Text and Industry*, edited by Joanne Entwistle and Elizabeth Wissinger, London and New York: Berg, 2012, 15–33.

Ephron, Nora. 'Serial Manogamy. My Cookbook Crushes', *The New Yorker*, 5 February 5 2006, https://www.newyorker.com/magazine/2006/02/13/serial-monogamy?utm_source=nl&utm_brand=tny&utm_mailing=TNY_SundayArchive_090521&utm_v=57338746&hasha=656be797c5db6a1e93f627913eda1202&hashb=deccbcc38ede43dc0362561f1b7d58220bc6835b&hashc=67555da96b9bbf4474ed422a67c03d47bdb77e2bed30a519f3ff4c38baac94a2&esrc=Archive_NL_page&mbid=mbid%3DCRMNYR012019&utm_term=TNY_SundayArchive (accessed 5 October 2021).

Evans, Caroline. 'The Ontology of the Fashion Model', *AA Files*, Vol. 63, 2011, 56–69.

Everette, Christina. 'In the Flesh Lady Gaga Dons Red Meat on Cover of Hommes Japan', *Daily News*, 7 September 2010, https://www.nydailynews.com/entertainment/gossip/flesh-lady-gaga-dons-raw-meat-cover-vogue-hommes-japan-article-1.438875

Fink, Beatrice. 'Enlightened Eating in Non-Fictional Context and the First Stirrings of Ecriture Gourmand', *Dalhousie French Studies*, Vol. 11, Fall/Winter, 1986, 9–21.

Finkelstein, Joanne. *Dining Out. A Sociology of Modern Manners*, New York: New York University Press, 1989.

Firestone, Mary. *Dayton's Department Store*, Arcadia: Chicago, 2007.

Fletcher, Kate. 'Slow Fashion', *Ecologist*, https://theecologist.org/2007/jun/01/slow-fashion (accessed 19 October 2021).

Frazer, Laura. 'The Inner Corset. A Brief History of Fat', *The Fat Studies Reader*, Esther D. Rothblum and Sondra Solovay, eds., New York: New York University Press, 2009.

Frazier, Nancy. 'Salvador Dali's Lobsters: Feast, Phobia and Freudian Slip', *Gastronomica. The Journal of Food and Culture*, Vol. 9, No. 4 (Fall, 2009), 16–20.

Freedman, Paul. 'Women and Restaurants in the Nineteenth-Century United States', *Journal of Social History,* vol. 48, no. 1, (2014), 1–19.

Fried, Rachel. 'Tommy Cash and Maison Margiela drop Haute Couture Carbs', *CR Fashion Book*, 21 March 2021, https://www.crfashionbook.com/fashion/a35903084/tommy-cash-maison-margiela-haute-couture-carbs/

Friedman, Vanessa. 'Let them Wear Cake', *The New York Times*, 21 February 2020, https://www.nytimes.com/2020/02/21/style/milan-fashion-week-prada-moschino.html (accessed 10 December 2021).

Gallaghar, Jacob. 'Goodbye Croc, Hello Gucci: How chefs became Style Icons,', *The Wall Street Journal*, https://www.wsj.com/articles/the-rise-of-the-sexy-chef-1525109908 (accessed 3 October 2021).

Ghandi, Shweta. Christian Dior's 1972 Cookbook will Inspire your Quarantine Cooking', 3 June 2020, https://settingmind.com/christian-dior-1972-cookbook-quarantine-cooking/ (accessed 16 October 2021).

Geczy, Adam. *Fashion and Orientalism: Dress, Textiles and Culture from the 17th to the 21st Century,* London and New York: Bloomsbury, 2013.

Geczy, Adam. *The Artificial Body in Fashion and Art: Marionettes, Models, and Mannequins*, London and New York: Bloomsbury, 2017.

Geczy, Adam and Vicki Karaminas. *Libertine Fashion: Sexual Rebellion, Freedom and Style*, London and New York: Bloomsbury, 2020.

Geczy, Adam and Vicki Karaminas. *Fashion and Art*, Oxford and New York: Berg, 2012.

Geczy Adam and Vicki Karaminas. *Critical Fashion Practice: From Westwood to van Beirendonck*, London and New York: Bloomsbury, 2017.

Geczy, Adam and Vicki Karaminas. *Fashion and Masculinities in Popular Culture,* London and New York: Routledge, 2017.

Geczy, Adam and Vicki Karaminas. *Fashion Installation: Body, Space and Performance*, London and New York: Bloomsbury, 2019.

Gernsheim, Alison. *Victorian and Edwardian Fashion: A Photographic* Survey, New York: Dover, 1963.

Gilligan, Sarah. 'Heaving Cleavages and Fantastic Frock Coats: Gender Fluidity, Celebrity and Tactile Transmediality in Contemporary Costume Cinema', *Film, Fashion and Consumption*, volume 1, number 1, 2012, 7–38.

Goldstein, Darra. 'Russia, Carême, and the Culinary Arts', *The Slavonic and East European* Review, Vol. 73, No. 4, October 1995, 691–715.

Goldstein, Dara ed. *The Gastronomica Reader,* Los Angeles: California University Press, 2010.

Goody, Jack 'Industrial Food: Towards the Development of a World Cuisine', edited by Carole Counihan and Penny Van Esterik, *Food and Culture. A Reader*, Third Edition, New York and London: Routledge, 2013, 72–90

Gordon, Bertram. *Second World War France from Defeat and Occupation to the Creation of Heritage*, Ithaca: Cornell University Press, 2018.

Griffiths, M. 'Paris Dressmakers', *Strand Magazine* 48, vol, VIII, July to December 1894., http://www.avictorian.com/fashion_paris_dressmakers.html (accessed 4 January 2022).

Griffin, Emma. 'Diet, Hunger and Living Standards During the British Industrial Revolution, *Past and Present*, 2028, Volume 239, issue 1, 71–111.

Gundle, Stephen. *Glamour. A History*, Oxford: Oxford University Press, 2008.

Gunew, Sneja. *Framing Marginality Multicultural Literary Studies*, Melbourne: Melbourne University Press, 1994.

Harris, Jennifer, Hyde, Sarah and Smith, Greg. *1966 and All That. Design and the Consumer in Britain 1960–1969,* London: Trefoil Publications, 1986.

Hauser, Arnold. *The Social History of* Art, 4 vols., London and New York: Routledge (1962) 1999.

Holgate, Mark. 'Schiapparelli Spring 2017 Couture', Vogue Runway*,* 23 January 2017, https://www.vogue.com/fashion-shows/spring-2017-couture/schiaparelli, (accessed 17 May 2021).

Howes, David and Marc Lalande. 'The History of Sensibilities: Of the Standard of Taste in Mid-Eighteenth-Century England and the Circulation of Smells in Post-Revolutionary France,' *Dialectical Anthropology,* Vol. 16, No. 2, 1991, 125–135.

Hulanicki, Barbara. *From A to Biba. The Autobiography of Barbara Hulanicki*, London: Hutchinson, 1983.

Hyman Gwen. 'The Taste of Fame: Chefs, Diners, Celebrity, Class,' *Gastronomica,* Vol. 8, no. 3, Summer 2008, 43–52.

James, Kenneth, *Escoffier: The King of Chefs*, London and New York: Bloomsbury, 2012.

Joseph, Abigail. 'A Wizard of Silks and Tulle: Charles Worth and the Queer Origins of Couture', *Victorian Studies*, Volume 56, no. 2, (Winter, 2017), 252–279.

Kauffman, Jonathan. *Hippie Food. How the Back-to-Landers, Longhairs and Revolutionaries changed the way we Eat*, New York: William Morrow, 2018.

Larocquetinker, Edward. 'New Editions, Fine and Otherwise,' *The New York Times Book Review*, 27 March 1938.

Leer, Jonatan. 'What's cooking, man? Masculinity in European cooking shows after "The Naked Chef",' *Feminist Review,* No. 114, 2016, 72–90.

Largerfeld, Karl. https://getrawenergy.co/karl-lagerfeld-eats/#.YLpMCV6xUl4 (accessed 3 June 2021).

Leach, William R. 'Transformations in a Culture of Consumption: Women and Department Stores, 1890–1925', *The Journal of American History*, Sept.1984, Vol. 71, No.2, 23–177. https://timesmachine.nytimes.com/timesmachine/1938/03/27/99538396.html?auth=login-smartlock&pageNumber=97 (accessed 12 October 2020).

Lee, Jeremy. 'Elizabeth David: All that is Good in British Cookery', *The Guardian*, 10 August 2018, https://www.theguardian.com/food/2018/aug/10/jeremy-lee-cooks-cook-elizabeth-david (accessed 8 October 2021).

Lévi-Strauss, Claude. *The Raw and the Cooked. Introduction to a Science of Mythology: 1,* translated by John and Doreen Whiteman, Middlesex: Penguin, 1964,

Levi, Jane. 'Charles Fourier Versus the Gastronomes: The Contested Ground of Early Nineteenth-Century Consumption and Taste', *Utopian Studies*, Vol. 26, No. 1, 2015, 41–57.

Lewis, Philippa. 'Stomaching the Salon: The Sense of Taste in *Le Tintamarre*'s "Boulangerie du Louvre" and Baudelaire's *Salon de 1846*', *Nineteenth-Century French Studies*, Vol. 42, No. 1/2, Fall/Winter 2013–2014, 35–50.

Low, Rachel. *The History of British Film 1929—1939*, vol. 5, London: Routledge, 1979, 91.

Lyon, Phil. *Good Food and Hard Times: Ambrose Heath's Contribution to British Food Culture in the 1930s and the War Years*, https://www.brepolsonline.net/doi/epdf/10.1484/J.FOOD.5.108964 (accessed 13 October 2013).

Mariani, John, F. *How Italian Food Conquered the World,* New York: Palgrave McMillan, 2011.

Marriott, Hannah. 'Fast Food Fashion: Moschino Accused of "Glorifying" McDonalds Logo', *The Guardian*, 13 July 2014, https://www.theguardian.com/fashion/2014/jul/13/moschino-glorifying-mcdonalds-logo-fashion (accessed 26 December 2021).

Mars, Valerie. *A History of the French in London: Liberty, Equality,* Opportunity, London: University of London, 2013.

Marshall, David. *Celebrity and Power: Fame in Contemporary Culture,* Minneapolis: Minnesota University Press, 1997,

Mathews, Rachel. 'Contemporary Fashion Tastemakers: Starting Conversations that Matter', *Catwalk the Journal of Beauty and Style*, volume 4, no.1, 2015, 51–70.

Matsumara, Hiroshi. 'La physiologie, la table et la modernité: de Brillat-Savarin au *Père Goriot*,' *L'Année balzacienne*, No. 19, 2018, 87–100.

McDonough William and Braungart, Michael. *Cradle to Cradle: Remaking the Way We Make Things,* New York: North Point Press, 2002.

Mennell, Stephen 'On the Civilizing of Appetite', *Theory, Culture and Society*, vol. 4, no.2 (1987), 373–403.

Mennell, Stephen *All Manners of Food: Eating and Taste in England and France from the Middle Ages to the Present*, Oxford: Basil Blackwell, 1985.

Meola, Kiki. 'Diet Secrets: Beyonce Reveals the Super strict Diet she Started at 218 Pounds Post Twins: I'm Hungry', *US Weekly*, 17 April 2019, https://www.usmagazine.com/celebrity-body/news/beyonces-coachella-diet-after-twins-no-sugar-carbs-dairy-meat/ (accessed 18 June 2020).

Metternich, Princes de, *Souvenirs de la Princesse Pauline de Metternich (1859–1871*), Paris; Plon, 1922.

McCabe, Joanne. 'Gaga Defend Homosexuals with Prime Rib Speech', 21 September 2010, https://metro.co.uk/2010/09/21/lady-gaga-defends-american-homosexuals-with-prime-rib-speech-519254/

McAfee Tierney and McNeil, Liz. 'How Jackie Kennedy Invented Camelot Just One Week after JFK's Assassination', *People*, 22 November 2017, https://people.com/politics/jackie-kennedy-invented-camelot-jfk-assassination/ (accessed July 10 2020).

McCormack, Rachel. 'Caviar, Explained: Where to Source the Very Best and How to Serve it', *Robb Report*, 16 December 2019, https://robbreport.com/food-drink/dining/what-is-caviar-where-to-source-the-very-best-and-how-to-serve-it-2884402/ (accessed 17 June 2021).

McLerran, Jennifer. 'Disciplined Subjects and Docile Bodies in the work of Contemporary Artist Jana Sterbak', *Feminist Studies*, (Autumn, 1988), Vol. 24, No. 3, 535–552.

McPhee, Peter. *Robespierre: A Revolutionary Life*, New Haven and London: Yale University Press, 2012.

Menon aka François Marin, *Les Dons des Comus, ou l'art de la cuisine, réduit en pratique*, Paris: Chex la Veuve Pissot, revised edition, 1750.

Mercier, Louis-Sébastien. *Le nouveau Paris*, Paris 1795, v. 4.

Merriman, John. *Ballad of the Anarchist Bandits: The Crime Spree that Gripped Belle Époque Paris*, New York: Nation Books, 2017.

Merriman, John. 'Dynamite Club: The Anarchists,' https://www.youtube.com/watch?v=vVGsoiE3zQQ

Metzner, Paul. *Crescendo of the Virtuoso: Spectacle, Skill, and Self-Promotion in the Age of Revolution,* Berkeley and London: University of California Press, 1998.

Michel-Thiriet, Philippe. *The Book of Proust,* trans. Jan Dalley, London: Catto and Windus, 1989.

Montanari, Masimo. *Italian Identity on the Kitchen, or Food and the Nation*, translated by Beth Archer Brombert, New York: Columbia University Press, 2013.

Muhlke, Christine. 'Paris is Losing it,' *The New York Times Magazine*, 1 May 2005, https://www.nytimes.com/2005/05/01/magazine/paris-is-losing-it.html (accessed 1 June 2021).

Notaker, Henry. *A History of Cookbooks: From Kitchen to Page over Seven Centuries*, Los Angeles: California University Press, 2017.

O'Neil, Claire. 'Food Photo Friday: Gaga for Food Fashion', *The Picture Show*, 3 December 2010, https://www.npr.org/sections/pictureshow/2010/12/03/131760743/fashionfood

Ozdamar, Mergim. 'United Coffeedom: The History of London's Coffee Houses', *Londonr*, 14 February 2019, https://londnr.com/united-coffeedom-the-history-of-londons-coffee-houses/ (accessed 11 August 2019).

Painter, George. *Marcel Proust* (1959), Harmondsworth: Penguin, 1990, 2 vols.

Palmer Lunn Architects, *Kensington Roof Garden Pavilion Internal Strip Out Works, Design and Access Statement, Vol. 1*, June 2020, https://www.rbkc.gov.uk/idoxWAM/doc/Other-2398023.pdf?extension=.pdf&id=2398023&location=Volume2&contentType=application/pdf&pageCount=1

Pankhurst Ferguson, Pricilla. *Accounting for Taste. The Triumph of French Cuisine*', Chicago and London, The University of Chicago Press, 2006.

Parkhurst Ferguson, Priscilla. 'A Cultural Field in the Making: Gastronomy in 19th-Century France,' *American Journal of Sociology*, Vol. 104, No. 3, November 1998, 597–641.

Parkhurst Ferguson, Priscilla. 'Writing of the Kitchen: Carême and the Invention of French Cuisine', *Gastronomica*, Vol. 3, No. 3, Summer 2003, 40–51.

Passanen, Melissa. 'Enough Saffron to Cover a Sixpence. The Challenge and Pleasures of Elizabeth David,' *The Art of Eating*, no. 61, 2003, https://artofeating.com/the-pleasures-and-challenge-of-elizabeth-david/ (accessed 8 October 2021).

Paz, Octavio. 'Eroticism and gastrosophy,' trans. Sara Klaren, *Daedalus,* Vol. 117, No. 3, 1988, 227–249.

Perullo, Nicola. *Taste as Experience: The Philosophy and Aesthetics of Food,* New York: Columbia University Press, 2016.

Picardie, Justine *Coco Chanel: The Legend and the Life*, London: Harper Collins, 2010.

Pike, Judith. 'Brillat-Savarin's Occidentalizing of the Orientalist Origins of French Cuisine,' *The French Review*, Vol. 84, No. 5, April, 2011, 936–953.

Pine, Julia. 'Breaking Dalinian Bread: On Consuming the Anthropomorphic, Performative, Ferocious, and Eucaristic Loaves of Salvador Dali', *Invisible Culture: An Electronic Journal for Visual Culture,* Issue 14: Aesthetics and Eaters – Food and the Arts, Winter, 2000, 83–105, www.rochester.edu/in_visible_culture/Issue_14/pdf/jpine.pdf (accessed 20 May 2021).

Pitte, Jean-Robert. *French Gastronomy: A History and Geography of a Passion* (1991), trans. Jody Gladding, New York: Columbia University Press, 2002.

Potter, Clarkson. 'Chef Alice Waters Memoir Tells Tales of Her Youth and Loves', *The Salt Lake Tribune*, 9 September 2017, https://www.sltrib.com/artsliving/2017/09/08/chef-alice-waters-memoir-tells-tales-of-her-youth-and-loves/ (accessed 10 December 2021).

Porter Benson, Susan. *Counter Culture: Saleswomen, Managers, and Customers in American Department Stores, 1890–1940*, Champaign: University of Illinois Press, 1987,
Press, Clare. *Wardrobe Crisis: How We Went from Sunday Best to Fast Fashion*, Melbourne: Nero, 2016.
Proust, *Remembrance of Things Past*, trans. C. K. Scott Moncrieff and Terence Kilmartin, Harmondsworth: Penguin, (1983) 1987, 3 vols.
Quant, Mary. *My Autobiography*, London: Header and Hodder, 2012.
Reinach Segre, Simona. 'The Meaning of Made in Italy in Fashion', *Craft + Design Enquiry*, edited by Kay Lawrence, Canberra: ANU Press, 2015.
Raymon, Noah. 'How a McDonalds Restaurant Spawned the Slow Food Movement', *Time*, 10 December 2014, https://time.com/3626290/mcdonalds-slow-food/ (accessed 21 December 2021).
Riley, Nick. 'U2 Bono Debuts Star-Studded "Beautiful Day" Cover and Shares powerful Speech', *NME News*, 8 June 2020, https://www.nme.com/en_au/news/music/u2-bono-debuts-star-studded-beautiful-day-cover-and-shares-powerful-speech-2684185
Rizzo, Mary. 'Embodying Withdrawal. Abjection and the Popularity of Heroin Chic', *Michigan Feminist Studies*, Special issue, Desire, Vol. 15, 2001, https://quod.lib.umich.edu/cgi/t/text/text-idx?cc=mfsfront;c=mfs;c=mfsfront;idno=ark5583.0015.004;g=mfsg;rgn=main;view=text;xc=1 (accessed 16 June 2020).
Robeiro, Aileen. 'Painting: Refashioning Art – Some Visual Approaches to the Study of the History of Dress', Geczy, in Adam Geczy and Vicki Karaminas (eds) *Fashion and Art*, London: Bloomsbury, 2012.
Sams, Lauren. 'Mary Quant. The Great Liberator', *Financial Review*, 12 March 2021, https://www.afr.com/life-and-luxury/fashion-and-style/mary-quant-the-great-liberator-20210215-p572mm (accessed 24 September 2021).
Schwartz, Erin. 'Everything you see Moschino Owes to Spaghetti', https://www.ssense.com/en-us/editorial/fashion/everything-you-see-moschino-owes-to-spaghetti (accessed 25 December 2021).
Secrest, Meryle. *Elsa Schiaparelli: A Biography*, New York: Knopf, 2014.
Senelick, Laurence. 'Consuming Passions: Eating and the Stage at the Fin de Siècle', *Gastronomica,* Vol. 5, No. 2, Spring 2005, 43–49.
Sévigné, Marie de Rabutin-Chantal, marquise de. *Receuil des lettres de Madame de Sévigné*, 9 vols., Paris: Libraires Associés, 1806.
Shrum, Wesley Monroe. *Fringe and Fortune. The Role of Critics in High and Popular Art*, Princeton, New Jersey: Princeton University Press, 1996
Shurtleff William and Aoyagi, Akiko. *History of Erwhon-Natural Foods Pioneer in the United States (1966–2011), An Annotated Bibliography and Sourcebook*, California: Soyinfo Centre, 2011.
Shoup, Mary Ellen. 'Homebaking Continues in 2021 Giving rise to Comfort and Wellness Trends', *Food Navigator-usa.com*, 22 March 2021, https://www.foodnavigator-usa.com/Article/2021/03/22/Home-baking-continues-in-2021-giving-rise-to-comfort-and-wellness-trends
Smith, E. *The Compleat Housewife, or, Accomplished Gentlewoman's Companion*, London: J. and J. Pemberton, 1739.
Smith, Gilly. *Taste and the TV Chef. How Storytelling Can Save the Planet*, [Bristol: Intellect], 2020
Smith, Natalie. 'Food and Fashion: Establishing a Critical Distance from the . . . Mess', in *Art and Food*, ed. Peter Stupples, Cambridge: Cambridge Scholars Press, 2014, 133–145.

Sover Arie and Ben-Meir, Orna. 'Humour Food and Fashion: The Use of Humour and Food in Fashion Shows', *European Journal of Humor Research*, 5, (1), 81.

Spang, Rebecca. *The Invention of the Restaurant: Paris and Modern Gastronomic Culture*, Cambridge MA: Harvard University Press, 2000.

Spang, Rebecca. 'L'Individu au menu: l'invention du restaurant à Paris au XVIIIe siècle', *Ethnologie française*, Vol. 44, No. 1, January 2014, 11–17.

Statetsen, Liana. 'Tommy Cash and Maison Magiela Collaborate on the Weirdest Merch Yet', *Vogue*, 18 March 2021, https://www.vogue.com/article/tommy-cash-maison-margiela-bread-slippers-collaboration

Steele, Valerie. *Paris Fashion. A Cultural History*, London: Bloomsbury, [1988,1998], 2017.

Steingarten, Jeffrey. 'Breading Bread', in Taylor Atrim, ed, *Food in Vogue*, New York: Abrams, 2017.

Steavensen, Wendell. 'The Rise and Fall of French Cuisine', *The Guardian*, 16 July 2019, https://www.theguardian.com/food/2019/jul/16/the-rise-and-fall-of-french-cuisine (accessed June 2021).

Stewart, Viviene 'The Way they Were: A Sydney Department Store in the 1920s', *Heritage Australia,* vol. 9, no. 4, Summer 1990, 20–23.

Sweney, Mark. 'Diet Coke Swaps Duffy for Puppets', *The Guardian*, 11 March 2010, https://www.theguardian.com/media/2010/mar/11/diet-coke-duffy-puppets (accessed 4 June 2021).

Saunders, Edith. *The Age of Worth, Couturier to the Empress Eugéne*, London: Longmans Green, 1954.

Suro, Davis Mary. 'Romans Protest McDonalds', *The New York Times*, 5 May 1986, https://www.nytimes.com/1986/05/05/style/romans-protest-mcdonald-s.html (accessed 15 December 2021).

Tadié, Jean-Yves. *Proust*, Paris: Gallimard, 1996.

Coats, Ta-Nahisi. 'The Largerfeld Diet', *The Atlantic*, 7 March 2012, https://www.theatlantic.com/health/archive/2012/03/the-lagerfeld-diet/254018/ (accessed 4 June 2021).

Taine, Hippolyte. *Notes on Paris*, translated by John Austin Stevens, New York: Henry Holt, 1875.

Taylor, Valerie. 'Banquet plate and Renaissance Culture: A Day in the Life', *Renaissance Studies*, Vol. 19, No. 5, November 205, 621–633.

Teulon, Fabrice. 'Le Voluptueux at le gourmand: économie de la jouissance chez la Mettrie et Brillat-Savarin,' *A Quarterly Journal in Modern Literatures*, Vol. 52, No. 3, 176–192.

Thesander, Marianne. *The Feminine Ideal*, London: Reaction, 1997.

Tinoco, Sarah. 'Jeremy Scott the Peoples Designer, Vlad Yudin (2015)', Review, *Critical Studies in Men's Fashion*, Vol. 3, Number 1, 2016, 51–54.

Titton. Monica. 'Afterthought. Fashion, Feminism and Radical Protest', *Fashion Theory, The Journal of Dress, Body and Culture*, Special Issue on Fashion as Politics: Dressing Dissent, Volume 23, Issue 6, 747–746.

Toffoletti, Kim *Cyborgs, Feminism, Popular Culture and Barbie the Posthuman Dolls*, London: I.B Tauris, 2007.

Trubek, Amy. *How American Cook Today,* Los Angeles: University of California Press, 2017.

Slade, Toby and Jensen, M. Angela. 'Letter from the Editors', *Fashion Theory the Journal of Dress, Body and Culture,* Special issue on Decoloniality and Fashion, 2020, vol. 24, issue 6, 809–814.

Trubert-Tollu, Chantal, Tétart-Vittu, Françoise, Martin-Hattemberg, Jean-Marie and Olivieri, Fabrice *The House of Worth 1858–1954. The Birth of Couture*, London: Thames and Hudson, 2018.
Turner, Alwyn W. *The Biba Experience*, London: Antique Collectors Club, 2007.
Veblen, Thorstein. *The Theory of the Leisure Class,* trans. Robert Hullot-Kentor, New York: Random House, 2001.
Velonté, Paolo. 'The Thin Ideal and the Practice of Fashion', *Journal of Consumer Culture*, 2019, Vol. 19 (2), 252–270.
Visser, Margaret. *The Rituals of Dinner: The Origins, Evolution, and Meaning of Table Manners*, Harmondsworth: Penguin, 1992.
Walhout, Hannah. 'Zac Posen on the Intersection of Food and Fashion and his new Cookbook', *Food and Wine*, https://www.foodandwine.com/news/zac-posen-new-cookbook (accessed 15 October 2021).
Wait, Thom. 'Tommy Cash Drop Maison Margiela Noodles and More Bizzare Merch', *Dazed* magazine, 18 March 2021, https://www.dazeddigital.com/fashion/article/52253/1/tommy-cash-drops-maison-margiela-noodles-bread-slippers-more-bizarre-merch
Wanders, Anne Teresia. *Slow Fashion*, Niggli: Berlin, 2009.
Weintraub, J. 'The Restaurants of Paris: A Translation from *Paris à table*,' *Gastranomica*, Vol. 14, No. 1, Spring 2014, 33–43.
Wertz, S. K. 'Taste and Food in Rousseau's *Julie, or the New Héloïse*', *The Journal of Aesthetic Education*, Vol. 47, No. 3, 2013, 24–35.
Whitaker, Jan *Service and Style. How the American Department Store Fashioned the Middle Class,* New York: St Martins Press, 2006.
Whitaker, Jan *The Department Store, History, Design, Display,* London: Thames and Hudson, 2011.
Widdicombe, Lizzie. 'Barbie Boy. How Jeremy Scott Remade Moschino for the Instagram Era', *The New Yorker*, 14 March 2016, https://www.newyorker.com/magazine/2016/03/21/jeremy-scotts-new-moschino (accessed 20 December 2021).
Wilson, Elizabeth. *Adorned in Dreams. Fashion and Modernity*, London: I.B Tauris, 1985.
Williams, Rosalind. H. *Dream-Worlds: Mass Consumption in Late Nineteenth Century France*, Berkley: University of California Press, 1982.
Zaryn, Cynthia. 'Portrait of a Marriage Julia Child Captured in Paul Child's Shimmering Photographs', *The New Yorker*, 2 December 2017, https://www.newyorker.com/culture/photo-booth/portrait-of-a-marriage-julia-child-captured-in-paul-childs-shimmering-photographs (accessed 6 October 2021).
Zola, Èmile. *The Kill*, translated by with an introduction and notes by Brian Nelson, Oxford: Oxford University Press, 2004.

Internet sources not otherwise listed

http://www.bbc.co.uk/britishstylegenius/content/21800.shtml (accessed 4 September 2021).
https://www.cameramoda.it/en/associazione/news/920/ (accessed 25 December 2021).
https://kasiacharko.wordpress.com/2013/08/03/the-rainbow-room-big-biba/ (accessed 4 September 2021).
https://fashion.mam-e.it/moschino/ (accessed 15 December 2021).
https://jannaludlow.co.uk/Biba/DT_Rainbow_Room_Roof_Gardens.html (accessed 4 September 2021).

'Gordon Ramsay 'using taxpayer-funded furlough scheme to pay sacked staff', https://www.mirror.co.uk/3am/celebrity-news/gordon-ramsay-using-taxpayer-funded-22114506

'Chanel's Supermarket Chic', https://www.nytimes.com/2014/03/05/fashion/chanels-supermarket-chic.html https://www.opentable.com.au/the-polo-bar

'Skinny Model Furor: Not All Fashion's Fault, Say Designers, Editors,' *Women's Wear Daily*, Vol. 193, Issue 21, 30 January 2007, http://web.a.ebscohost.com.ezproxy1.library.usyd.edu.au/bsi/detail/detail?vid=0&sid=743b296d-e3dd-4361-b3af-01592c40fd12%40sdc-v-sessmgr01&bdata=JnNpdGU9YnNpLWxpdmU%3d#AN=23978126&db=bsu

'A Stitch in Time', S1, E6: Marie Antoinette, https://www.youtube.com/watch?v=fN4RQiYPSqM

'Elsa Schiaparelli: Fashion Visionary', Legacy.com, 13 November 2013, https://www.legacy.com/news/elsa-schiaparelli-fashion-visionary/

'*Dizzy Dali Dinner*', 1941 News reel. YouTube, 14 September 2006, https://www.youtube.com/watch?v=vg6i4E0Woak (accessed 20 May 2021).

St Regis Magazine, in Dalí in New York, *Dalí Universe*, 20 November 2017, https://www.thedaliuniverse.com/en/news-dali-new-york

The Meat of the Matter: A Neo-Aristotelian Analysis of Lady Gaga's 'The Prime Rib of America' Address, https://alicieinwonderland.wordpress.com/2011/09/22/the-meat-of-the-matter-a-neo-aristotelian-analysis-of-lady-gagas-the-prime-rib-of-america-address/

Lady Gaga, *Lady Gaga's Portland Speech*, YouTube, https://www.youtube.com/watch?v=MoqOvFJ5-0c

Kate Moss Regrets Nothing Tastes as Good as Skinny Feels', *BBC News*, 14 September 2018, https://www.bbc.com/news/newsbeat-45522714 (accessed 1 October 2021).

https://london.doverstreetmarket.com/rose-bakery (accessed 1 October 2021).

'The Rise of the Bad Boy Chef', *Combatant Gentlemen*, 22 November 2015, https://combatgent.com/blogs/unhemmed/bad-boy-chefs (accessed 10 October 2021).

INDEX

Page numbers in *italic* refer to illustrations.